Translation Practices Explained

Translation Practices Explained is a series of coursebooks designed to help students and teachers of translation, particularly self-learners.

Each volume focuses on a specific type of translation, in most cases corresponding to actual courses available in translator-training institutions. Special volumes are devoted to professional areas where labour-market demands are growing: court interpreting, community interpreting, European-Union texts, multimedia translation, text revision, electronic tools, and software and website localization.

The authors are practising translators or translator trainers in the fields concerned. Although specialists, they explain their professional insights in a manner accessible to the wider learning public.

Designed to complement the *Translation Theories Explained* series, these books start from the recognition that professional translation practices require something more than elaborate abstraction or fixed methodologies. The coursebooks are located close to work on authentic texts, simulating but not replacing the teacher's hands-on role in class. Self-learners and teachers are encouraged to proceed inductively, solving problems as they arise from examples and case studies. The series thus offers a body of practical information that can orient and complement the learning process.

Most volumes include activities and exercises designed to help self-learners consolidate their knowledge and to encourage teachers to think creatively about their classes. Updated reading lists and website addresses will also help individual learners gain further insight into the realities of professional practice.

Anthony Pym
Series Editor

Legal Translation Explained

Enrique Alcaraz Varó
and
Brian Hughes

ST JEROME

PUBLISHING

St. Jerome Publishing
Manchester, UK & Northampton, MA

Published by St. Jerome Publishing
2 Maple Road West, Brooklands
Manchester, M23 9HH, United Kingdom
Tel +44 161 973 9856 / Fax +44 161 905 3498
stjerome@compuserve.com / http://www.stjerome.co.uk

ISBN 1-900650-46-0 (pbk)
ISSN 1470-966X (*Translation Practices Explained*)

Printed and bound in Great Britain by
T. J. International Ltd., Cornwall, UK

Cover design by
Steve Fieldhouse, Oldham, UK (+44 161 620 2263)

Typeset by
Delta Typesetters, Cairo, Egypt. Email:hilali 1945@hotmail.com.eg

British Library Cataloguing in Publication Data
A catalogue record of this book is available from the British Library

Library of Congress Cataloging-in-Publication Data
Alcaraz Varó, Enrique, 1940-
  Legal translation explained / Enrique Alcaraz Varó, Brian Hughes.
      p. cm. — (Translation practices explained, ISSN 1470-966X)
Includes bibliographical references and index.
  ISBN 1-900650-46-0 (pbk. : alk. paper)
  1. Law—Translating. 2. Law—Language. I. Hughes, Brian, 1951- II.
Title. III. Series.
  K213 .A418 2002
  340'.1'4—dc21

                                    2002004952

Foreword

This book is designed principally to cater for the needs of students who are taking their first steps in the translation of legal English. Our aim has been to provide readers with practical guidelines; the emphasis is on the identification and solution of problems that actually arise in this area of specialized translation. With this in mind, we have grouped the contents into four main blocks, each of which is further subdivided into two chapters. Blocks one and two provide a basic introduction to the linguistic and legal backgrounds; blocks three and four suggest methodological approaches to this type of translation.

Block one (Chapters 1 and 2) deals with legal English as a linguistic system and contains pointers to the leading features of that system. The main points discussed are the 'Plain English Campaign', the stylistics of legal language, the classification of legal vocabulary and the analysis of lexical vagueness and syntactic ambiguity, with the needs of the translator uppermost throughout.

The second block (Chapters 3 and 4) is essentially an outline of the specific features of the Anglo-American legal system. It also contains a brief account of the differences between that system and the continental or 'civil law' systems prevalent in most European countries. Among the matters dealt with are the sources of law (common law, equity, statute law and case law), the court structure and the rules of procedure in civil, criminal and administrative cases.

Chapters 5 and 6, which comprise the third block, are devoted to questions of translation method. Here the concept of text genre is first introduced and explained, then applied to an exploration of written and oral genres, specialist legal and professional genres such as judgements, contracts, wills or the examination of witnesses, academic genres like articles on the law published in specialist journals, and popular genres with an indirect bearing on the law, such as thrillers and courtroom dramas.

Finally, block four, made up of Chapters 7 and 8, completes the methodological picture with analysis of the linguistic and stylistic resources available to the translator of legal texts. The issues covered in this section include the need for awareness of semantic fields and collocations, ways of dealing with problems of syntax (e.g. thematization, complex noun phrases in English, the use of double conjunctions in legal phraseology), and the practical application to legal translation of familiar techniques such as transposition, modulation and expansion.

We would like to take this opportunity to acknowledge the generous help with technical matters provided by Dr Frank Southworth of the School of Law at the University of the West of England, Bristol. On countless occasions during the writing of this book we have benefited from Dr Southworth's invaluable advice on matters of terminology and have drawn on his lengthy experience as a barrister and part-time judge to refine on our comments on English law. Any errors of legal definition or procedure that may have crept into the text are, of course, entirely the responsibility of the authors and not of our adviser.

Enrique Alcaraz Varó
Brian Hughes

Alicante, Spain, 2002

Editor's Acknowledgements

We would like to thank Marta Vallinoto, Jan Janssen, Marcià Riutort, Jorge Seca, Ignasi Fernàndez and Angelita Rabe for their work on the terms in German. The French terms were put together by a team working in the MA in Translation with Language Technology at the University of Wales Swansea: Rachel Carrée, Karine Humbert, Sandrine Perkins, Joanna Thomas and David Wooldridge were supervised by Nigel Addinall. To all of whom, our sincerest thanks for fighting what will always be a losing battle against the incommensurability of legal systems. The terms offered here should not be taken as fixed equivalents. Those that fail to match, or the lacunae that invite doubt and research, can only remain bookmarks for a future multilingual glossary.

Contents

Foreword

Acknowledgements

1. Some Pointers to the Linguistics of Legal English

1. Introduction: Legal English and the rise of English for professional purposes

A few decades ago, any non-native speaker of English who progressed beyond training in basic 'communicative English' would probably have been offered a course on advanced grammar, vocabulary building and an introduction to some at least of the classic authors of English and American literature. In the universities, the concentration on historical and cultural aspects of English would be even greater, and most specialists would complete their degrees without having taken much, or perhaps any, notice of the major role of English as the international language of trade, marketing, tourism, legislation and policy-making. There was even a certain consensus in academic circles that such matters were beneath the notice of teachers of English in institutions of higher learning, or that they could be learned later if at all.

It would be easy to criticize this attitude as snobbish, impractical or misguided, but to do so would be to overlook the radical change that has occurred in very recent times in the role of universities. When the lines of demarcation between the academy and the market were relatively clear, and the prospects of long-term unemployment were, at least for graduates, comparatively rare, it was natural enough that the people responsible for planning the syllabus of university courses should place the stress on the study of English, or any other subject, for its own sake. Indeed, many teachers express concern at what looks like the increasing Philistinism of the market-driven 'global village' so dear to entrepreneurs and university managers alike. To them, it seems more important than ever that universities should continue to offer degree courses in modern languages that place the systematic study of the works of the great authors and of the history of language at the core of the curriculum. All business and no cultural awareness makes Jack a bore as well as a dull boy.

Nevertheless, there is ample scope for developing courses catering for either emphasis, as the recent phenomenal expansion of Applied Languages degrees has shown. It is time to move on from the debate over Shakespeare or shipping documents, Tennyson or technology, Chaucer or the cheese industry, Langland or legal English. The modern world emphatically needs both. The enhanced status of English as the dominant world language has led to an increased demand for the training of competent specialists able to mediate between it and other languages in a wide variety of fields. It is in this context that the prominence recently given in the universities to Translation Studies is best understood.

Over the past two decades, courses in Applied Languages have become increasingly popular in universities. Here in Europe, as the impact of the institutions of the European Union makes itself increasingly felt, universities offer an ever-growing number of degree courses combining the study of modern languages with modules on business studies, economic history, politics and European law. At the same time, universities everywhere have been developing international relations both as a subject area and as a focus for student exchange and recruitment. This has meant an increasing tendency to offer places both to overseas students specializing in combined courses of this type and to those whose area of specialization requires a Modern Languages component.

Naturally enough, given the prominence of English as *the* world language of contemporary communication and trade, there has been a phenomenal increase in the teaching of 'the other Englishes', i.e. 'English for special (or specific) purposes' (ESP), or 'English for professional purposes', as some prefer to call it. Inevitably, this tendency toward greater specialization in the teaching of English, together with the widespread adoption of modularization in the institutions of higher education, has had an enormous impact on Translation Studies, which has blossomed over the same period. General and literary translation remain key areas of these studies, but among students and teachers there is a perception that professional openings for translators are increasingly conditioned by market trends. International organizations and institutions, government departments and agencies, multinational corporations, import-export firms, the media, the film and tourist industries, information technology and the vast web of activities of every kind spun by the Internet all provide opportunities for translators. However, more often than not candidates for jobs in the field are expected to have received training in one or more specialist areas (commercial translation, medical translation, scientific and technical translation, legal translation, and so on).

The legal profession has played an undeniably significant role in the advances made in international cooperation and business. When money moves, lawyers move with it. But that is not all. The drafting and continual modification of international treaties such as those that underlie the European Union provide legal work with obvious multilingual implications. And contemporary protocols governing international cooperation in the clampdown against organized terrorism, drug-smuggling and the impunity of dictators depend to a very large extent on coordinating the efforts of administrative bodies, courts, police forces and lawyers, all of whom depend inevitably on the assistance of competent translators. At this early stage of the new millennium, legal translation is thus a basic requirement in both the public and private sectors of the international community. Further, this international community accords an important place to the English-speaking countries and their systems of law.

2. The aims of this book

Legal Translation Explained has been written with the above international context in mind. Our aims are to identify some of the common problems faced by translators of English legal texts into other languages and, where possible, to suggest ways round these difficulties. Chapters 7 and 8 in particular provide detailed guidance on linguistic questions raised by the possible translations of terms of English law.

Obviously the first stage in successful translation is to understand the source text fully. This is then followed by the production of a target text. In practice, many kinds of target texts are possible, ranging from a summary to a word-for-word gloss for philological purposes. In this book, however, we shall make the normalizing assumption that the translator is looking for an equivalent for each part of the source text, word for word, phrase for phrase or concept for concept. We shall also assume that the translation is to be of the 'domesticating' kind, designed to sound as natural as possible to the target-culture reader, even though there are clearly situations and clients that require alternatives such as the use of loan words or the invention of neologisms. For example, the phrase 'judgement for the plaintiff' is to be understood as conveying the idea that the court's decision favours the party who brought the suit, and the translation should be in the standard form of words that indicates that the plaintiff wins and/or the defendant loses. In Spanish this would give *fallo estimatorio de la demanda* or *fallo condenatorio*; in French we might say *jugement donnant gain de cause au demandeur*; and in German *ein Urteil im Sinne des Klägers*, among other possibilities. Throughout this book, such English terms are glossed either in English or in these other languages (more in Spanish, since that is the authors' immediate context). It should be clear, however, that there is rarely one-to-one correspondence in such matters, and that the one idea can often be expressed in several different terms or phrases in the one language. For reasons of space, our glosses cannot present this true variety; they should be taken as no more than suggestions or quick aids to comprehension. For further equivalents, students are advised to consult standard reference works in their language or, better, to locate official parallel texts (texts on the same topic and in the same genre, but in the language into which one is translating). Many good parallel texts can be located on the Internet, and in many cases they will be a more reliable guide to standard functional equivalents than will the simple terms given in this book.

The need to use the standard target-language terms means that translators must familiarize themselves with the somewhat arcane vocabulary of the law. This is more easily achieved when they know what to expect of legal texts in general. We suggest three steps in this process: the study of the legal systems, bottom-up linguistic processing, and top-down linguistic processing.

(a) The legal systems

Clearly there is no requirement for translators to be experts in the law, but equally obviously they need a good working knowledge of the main outlines of both the Anglo-American system of law and the legal system of the other language in play. In Chapters 3 and 4 we examine the leading features of the British system, particularly in relation to the three major sources of English law (common law, equity and statute law).

(b) Bottom-up linguistic processing

By this we mean the process of understanding a text starting with the smallest units of meaning (phonemes and morphemes) and gradually relating them to the units situated above them on the scale until the entire text has been compre-hended. From this point of view, full understanding of the text is the last link in a long chain of partial meanings gradually increasing in length and complexity as the decoding process advances. These issues are dealt with in this chapter and the following one.

(c) Top-down linguistic processing

This model is the corollary of the previous strategy of text interpretation. In this case, the process of understanding begins with the identification of large blocks of text viewed not as piecemeal chunks of meaning, but as instances of text types or genres – in our case, legal genres, such as contracts, judgements and statutes. The advantage of this approach is that translators can operate half-intuitively on the basis of pragmatic expectations as to the likely function and meaning of the text. The final version emerges from a gradual process of con-firmation or elimination until uncertainty ideally disappears. This model assumes that the native speaker of a language brings their previous knowledge and expe-rience to bear on the original text as a grid or framework into which the actual linguistic content is to be fitted. Familiarity with the legal genres provides the translator with a handy tool for rough-hewing the original, and the translation can then be shaped and refined on. A detailed study of this process will be found in Chapters 5 and 6.

3.   The leading features of legal English

Like its counterparts in other languages, legal English is a complex type of discourse. As we shall see in section 4, native speakers of English have recently reacted against the perceived obscurity of the language of the law. The 'Plain

English Campaign' has had some effect on the legislature and the judiciary, which have been forced to clarify and simplify legal language, or at least those parts of it that ordinary people need to understand in order to use the system to defend their rights and settle their differences. However, many lawyers continue to argue, with some justification, that technical accuracy is an essential prerequisite of good justice, and that if linguistic precision is watered down to suit the demands of an uncomprehending majority, legal certainty will all but disappear. There is a danger, in other words, of throwing out the baby with the bath-water. For this reason, it is unlikely that the 'Plain English Campaign' can go much further than ensuring that the court forms used by prospective litigants, or the style used by judges in explaining technical matters to the parties, are phrased as simply as is compatible with good law. Generally speaking, translators should expect to face some quite daunting linguistic tasks in preparing their versions of legal originals.

The following is an overview of some of the main features of legal English:

(a) Latinisms

Despite the native origins of many of its most characteristic terms, legal English has not entirely escaped the influence of Roman law and the Latin in which it was administered. It is not difficult to see why. In the first place, English law grew out of a system that evolved in the Middle Ages when Latin, bolstered by the power and prestige of the Roman Church, was the *lingua franca* throughout Europe for written texts and for intellectual exchanges. Secondly, Roman law was a coherent written system that, for centuries, had been developing over a wide area of Europe and had the force of an institution. It was inevitable, therefore, that some of its precepts and formulations should become enshrined in the texts and the professional speech of English lawgivers who shared a common culture with their colleagues elsewhere. Even today the famous tag *Nulla poena sine lege* ('No punishment except in accordance with the law') is found in the writings of British lawyers as well as in those of their Continental colleagues. Among hundreds of Latin phrases in common legal use, we have selected the following examples as a reminder that translators cannot always assume that Latin can be left untranslated. The decision as to whether to translate or not must be made in accordance with standard practice among the members of the legal community in the target-language system:

> writ of *fieri facias [fi. fa.]* ' *you may cause it to be done*' (*auto de ejecución de una sentencia*, perhaps *bref de fieri facias, Pfändungs-anordnung, Vollstreckungsbefehl*)
> *prima facie* "*at first sight*" (*a primera vista, légitime, beim ersten Anschein*)
> *bona fide* (*de buena fe, de bonne foi, in gutem Glauben*)

> *bona fide* error (*error involuntario, erreur de bonne foi, fahrlässiger Fehler*)
>
> *res judicata* (*res judicata, cosa juzgada, affaire jugée, rechtskräftig entschiedene Sache*)
>
> *restitutio in integrum* 'restoration to the original position' (*restitución o devolución íntegra, restitution, Wiedereinsetzung in den vorigen Stand, Wiederherstellung des ursprünglichen Zustands*).

In some cases English makes use indistinctly of either the original Latin phrase or a calque, e.g.:

> *onus probandi*/burden of proof (*carga de la prueba, charge de la preuve, Beweislast*)
>
> *mors civilis*/civil death (*muerte civil, mort civile, bürgerlicher Tod, Verlust der Rechtsfähigkeit*)

(b)   Terms of French or Norman origin

Here again the terms concerned are survivals from the earliest stages of development of English law. Following the successful Norman invasion of 1066, the new masters of the country brought their own customs and language with them and justice was administered in their native Norman French. Even the royal seal carries a French motto (*Dieu et mon droit*) as does the badge of the Knights of the Garter, the highest order of English knighthood (*Honni soit qui mal y pense*). Here are some examples:

> profit à prendre (*el usufructo, los objetos extraídos, los beneficios conseguidos, profit à prendre, Recht, die Nutzung aus einem fremdem Grundstück zu ziehen*)
>
> chose (*objeto, cosa, objet, propiedad personal, Sache*)
>
> feme sole: (*mujer soltera, femme non mariée , unverheiratete Frau*)
>
> lien (*derecho prendario, derecho de retención, embargo preventivo, droit de rétention, Pfandrecht*)
>
> on parole (*en libertad condicional, en liberté conditionnelle, gegen Ehrenwort freigelassen*)

As is well known, among the many forces that shaped the English language, the French influence after the Norman Conquest was paramount. As a result, thousands of English words are Old French or Norman in origin, and the rules of word-formation have been profoundly marked by this contact. Our list could therefore be wearyingly long, but for practical purposes it is worth noting that many legal terms ending in '-age' came into the language via French and bear the meaning of some specific service, right or duty, including the notions of indemnity, prize, reward, contribution, and so on. Here are some of the most common:

> salvage (*salvamento, premio por salvamento, prime de sauvetage, Bergung, Bergungsgut*)
> average (*avería, contribución proporcional al daño causado por la avería, averies, Havarie*)
> beaconage (system of beacons or markings at sea to guide navigation, payments made for the maintenance of the beacons)
> towage (*remolque, derechos por remolque, droits de remorquage, Schleppen, Schlepplohn*)
> pilotage (*practicaje, derechos de practicaje, droits de pilotage, Lotsen(dienst)*)
> demurrage[1] (*estadía, demora, penalización/gastos por estadía/demora, surestarie, Überliegezeit*)
> anchorage (*fondeadero, derechos de anclaje, derechos que se pagan por fondear, droits de mouillage, Ankern, Ankerplatz, Ankergebühr*)
> damage (*daño, desperfecto, perjuicio, dégâts, Schaden, Beschädigung*)
> damages (*[indemnización por] daños y perjuicios, dommages-intérêts, Schadensersatz*)

(c) Formal register and archaic diction

English legal language is no exception to the universal tendency toward stiffness and formality that marks this form of discourse, a tendency heightened by the unusual density of old-fashioned syntax and antiquated vocabulary. In part, this is due to the preservation of terms of art that were coined many centuries ago. As we have said, lawyers are reluctant to depart from these terms precisely because, having fallen out of ordinary use – if, indeed, they ever really belonged to it – they are less prone to semantic change and so have the advantage of clarity and certainty to those who understand them. It should also be remembered that, in the nature of legal process, references are constantly being made to very old texts, such as judicial decisions, wills, contracts or venerable textbook definitions, which are quoted in support of legal arguments about the continuing validity of rules, doctrine or precedents.

Naturally enough, the syntax of contemporary judgements, deeds and statutes, though highly formal, is not strictly speaking archaic. In texts of these kinds translators will not find grammatical dinosaurs like the old '-th' ending of verbs in the third person singular of the present tense, nor the liberal sprinkling

---

[1] Compare 'demurrer' (a pleading that accepts the opponent's point but denies that it is relevant to the argument) and the formal verb 'demur' (a pleading that accepts the opponent's point but denies that it is relevant to the argument), e.g. 'The judge demurred to that part of counsel's argument'. Originally from Fr. *demourer* (to remain, to stay, to spend time).

of 'doth', 'does' or 'did' preceding the infinitive which, in older English, was a regular, non-emphatic alternative to the simple present and past. But they must expect occasionally to have to deal with these and other syntactic oddities when the text for translation quotes passages from older writers. For example, the following is an extract from a deed: "This indenture made the ninth day of May 1887... *witnesseth* that..." (attests or affirms that...). Even nowadays we occasionally come across antique-sounding phrases and constructions like "an action *sounding in* damages" (i.e. one brought by an unpaid creditor for damages rather than simply to recover the debt); or "it does not *lie in the defendant's mouth* to say that..." (the defendant does not have the competence or right to say that...); or, as an alternative to the preceding phrase, "the defendant *cannot be heard to say*...". It is extremely unlikely that phrases of this type would now be heard outside of a courtroom, though some of them were once common enough.

Along the same lines, Garner (1987) lists lexical choices marking the stiff formality, or downright pedantry, of some members of the legal profession. Some insist on using the longer rather than the shorter word, or the older rather than the newer, e.g. 'imbibe' rather than 'drink', 'inquire' instead of 'ask', 'peruse' in preference to 'read', 'forthwith' as an alternative to 'right away', 'at once' or 'immediately', and so on. Few people nowadays would see the point of preferring 'impugn' to 'challenge' in the sentence 'An attempt was made to *impugn* the validity of a private Act of Parliament'. It is hard not to see a certain amount of smugness, sexism or old-school-tie exclusiveness in the habit of judges who refer to their judicial colleagues of the same rank as 'brethren' or 'brother judges'. In such cases it is very unlikely that other languages will possess a matching pair or a precise means of striking the equivalent note. If this is so, translators are perfectly entitled to act as though the term used had been the standard one, since all that will be missing from their versions will be the rather embarrassing and wholly meaningless tone of self-satisfaction.

However, markers of politeness and respect are part of every language, and we are very far from holding that translators are exempt from the rules of social etiquette or that they are free to coarsen the tone of highly formal originals. The contrary is true, but the sensible tactic would appear to be to follow the rules of register in situations that demand courtesy and deference. In the superior courts, British judges refer to their fellows as 'my learned friend' or, in the House of Lords, 'my noble and learned colleague' and, collectively, 'your Lordships'. Spanish judges are normally called *su señoría*, whatever court they are sitting in, and they might well refer to their colleagues as *mi docto colega* or address them collectively as *sus señorías*; and these, we would argue, are neither inaccurate nor socially absurd equivalents to the English terms. What the translator should not do is promote non-British judges to the ranks of the British aristocracy in translating into English, nor lower the register to street levels when translating out of it. Similarly, usable equivalents can almost certainly be found for the solemnity with which counsel request permission to speak by using phrases like 'With your Lordship's permission' or 'If it please the court' (*con la venia, si Monsieur le juge permet, Mit der Erlaubnis des Gerichts*).

(d) Archaic adverbs and prepositional phrases

A special case of fossilized language is the persistence in legal English of compound adverbs based on the simple deictics 'here', 'there', 'where' and so on, often referring to the text or document in which they appear or to one under discussion. Common examples include the following:

> hereinafter (*in what follows, below, en adelante, en lo sucesivo, más abajo, ci-après, nachstehend, im nachstehend, im folgenden*)
> thereunder (*by virtue of which, subsequently, below, en virtud del mismo, selon lequel, en-dessous, unten, unter, nachstehend*)
> hereby (*as a result of this, por la presente, par la présente, hiermit*)
> thereby (*por ello, por cuyo motivo, de ce fait, dadurch*)
> whereby (*because of which, por donde, por lo cual, grâce auquel, selon lequel, par le fait que,* perhaps *mit dem, mit dessen*)
> thereunto (*in the document or place referred to, al mismo, al documento aludido, hasta dicho lugar,* perhaps *dans le document cité, bereits genannt/erwähnt*)

A similarly archaic or solemn tone is achieved by the use of prepositional phrases like those listed below, which abound in legal texts:

> pursuant to (*en cumplimiento de, conformément à, gemäss, zufolge, im Sinne von*)
> without prejudice to (*sin perjuicio de, sans préjudice de, ohne Schaden für*)
> subject to (*sin perjuicio de lo dispuesto en, sous réserve de, unterworfen, abhängig von*)
> at the motion/instance of (*a propuesta de, sur la demande de, auf Veranlassung von*)
> notwithstanding (*no obstante, a pesar de, ce nonobstant, ungeachtet, unbeschadet, trotz, abweichend von*)

(e) Redundancy ('doublets' and 'triplets')

The well-known fastidiousness of lawyers frequently takes the form of reduplication, in which two, and sometimes three near synonyms are combined. In some cases, translators may find similar combinations ready to hand in their own languages. Otherwise, they will have to decide whether, on the whole, the English expression implies a genuine distinction, in which case a fairly literal rendering seems appropriate, or an emphasis, in which case the addition of an adjective or adverb conveying the notion of generality could well be the best solution. For example, from the list below, 'without let or hindrance' might be translated as though the original said something like 'without any impediment whatsoever', whilst 'null and void' could be rendered as 'utterly void, void *ab initio*', etc. There is, of course, the possibility that the original phrase contains a mere tautology exhibiting neither subtlety nor rhetorical aptness, i.e. what is sometimes called ' a distinction without a difference'. If this is the translator's conclusion, there would seem to be two options open: silent simplification by dropping the less general term, or simple reproduction. Lawyers, after all, are not always breathtakingly compelling speakers or writers, and it is likely that most languages would tolerate literal renderings of rather weak pairings like 'final and conclusive', even if conscious stylists would not applaud them. On the other hand, the doublet 'alter and change' is a candidate for simplification to the equivalent of 'alter' or, alternatively, to some such treatment as 'alter in any way'. In view of the considerable variety of possible solutions, we shall leave it to readers to make up their own minds about the best way of dealing with the following common examples:

false and untrue	have and hold	full, true and correct
sole and exclusive	each and every	rest, residue and remainder
request and require	without let or hindrance	give, devise and bequeath
seriously and gravely	fit and proper	nominate, constitute and appoint
alter and change	mind and memory	cancel, annul and set aside
final and conclusive	full and complete	
null and void	fair and equitable	
known and distinguished as	aid and abet	
force and effect	aid and comfort	
last will and testament	goods and chattels	

(f) Frequency of performative verbs

In speech act theory, performative utterances are those by which the state of affairs expressed by the words comes into being, or those that commit the speaker to carrying out or performing the actions expressed by the words (Austin 1962). For instance, when a court gives judgement on an issue, the decision comes into effect through the very act of pronouncing the operative words, or signing and delivering the document that contains them. Performative verbs are those that constitute the nucleus of such statements or declarations. The number of such verbs in a given language is necessarily quite small, but given the binding nature of legal relationships and judicial decisions, verbs of this type are used particularly frequently in legal texts and contexts.

Among the most common performative verbs are 'agree', 'admit' (recognize, allow), 'pronounce' (declare), 'uphold' (maintain, affirm), 'promise', 'undertake' (contract or commit oneself), 'swear' (promise), 'affirm', 'certify', 'overrule' (disallow) and so on. The simple verb 'do' has a performative function – as well as legal connotations – when it is uttered by the spouses at the marriage ceremony in answer to the question, 'Do you, X, take Y to be your lawful wedded wife/husband...?' Here are some common legal performatives:

> Both parties to the contract hereby *agree* to the following conditions....
> The Board of Trustees does hereby *confer* upon John Smith the degree of...
> An Act to *amend*...
> *Be it enacted*...
> I hereby solemnly *swear* to tell the truth, the whole truth and nothing but the truth.

Performative verbs can also appear in the past tense, although they are no longer truly performing the operation in such cases:

> The doctor *pronounced* the victim dead at the scene.
> The Court of Appeal so *held* when dismissing an appeal by the defendant.

There are many more examples of performative verbs in Chapter 4, where we deal with legal genres such as contracts, powers of attorney and wills.

(g) Changing registers: Euphemisms and contemporary colloquialism

Legal language may define a firearm (*arma de fuego, arme à feu, Schusswaffe*) as 'a lethal barrelled weapon of any description from which any shot, bullet or other missile can be discharged'. In an elaborately formal discourse type like this the use of euphemisms is almost inevitable, especially in those areas of law concerned with the harsher or more unsavoury aspects of criminal and other unlawful activity. And in the traditionally staid or puritanical moral climate of the English-speaking countries, linguistic reticence is particularly noticeable, as one would expect, in the drafting (writing) of the laws dealing with sexual offences. There are, for example, a number of offences of 'indecency', but while most people would probably agree that this general term is formal rather than actually euphemistic, the same cannot be said of the standard definitions of 'indecent exposure' or 'gross indecency'.

'Indecent exposure' is almost always committed by a man who exposes what is technically called 'his person' in a public place. One can think of a number of bad reasons, but no good ones, why 'person' is used here instead of 'penis'. Certainly, in more forthright jurisdictions, that or 'sexual organs' would be the term chosen, and translators untrammelled by the coyness that affects the British legislators could certainly plump for either of them. No doubt some translators will find similar restraints operating in their own languages, but it is likely that, in at least some cases, an equivalent like 'exhibitionism' will be available as the name of the act.

The term 'gross indecency' is even more clearly euphemistic, since it refers to explicit sexual acts, including 'buggery' (anal penetration) performed in public places. Literal translation of the term is unlikely to suggest this, so that, depending on the linguistic habits of the target audience, translators may have to be guided by the definition of the offence rather than the mere name. We are aware that there are theorists who insist that legal terms of art must be translated as literally as possible and that it is not the business of the translator to explain the implications of the source language terms to the new audience. However, it is our view that this seemingly high-minded restriction can all too easily become an excuse for unprofessional indifference to the implications for recipients of the actual words used. The intended audience surely has a right to expect the translator to avoid vagueness and misleading suggestion. And in any case there is no better justification for providing muddled or confusing versions of the terms we are discussing than there would be in the case of 'simpler' or more familiar offences like fraud (*estafa, fraude, Betrug*), theft (*robo, vol, Diebstahl*), burglary (*robo con escalo, vol avec effraction, Einbruch[sdiebstahl]*) or murder (*asesinato, meutre, Mord*).

A euphemism that tends to amuse non-English-speaking students of legal translation is the solemn announcement following the discovery of a crime (often a murder) that 'a man is assisting police with their enquiries'. Of course there are excellent procedural reasons for choosing this form of words, and it would be wrong to sneer at any means used to protect the reputation of the innocent or to uphold the democratic principle of the presumption of innocence. But there is no escaping the linguistic fact that literal renderings of this phrase into other languages would most probably lead the audience to believe that Sherlock Holmes had come again, or that Scotland Yard had fallen on hard days and had to call upon the services of members of the general public to help solve its cases. Once again, the translator would be strongly advised to follow the natural habits of the target audience and go with a version indicating that 'police are interrogating a suspect', or words to that effect.

Euphemism of a different kind is found in traditional and rather ornate expressions like the following, all of which invoke royal or divine intervention to describe what are essentially mundane though no doubt unfortunate situations:

Detention during Her Majesty's pleasure. Phrase used to mean detention for an indefinite period; in the case of adults found 'not guilty by reason of insanity', detention is in an approved psychiatric hospital; for persons below the age of 18 found guilty of murder, detention is in a young offender institution. The expression is also euphemistic because of the use of the milder word 'detain/detention' in preference to 'imprison/imprisonment' or 'confine/confinement'.

Act of God (*caso fortuito o de fuerza mayor, force majeure, höhere Gewalt*). Expression most often found in contract law and insurance cases to refer to a natural disaster, or to a calamity attributable to the forces of nature, that could neither have been foreseen nor guarded against. If found proved in the judgement, it destroys the claim. The piety of the phrase is likely to be of little consolation to the losing claimant.

Standing mute by visitation of God. Another case in which a cloak of supposedly religious reverence is thrown over the accused's physical or mental incapacity to answer the charge. The phrase is used when the accused is refusing to plead to the charge and the jury must decide whether he or she is 'mute of malice', i.e. out of sheer contumacy, or 'by visitation of God', i.e. through some physical or mental impairment of his or her faculties. The jury, in other words, has to decide whether the prisoner is fit or unfit to plead

However, no form of discourse can feed off the past alone, and translators will come across occasional signs of a more contemporary idiom creeping into both the speech and the writings of lawyers. Examples of this newer note follow. They are all to be found in the authoritative Blackstone (Murphy et al. 1998), a pillar of the establishment by no means given to frivolity. It will be noticed that some of these new or relatively new terms of current English law are not just informal but actually on the borderline between familiar colloquialism and slang – a sign, perhaps, that the streetwise tones of the marketplace are starting to make inroads into the patrician accents of the courtrooms:

Hacking (*piratería informática, piratage informatique, unerlaubtes Eindringen in Datenfernübertragungsnetze*). Often malicious. Like many terms relating to information technology, frequently found untranslated in many languages.

Insider trading (*delito de iniciados, tráfico con información privilegiada,* *délit d'initié, Insider-Geschäft, illegaler Aktienhandel auf Grund inner-betrieblicher Informationen*). Stock-exchange term originally, although the idea of an 'inside job' has been long familiar to detectives.

Money laundering (*blanqueo de dinero, blanchissage d'argent, Geldwäsche*). The everyday metaphor makes this an obvious candidate for literal translation, at the translator's discretion.

Mugging (*atraco, tirón, robo callejero con amenazas y agresiones, vol à l'arraché, Raubüberfall*). A term now familiar in magistrates' courts and which has many counterparts in earlier stages of British society. Most contemporary target-language terms for street attacks involving small-time robbery will serve the purpose.

Rogue (*pícaro, bribón, pillo, delincuente, impostor, fripon, Gauner*). As a noun, a slightly Victorian term, still used by some judges. In attributive use, probably influenced by 'rogue elephant' it is now found in 'rogue trader' (*operador fraudulento en Bolsa, opérateur véreux, Gauner der Wertpapierhändler,* in the case of Nick Leeson).

Stalking (*acoso, acecho, persecución obsesiva o psicopática, traque, Stalking*). Term describing a peculiarly contemporary form of neurotic or psychopathic behaviour, usually that of a male who pesters a female victim by following her about, communicating with her against her will and terrorizing her with unwanted attentions or veiled threats. Now a recognized offence, though translators should distinguish it from more common forms of sexual harassment.

Tip-off (*chivatazo, dénonciation, Warnung, Hinweis*). Once thieves' cant and police slang, this term has now found its way into judges' handbooks.

4. 'Legalese' and 'The Plain English Campaign'

So far we have been examining some of the specialist terms actually used by lawyers in the course of business. But in dealing with texts concerned with court proceedings translators will often face a considerable mixture of styles and registers. There is the legalese of the professional lawyers, the everyday language of lay witnesses and litigants, the slang of the police and the criminal underworld and the often extremely technical jargon of the reports and testimony of expert witnesses who may be doctors, surgeons, forensic pathologists, bankers, brokers, architects, builders, technicians, engineers or members of any profession whatever, depending on the facts of the case. In other words, by no means every term in a legal text for translation belongs to the law itself, and in fact it is often the technical issues at stake that give translators most trouble.

  The technicalities of legal vocabulary present a serious challenge to the translator or interpreter, while the tortuous syntax and the antiquated diction favoured by many lawyers are equally baffling to those unfamiliar with forensic method. It is arguable that a justice system genuinely concerned to safeguard ordinary people's rights should find some means of administering the law in a language that those people can understand, and this is precisely the aim of the pressure groups and lawyers who are behind the 'Plain English Campaign'.

Nevertheless, it is doubtful whether this attempt at simplification can ever be more than a cosmetic operation designed to reassure the general public. In the first place lawyers, like members of any other profession, are trained in the mysteries of their trade and tend to perpetuate the language used by their predecessors and teachers before them. Second, the scientific basis of the law is enshrined in the texts of the past (statutes, procedural rules, guidelines, decided cases, judgements, pleadings, counsel's arguments, and so on) and to ask contemporary lawyers to write and speak as if these texts had never been is as absurd as asking a philologist to strike out of their vocabulary any term no longer current after, say, 1980. We would not thank our solicitors for fighting with one hand tied behind their backs while they are representing our interests. Third, the most cogent reason given by lawyers who stress the impossibility of making wholesale changes to traditional terminology is that the great advantage of the terms to which exception is most often taken is precisely that they are clear and precise. The more precise and unambiguous the terms, they argue, the greater the degree of legal certainty. And it is legal certainty that enables courts to protect the rights of ordinary citizens and therefore provides the best guarantee that justice will be done in the end.

On the other hand, it would certainly not be impossible for lawyers to improve and simplify their syntax, which is proverbially daunting and obscure. Here, the unwillingness of lawyers to pare down their rhetoric, trim their grammar and lighten up their style has more to do with tactics than technique. To put it bluntly, and somewhat cynically, it is well worth their while to keep their clients in the dark. As Jonathan Swift put it long ago, "If my Neighbour hath a mind to my Cow, he hireth a Lawyer to prove he should have it of me". Clearly if the neighbour thought he could convincingly argue his own case, he would save himself the expense of the lawyer's fee and, with luck, get my cow into the bargain. Moreover, lawyers themselves recognize that their language is sometimes not far short of mystification and that it involves them in a power game. The following comment by an author on the subject is of particular interest to legal translators:

> The need to develop the 'special' skills of a lawyer has the effect of excluding non-lawyers from entering into legal discourse, with, it is argued, consequent limits upon the ability of citizens to gain access to justice

[...]. Getting past the camouflage is one of the major problems lawyers face in reaching an accurate understanding of a foreign legal system. (Holland 1991:88-9).

5.   The classification of legal vocabulary

Probably the greatest single difficulty encountered initially by legal translators is the unfamiliarity of the vocabulary characteristic of this type of discourse. Unfortunately there is no way round this problem except the deliberate process of learning. There is no magic wand one can wave. Nevertheless, it is possible to find some semblance of system in the legal lexicon, and this is the point of the present introductory section. Fuller discussion of the points raised here will be found in Chapter 7, which deals with problems of translation as they relate to vocabulary.

As a first step, the lexical items found in any given language can be divided into two groups: symbolic (or representational) items and functional items. The latter type consists of grammatical words or phrases that have no direct referents either in reality or in the universe of concepts, but which serve to bind together and order those that do. Examples from the legal sphere are 'subject to', 'inasmuch as', 'hereinafter', 'whereas', 'concerning', 'under' and 'in view of'. Deictics, articles, auxiliaries, modals and other purely syntactic and morphological markers also belong with this group, as do other more complex units like 'unless otherwise stated', 'as in section 2 above', 'in accordance with order 14' and similar phrases (Harris 1997).

The symbolic or representational group, on the other hand, includes all the terms that refer to things or ideas found in the world of reality, physical or mental. Legal terms of this type may be one-word units ('tort', 'court', 'law', 'right', 'adjudge', 'contract', 'misrepresentation', 'guilty', 'liable', etc.) or compound units ('serve proceedings', 'bring in a verdict', 'evidence in rebuttal' 'tenant from year to year', 'statute-barred claims', 'beyond reasonable doubt', and many others). This group may be further subdivided into three subgroups for any given specialist lexicon: purely technical vocabulary, semi-technical vocabulary, and shared, common or 'unmarked' vocabulary. Let us briefly examine each of these groups in turn.

(a)   Purely technical terms

For our purposes, technical terms are those that are found exclusively in the legal sphere and have no application outside it. Examples include 'barrister', 'counsel' when used as an uncountable noun unaccompanied by an article, 'solicitor', 'estoppel', 'mortage', 'breach of official duty', 'serve proceedings', 'refuse leave to appeal', 'bring an action', and so on.[2] Lexical units of this type are distinguished from the others in that they are monosemic and have long remained semantically stable within their particular field of application. For the same reasons, they may be said to be the least troublesome terms for a translator to deal with. Arguments may arise about the best way of translating 'estoppel', 'liferent' or 'usufruct', but there can be no dispute about their meanings or their purely legal function. On the other hand, they are crucial terms in the contexts in which they occur, since the rest of the text cannot be dealt with until they have been understood and catered for.

Because these terms are identified so intimately with the system that spawned them, some commentators believe they are true terms of art and cannot be translated, but only adapted. It is certainly true that the jury system, for instance, is a native English growth that has later been adopted by other legal systems, sometimes with the name included. Similarly, the concept of 'tort' has made itself known to non-English jurists under a variety of names (*agravio extracontractual, derecho de daños, préjudice, unerlaubte Handlung*, etc.). And 'estoppel' and 'trust' are often left untranslated in essays on comparative law by those who are either unsure of their scope, reluctant to accept the full equivalence of *doctrina de los actos propios, Rechtsverwirkung* and *fideicomiso, fidéicommis, Treuhandverhältnis* or determined not to relinquish the snob value of the eye-catching anglicism. Whatever decision the translator makes, or is forced to make, there is no question that the term in question is recognized as a full-blown legalism that has to be assimilated and dealt with in the translation.

(b) Semi-technical or mixed terms

This second group consists of words and phrases from the common stock that have acquired additional meanings by a process of analogy in the specialist context of legal activity. Such terms are therefore polysemic, unlike those belonging to the first group. For the translator, terms belonging to this group are more difficult to recognize and assimilate than wholly technical terms. For a start, they are much more numerous and their number is constantly growing as the law changes to meet the developing needs of society. Moreover, they are semantically more complex, involving the translator in a wider range of choices, since group-one words in one language may be translatable by group-two terms in another (e.g. the term 'estoppel' mentioned in the preceding paragraph). Even without that difficulty, translators dealing with terms of this kind face

---

[2] 'barrister' *(abogado, avocat)*, 'counsel' *(abogado, letrado)*, 'solicitor' *(representante legal, approx. procurador)*, 'estoppel' *(doctrina de los actos propios)*, 'mortage' *(hipoteca)*, 'breach of official duty' *(prevaricación)*, 'serve proceedings' *(notificar la incoación de la demanda, emplazar al demandado)*, 'refuse leave to appeal' *(inadmitir un recurso)*, 'bring an action' *(ejercitar una acción)*.

the familiar dilemma raised by connotation, ambiguity, partial synonymy and the fact that the precise nuance is often context-dependent. An example is the word 'issue' found in the following sentences:

(a)   'The testator died without *issue*', i.e. 'offspring, children' (*descendencia, descendence en ligne directe, Nachkommen*).

(b)   'The parties could not agree on the *issue*', i.e. 'disputed point' (*cuestión, question, Streitpunkt*).

(c)   'The passport was *issued* by the Liverpool office', i.e. 'give out' (*expedir, délivrer, herausgeben*).

(d)   'Parties must wait for process to *issue* from the court', i.e. 'be served' (*notificarse,*perhaps *être notifié, bekanntgeben*).

(c)   Everyday vocabulary frequently found in legal texts

This third group, which is naturally the most numerous, consists of terms in general use that are regularly found in legal texts but, unlike the previous group, have neither lost their everyday meanings nor acquired others by contact with the specialist medium. Given the generality of this definition, it is rather difficult to provide telling examples, since virtually any non-technical term will do. However, on the basis of relative frequency of occurrence, the point may be illustrated by terms such as 'subject-matter', as in 'the *subject-matter* of the contract', 'paragraph', as in 'Section 2, subsection 12, *paragraph* (b) of the Act', or 'summarize', as in 'The judge *summarized* the facts of the case'. It may occasionally happen, as with the previous group, that a group-three word is best translated by a group-one or group-two equivalent as a matter of traditional usage, e.g. English 'system' will normally be Spanish *sistema*, but 'legal system' is best rendered as *ordenamiento jurídico*. In this case, *sistema legal* would not be incorrect, but the expected term is the group-one *ordenamiento*.

6.   Some leading features of the morphology and syntax of legal English

For the translator, the second major source of difficulty in legal English is the peculiarity of its morphology and syntax. Our aim in this section is simply to draw attention to some of the most significant grammatical features of the type. In Chapter 8 we shall discuss the issue more fully and provide some pointers to the solution of particular translation problems.

(a)   Unusually long sentences

One section of the British Drug Trafficking Act is a single highly complex sentence of over 250 words in length. It is typical of the syntax of British statutes both in this and in the complexity of its layout, with multiple subordination and postponement of the main verb until very late in the sentence. Writers report similar findings after analysis of pleadings and private law documents like leases and contracts. By contrast, Continental law statutes tend to be made up of much shorter sentences with far fewer members and hence a more predictable syntactic development. European private law documents, however, are at least as complex as their British counterparts. For instance, notarized powers of attorney as produced by Spanish, French and Italian authors are notoriously boiler-plated and generally ill-punctuated, as are pleadings and other pre-trial documents drafted by lawyers in these languages. Translators of these texts must therefore choose between retaining the format (at the risk of incomprehensibility or added ambiguity) and undertaking vigorous breakdown of inconveniently long sentences into their component parts prior to translation. Whichever course is taken, target audience expectations should clearly be paramount for the translator.

(b) The anfractuosity of English legal syntax

Our example from the Drug Trafficking Act illustrates another leading feature of the morphology of legal English, namely the abundance of restrictive connectors. As we shall see more fully in Chapter 8, this density of subordination and parenthetic restriction is particularly frequent in the texts of laws and of contracts, and gives them their characteristic air of complexity (Bhatia 1993:116). For the moment, we shall simply point out that the following are among the commonest conjunctions and prepositional phrases of this type found in legal English: 'notwithstanding', 'under', 'subject to', 'having regard to', 'relating to', 'on', 'pursuant to', 'in order to', 'in accordance with', 'whereas', and many more.[3] Garner (1991) has this feature in mind when he remarks on the 'anfractuosity' of English legal style.

(c) Abundant use of the passive voice

This is a pet hate of proponents of 'Plain English' but need not trouble the translator. Though it is undoubtedly true that one common effect of the passive mood is to suppress the identity of the agent responsible for the performance of

---

[3] 'notwithstanding' *(pese a, no obstante, sin embargo de)*, 'under' *(a tenor de lo dispuesto en, conforme a, en virtud de, de conformidad con, de acuerdo con, al amparo de, según)*, 'subject to' *(salvo, sin perjuicio de)*, 'having regard to' *(visto, habida cuenta de, considerando)*, 'relating to' *(relativo a, en relación con, en lo que atañe a)*, 'on' *(respecto de, relativo a)*, 'pursuant to' *(en cumplimiento de, en virtud de, a tenor de lo dispuesto en)*, 'in order to' *(para, con el fin de, a fin de que)*, 'in accordance with' *(de acuerdo a/con, siguiendo instrucciones de, en virtud de, de conformidad con)*, 'whereas' *(considerando que)*.

the act, this is often exactly the point of the construction, e.g. when the import
of the statement is universal ('No submissions [by any party] *will be accepted*
after *the date stated*') or when the implied subject is too obvious to need stating
('Payment *must be made* within seven days' or 'The accused *was found guilty*').
Within target-language norms, it is usually easy to preserve the equivalent effect in translation, thus keeping the stress on the action, rule or decision rather
than on the personality of the doer. Nevertheless, the Securities Exchange
Commission (SEC) is one example of an official body that is sensitive to the
appearance of obscurity that over-use of the passive can convey. A good example of how clarity of statement can be achieved by the switch from passive to
active, and from impersonal to personal (second-person address directed at the
reader) is provided by the following case of rewriting of one of the sentences in
a prospectus:

> **(Old version):** No person has been authorized to give any information
> or make any representation other than those contained or incorporated
> by reference in this joint proxy statement/prospectus, and, if given or
> made, such information or representation must not be relied upon as hav-
> ing been authorized.

> **(New version):** You should rely only on the information contained in
> this document or that we have referred you to. We have not authorized
> anyone to provide you with information that is different.

(d) Conditionals and hypothetical formulations

In texts like statutes, contracts and handbooks containing procedural rules, many
possible situations, factual scenarios and exceptions must be provided for. The
result is that the language in which they are written, and legal language generally, is unusually rich in syntactic indicators of condition and hypothesis, which
may be positive ('if', 'when', 'where', 'whenever', 'wherever', 'provided that',
'in the event that/of', 'assuming that', 'so long as', 'should' and many others)
or negative ('unless', 'failing', 'should... not...', 'except as/where/if', 'but for',
and so on). Translators should be especially vigilant to ensure that they deal
adequately with complex conditions, which may include double or triple hy-
potheses and mix positive with negative possibilities, as in the following passage:

> *Where either party fails to perform* their side of the bargain, then, *sub-
> ject to clause 15* above, *if notice of non-performance is given* in writing
> by the injured party within seven days, or, *in the event that communica-
> tion is impossible* until the ship reaches a port of call, as soon thereafter
> as is practically possible, the injured party shall be entitled to treat the
> contract as discharged *except as otherwise provided* in this contract.

(e)   The simple syntax of plain judicial narrative

We have seen that the syntax of statutes, contracts and pleadings can be extremely dense and complex. However, the opposite style of discourse is commonly found in the judicial summary of the particular facts of a case. Here, the chosen style is commonly plain to the point of baldness and the dominant structure is paratactic, in keeping with the aim of this part of the text, which is to lay out simply and clearly the issues on which the judgement depends.

Odd though it may seem, this forthright form of English writing may present difficulties for the translator, whose language may not tolerate the quickfire staccato of 'subject+verb+object', the dearth of connectors and the reiterative use of pronouns and deictics natural in everyday English. In other words, while complex sentences may need breaking down for translation, simple sentences may need building up (we shall deal more fully with this issue in Chapter 8). An instance of the problem is the following passage from the 'facts as found' section of a judgement. We have used italics for the subjects of each of the sentences, and the repeated references to 'the ship' and 'she', to draw attention to the possible need for translators to supply connectors and perhaps adjust the anaphoric and cataphoric layout of the original in their versions:

> HIS LORDSHIP said that *M-Vatan* was an ultra-large crude carrier 370 metres in length and 64 metres in beam. *She* was probably the largest *ship* ever salved. In July 1985 *she* was on charter to the National Iranian Tanker Co, engaged on a shuttle service between the oil loading terminal at Kharg Island and Sirri Island. On July 9 *she* was struck by a missile which caused a fire. *The ship* was almost fully laden with crude oil owned by the National Iranian Oil Co (NIOC). *The explosion* blew a large hole in the *ship*'s side. Burning oil flowed out of *the ship*. *The salvors' tug*, Salveritas, was at anchor about 48 miles from the casualty. *The services rendered* involved fire-fighting and 200 miles' towage to anchorage off Sirri Island.

(f)   Active and passive parties in legal relationships: the suffixes -er (-or) and -ee

Most legal activity is concerned with the creation, exercise and extinction of rights and with disputes concerning those rights, and in most of these situations there are two parties. In criminal cases the two parties are the state (or the Crown, in British practice) and the accused, or the prosecution and the defence. In civil proceedings they are the plaintiff (or claimant) and the defendant, or the applicant (or petitioner) and the respondent, and on appeal they are the appellant and the respondent (or, less usually, the appellee). In proceedings the court adjudicates between the rival claims of the two sides or adversaries. Hence the generic name of 'adversarial procedure' for this state of affairs, rather than the 'inquisitorial procedure' characteristic of the examining magistrate or 'investigating judge' (*juez de instrucción, juge d'instruction, Untersuchungsrichter*) found in Continental criminal law.

On the other hand, a feature of legal relationships created at the will of the parties is the use of the suffixes '-er' (or '-or') and '-ee' added to the appropriate verb to form the names, respectively, of the active and the passive parties. For example, the party who *grants* a right is the 'grantor' and the person who receives it is the 'grantee'. In contracts, where each party both gives and receives a promise, both parties are 'promisor' and 'promisee' vis-à-vis their opposite number. And the same holds true of verbs like 'lease' ('lessor'/'lessee') 'bail' ('bailor'/'bailee'), 'mortgage' ('mortgagor'/'mortgagee'), 'license' ('licensor'/'licensee'), 'assign' ('assignor' /'assignee') and 'draw' ('drawer'/ 'drawee').[4]

However, this is not an automatic feature of word-formation. For one thing, care sometimes has to be taken with the semantics of the active and passive senses. For instance, in the case of 'mortgage', the verb means 'to offer property as security for the repayment of a loan', so that the 'mortgagor' is the debtor and the 'mortgagee' the creditor, and not the other way round. Moreover, there are cases where one of the pair is in common use while its fellow is not: 'payee', for instance, is more often matched with 'drawee' than with 'payer'; the counterpart of 'debtor' is 'creditor' rather than 'debtee'; 'licensing body' and 'rightholder' are more common than 'licenser/licensor', and so on.

---

[4] 'grantor' *(mandante)*, 'grantee' *(mandatario)*
'promisor' *(prometiente)*, 'promisee' *(receptor de una promesa)*
'lessor' *(arrendador)*, 'lessee' *(arrendatario)*
'bailor' *(depositante)*, 'bailee' *(depositario)*
'mortgagor' *(deudor hipotecario)*, 'mortgagee' *(acreedor hipotecario)*
'licensor' *(cedente, titular del derecho)*, 'licensee' *(cesionario, derechohabiente, titular de la licencia)*
'assignor' *(cedente)*, 'assignee' *(cesionario, derechohabiente)*
'drawer' *(librador, girador)*, 'drawee' *(librado, girado)*.

2. Equivalence and Interpretation

1. The question of equivalence in Translation Studies

Translation Studies has set itself the task of building models aimed at explaining what goes on during the process of translation. A very basic model of this process was suggested in Chapter 1 above. Put at its most embarrassingly simple, this consists of the following three stages:

1) A thorough understanding of the ideas of the source text and the means by which these ideas have been achieved and expressed;

2) The attempt to express these ideas in linguistically equivalent terms in the target language;

3) The proviso that, other things being equal, the criterion of 'naturalness' of target-language expression is to preside over any other in attaining the equivalence referred to in stage (2), 'naturalness' being understood to mean the avoidance of strain or the forcing of sense or syntax.

We are aware that this may sound simplistic amid the sophistications of current theories of translation, and that questions of equivalence are especially problematic in the field of legal translation. For obvious reasons, the conceptual analysis of equivalence (Rabadán 1991) has tended to vary with the theories prevalent, or fashionable, at different stages of linguistic studies. Thus, for Nida (1975), semantic equivalence is an essential prerequisite for effective translation. More recently, linguistic pragmatics has added new variables to the study of the phenomenon of equivalence, notably the idea of contextualized meaning (Alcaraz 1996:104). For this school, semantics (and hence syntactic choices) includes what is implied, assumed or tacitly understood by those involved in the context of utterance. For our purposes, this is clearly helpful in the translation of oral genres like the examination of witnesses and is relevant to our understanding of the sensitive issue of 'leading questions' during this process. Another useful analytical tool developed by the proponents of linguistic pragmatics is the idea of genre or text-type, which in our view can be of substantial help to the translator (see Chapter 5 below).

Even if one denies translators any truly creative role in text production, they must be regarded as (saving mishaps) expert wielders of words, cunning artisans who devise, exploit and perfect techniques of adaptation and adjustment in their quest for elusive, and no doubt occasionally illusory equivalents. For the practicalities of legal, or indeed of any form of translation, we have found much that is helpful in the techniques described by Vázquez Ayora (1977) (cf. Fawcett

1997). Discussion and application of these techniques, particularly transposition, modulation and expansion, will be found in Chapter 8.

2. Judges and translators. Interpretation and construction. The elusiveness of meaning

Words strain,
Crack and sometimes break under the burden,
Under the tension, slip, slide, perish,
Decay with imprecision, will not stay in place,
Will not stay still.

                    T.S. Eliot: *Four Quartets*, 'Burnt Norton', V

Like translators, all practising lawyers, and judges most specifically, are professionally engaged in the task of interpreting the meaning of texts, and of particular words in particular texts. To interpret, in general, is to assign a meaning to a word, phrase, clause, sentence or utterance, and, where two or more meanings are possible, either to decide between them or to declare the utterance indeterminably ambiguous. For the translator, the purpose of interpretation is to decide on the closest possible linguistic equivalent in the target language, while for the judge it is to match up the resulting propositions against the definitions established in existing law. The difference, of course, is that the translator's work is over once the semantic hurdle has been negotiated, whereas the judge must go on to apply the results of the linguistic analysis and announce a decision in accordance with the rules and principles of law.

We are not talking here only of so-called 'legal subtleties', though they come into it. For example, a court case came down to the judge's decision that the general sense of the expression 'unmarried' is 'never having been married', so that it may be construed as 'not having a husband or a wife at the time in question'. If one wishes to be absurd, one can very easily take that decision and expand it in a number of probably frivolous directions: babies and horses are technically 'unmarried'.

It is instructive to compare the linguist's view of semantic equivalence with the ideas on the same subject prevalent in the legal profession. Lawyers, or British lawyers at any rate, are much given to invoking the 'ordinary meaning' of words whenever a particular issue is seen to turn on semantics. Yet as a group they seem reluctant to accept that this appeal ought, in principle, to commit them to adopting standard or everyday English in *all* their professional business, and not just when it suits them. British lawyers are not alone in this. A remarkable number of Spanish lawyers, for instance, seem unaware that the legal sense of *excepción* (special defence or bar to trial, action or right of action) is quite alien to most speakers of the language or distinct from the 'normal' usage. To return to English usage, any non-lawyer who has ever tried to follow the tortuous logic of the successive definitions of 'constructive manslaughter' can see that what is shifting is not really the meanings of words, but the set of possible circumstances the designated terms were originally thought to cover.

This, of course, is the major problem with legal translation. In most other fields, a translator can usually assume that when a decision has to be made about the equivalent for a given term, there will be a definite consensus as to its range among experts in the source context. In legal texts, however, terms are continually being redefined, as social developments overtake past practice and thus force legislation to change, simply in order to keep abreast of new standards of acceptable and unacceptable behaviour. This, in turn, affects judicial perceptions of what the legislators had in mind when they originally defined certain terms (or rather, when they happened to use particular words to define specific types of conduct). And since judges are loath to relinquish these established terms, a certain amount of semantic forcing is the inevitable result, as our 'constructive manslaughter' example shows.

From the point of view of the translator, as our quotation from Eliot suggests, words themselves seem to shift. They always do, of course, and in the fullness of time our dictionaries will cease to be of any use to us, except as historical documents. But the problem sometimes is that lawyers do not like dictionaries, or, more accurately, they do not approve of the use of dictionary definitions to explain conduct that they consider to be more precisely expounded in statutes, in decided cases and in accordance with the principles of legal construction. Dictionaries, to the average person, are a sort of monument to the past; to lawyers they are an unwelcome reminder of the future and are normally barred from courtrooms.

Blackstone (Murphy et al. 1998:1404) provides us with the example of a jury that, so to speak, took the law into its own hands by requesting the jury bailiff to supply it with a dictionary. The case involved a charge of 'grievous bodily harm' (*lesiones graves, coups et blessures, schwere Körperverletzung*) and despite – or perhaps because of – the judge's direction, the jury had not grasped the precise legal sense of 'grievous'. They therefore asked the bailiff, who was standing guard outside the room where they had retired to consider their verdict, for a dictionary, and the officer, without consulting the judge, provided them with one. Amazingly it took a decision by the Court of Appeal to decide that a jury had the right to look up a word in a dictionary. Even then, the court made it clear that it took a dim view of the jury's request, which it regarded as 'irregular'. In the context it is clear that the Court of Appeal was not referring only to the 'irregularity' of the jury being handed a suspicious object by the bailiff without the judge's knowledge, which one could have understood might be questionable. It was the fact that the jury had requested a *dictionary* that was 'irregular', since it indicated their intention of 'conducting a private enquiry'.

The question raised in the mind of lay persons (e.g. translators) by this unfortunate incident is what exactly judges and lawyers mean when they talk of the 'ordinary sense' of words. If dictionaries are viewed with suspicion, what must courts make of translators?

However, lawyers are not the only ones who distrust words and develop strategies to protect their meanings. All of us are aware of the need to negotiate meaning, even in ordinary exchanges, and there are many ways in which we can show our awareness of ambiguity, uncertainty or indefiniteness. Obvious examples include syntactic forms like 'Don't you think...?', 'I think you said that...', the blunt 'What exactly do you mean?' or the slightly more subtle rhetorical question (such as the last sentence of the preceding paragraph). However, the area of modern grammar known as 'pragmatics', part of which studies the phenomenon of dynamic meaning creation in human conversation, has shown that strategies of this type aimed at confirming hunches, eliciting clarification or coaxing our listeners into adopting a particular point of view need not be formulated as questions. Phrases commonly used with this aim in mind include, for instance, '[I have] no doubt you believe', 'as you can probably see', 'as we all know', and so on. In the last example, implication, assumption or presupposition are at their strongest and most insidious: there are very few things indeed that 'we all know', so the speaker here is clearly indulging in the ancient rhetorical or persuasive device of *begging the question*, i.e. assuming what is supposed to be proved.

Judges are no less sensitive than other people to implication and presupposition. Like everybody else, they consider context when the parties to a suit base their arguments on conflicting interpretations of the same rule or doctrine. As Solan (1993:140) puts it, "Our knowledge of words (known by linguists as the 'lexicon') provides an arena in which the fundamental legal battles are fought". This is what is meant, judicially, by interpreting legal terms in accordance with the 'habitual' or 'ordinary' meaning of words, as in the following instance:

> In his Lordship's view the ordinary meaning of the word 'disputes' or
> the word 'differences' should be given to those words in the arbitration
> clauses. (*The Times* 29.3.1990:36)

In a sense, then, judges briefly become linguists and philologists when they make such decisions. This happened, for example, when Lord Diplock somewhat testily reproved the legal profession for having accepted for over two centuries the terms *'actus reus'* (forbidden act) and *'mens rea'* (the relevant criminal mental element) in determining the elements of criminal conduct. His Lordship pointed out that *'reus'* is a noun and not an adjective, that English lawyers have consistently misapplied the Latin phrase and that "it would, I think, be conducive to clarity of analysis of the ingredients of a crime that is created by statute, as are the great majority of criminal offences today, if we were to avoid bad Latin and instead to think and speak [...] about the conduct of the accused and his state of mind at the time of that conduct, instead of speaking of 'actus reus' and 'mens rea'" (in *R v Miller* [1981], House of Lords). All that can be said in this particular case is that Lord Diplock's criticism of dog-Latin came too late to prevent the linguistic evil he desired to uproot: students of law in the English-speaking countries continue to be taught that crime consists of a combination of the '*actus reus*' and '*mens rea*'. Though the term '*actus reus*' is not listed in all the standard dictionaries of the English language, it is always found in the specialist dictionaries compiled by lawyers.

A quite different matter is judicial ruling on the meaning to be attached to specific terms used in statutes or in the texts of contracts as agreed between the parties. These decisions fall within the province of judicial determination and often constitute the whole basis of the cases referred to the courts. In fact, of all the cases brought to the attention of the courts, a very large majority never reach the stage of the 'trial proper', since rulings on preliminary points of law effectively put an end to the claims of one of the parties to the suit. We should therefore briefly consider the principles on which such judicial 'interpretation' or 'construction' (from 'construe') is based.

According to the standard dictionaries, to 'interpret' a term means to 'elucidate or explain its meaning' whereas to 'construe' a word or expression means to 'assign a definite sense' to one that is ambiguous, vague or indeterminate, i.e. to take it in a specified way. To some jurists, this means that 'construction' is a more linguistic task, while 'interpretation' is more ideological. In other words, 'construction', like the Latin *constructio* from which it derives, is an attempt to conduct a linguistic analysis aimed at deducing the textual meaning of a word, phrase or clause from the surrounding utterance. The entire context, mediate and immediate, is borne in mind, including word position, the author's linguistic habits (if known), punctuation, contemporary dictionary definitions, relevant scientific and cultural criteria, etc. Explanations derived from 'interpretation', on the other hand, have more to do with scientific or academic theories, specific training, beliefs or precedent.[1] A recent article on the topic conveniently uses both the terms we have been examining in a way that suggests that,

---

[1] One of the issues canvassed in the year 2000 presidential campaign in the USA concerned the appointment of Supreme Court justices. In the course of a debate between the two leading candidates, Mr Bush stated that he would favour the appointment of 'constructionists' rather than judges who would 'interpret' the Constitution to 'make political policy'. The conservative Bush understood 'construction' to be a more or less literal reading of the laws, rather than the can-of-worms 'interpretation', which would be less foreseeable in its social effect.

while the 'construction' is linguistic, the 'interpretation' is intended to update the statute:

> Damages under the Federal Electronic Fund Transfer Act: a proposed *construction* of sections 910 and 915'. *Interpretation* of Arbitration Act 1979, section 1(5) (6). (Downs 1985:5-26, italics ours)

However, for practical purposes the two terms 'construe' and 'interpret' are best treated as close synonyms. Indeed, law dictionaries tend to define each of these words in terms of the other, so that 'construction' is defined as 'interpretation' and vice versa (see, for instance, Bird 1990; Curzon 1990; Martin 1990). Judges may, of course, invoke the rules of equity in certain circumstances to prevent abuse and provide pragmatic judgements, as in the following example, in which a penalty clause in a contract was deemed unfair:

> In *Clydebank Engineering [1905] AC 6* Lord Halsbury emphasised that the court must construe such a clause according to the real nature of the transaction and that the mere use of 'penalty' or 'damage' would not be conclusive as to the parties' rights.

In theory, the rules of judicial construction of disputed or unclear terms are the same for statutes as for any other kind of document. The main rules are as follows:

(a)   *The literal rule*: Words that are reasonably taken to have a single meaning are to be given that meaning, however anomalous the result (e.g. Shakespeare leaving his 'secondbest bed' to his wife in his will).

(b)   Documents and statutes are to be construed *as a whole*, the idea being that internal inconsistencies will thus be avoided.

(c)   *The golden rule*: Ordinary words are to be given their ordinary meanings and technical terms their technical meanings, unless the outcome is absurd. For example, 'ticket' means the cardboard or paper slip or voucher issued to passengers by a travel company when the context is some form of travel, while the same word means the written notice of a fine issued by the police or an authorized official when the context is that of a parking fine. But 'estoppel' always and only means the legal principle defined by courts.

(d)   *The mischief rule*: When the aim of a statute is to cure defects in the law, any ambiguous terms are to be construed in such a way as to favour that outcome.

(e)   *The 'ejusdem generis' rule*: When a document contains a list of specific items belonging to the same class followed by general words, the general words are to be interpreted as referring to other items of the same class (*ejusdem generis*). For example, if a law refers to 'cows, pigs, goats and other animals', the phrase 'other animals' means other farm animals, and does not include, for instance, goldfish, foxes or crocodiles.

(f)   The rule '*expressio unius est exclusio alterius*', i.e. 'the inclusion of the one signifies the exclusion of the other'. This is the corollary of the previous rule, and means that if specific words in a list are not followed by other general ones, the list is to be regarded as exhaustive, e.g. 'weekends and public holidays' excludes working weekdays.

These rules seem fairly clear and in accordance with common sense. In any case translators of legal texts are unlikely to be tempted to interpret ambiguous terms or phrases; they will probably reproduce the ambiguity as literally as possible and leave the matter up to the parties concerned. However, it is worth adding that, despite the theoretical principles we have just outlined, judicial approaches to construction often vary depending on whether the disputed terms are found in statutes or in private documents like deeds or contracts. In dealing with Acts of Parliaments, judges are extremely unwilling to depart from literal readings of the text approved by the legislature. They often comment that if legal rules are to be changed, it is the task of the legislators rather than the judiciary to change them. An excellent example of this convention is the case of *Air-India v Wiggins*, where the leading opinion in the House of Lords held that if the literal words of the law as they stand make intelligible sense if read in a certain way, that is how they must be read. The implication is that a court is only justified in interpreting Parliament's words against the obvious sense indicated by ordinary grammar and logic if the obvious sense would lead to an absurd or contradictory conclusion. In other words, judges, unlike many lay people, assume that MPs know what they mean and mean what they say when they formulate laws. More importantly, the courts only require the words of the legislators to be intelligible and meaningful; they do not necessarily expect those words to represent good sense or the reasonable person's idea of justice.

In common-law construction, on the other hand, courts tend to be more forthright in their law-giving function. Contracts and other private arrangements between individuals fall to be interpreted in accordance with the usual rules of law, the norms of decided cases (*jurisprudencia*), the ordinary meanings of words, and common business practice, including local or regional rules or habits of trade. Also, as Lord Denning commented in *Lewis v Averay* [1972], when judges are engaged in determining the true construction of a contract, "we do not look into the intentions [of the party], or into his mind to know what he was thinking [...]. We look at the outward appearances." Moreover, in modern times Parliament increasingly frequently intervenes to clarify the sense in which particular terms are to be interpreted in common business practices, such as contracts, credit or hire-purchase arrangements, mortgage agreements and so on. This can be seen in statutes such as the Unfair Contract Terms Act, the Sale of Goods Act, and the Consumer Credit Act.

There is one rule of construction, or 'canon of interpretation', that is specifically aimed at producing a result that most people would probably consider fair, in the ordinary sense, rather than strictly legal or logical. This is the 'rule of lenity', which holds that any lexical vagueness or syntactic ambiguity is to be interpreted against the drafter in both civil and criminal law. (Spanish translators might compare the contemporary rule whereby, in the event of conflict between the older and the newer versions of the Penal Code, whether affecting procedure or prescribed punishment, the accused is always entitled to the more favourable interpretation.)

Within the general scheme outlined, let us examine some of the difficulties the translator might be asked to deal with in interpreting legal texts. We shall begin with problems deriving from lexical vagueness and syntactic ambiguity.

3. Lexical vagueness (I)
Definition, extension and intension

In the context of legal documents, specific definition is one of the chief means by which the precise meaning of a lexical unit is determined and legal certainty is guaranteed. With this end in view, many legal texts, such as statutes, contracts, deeds and warranties, commonly contain clauses, appendices, riders (additional clauses) or schedules (annexes) that provide definitions of the main terms involved or representative lists of the principle items caught by the agreement. The following is an example of a statute (the Further Education Act 1985) that clarifies the sense in which some of its basic terms are used:

(10) In this section 'rate fund'

(a) in relation to the Inner London Education Authority *means* any fund for which a precept is issued by the Greater London Council;

and (b) in relation to any other local education authority, *means* the county fund or general rate fund;

and 'year' *means* a period of twelve months ending with 31st March. (emphasis added)

Etymologically, 'define' is derived from the Latin *de* (from, of, concerning, relating to) and *finis* (end, limit), so that the original sense of the verb is to set limits. Old authorities distinguish between the *definiens* (defining phrase or clause) and the *definiendum* (objective of definition). The *definiendum* can be further subdivided into a 'generic' and a 'specific' feature, as in the following examples:

> **Estoppel:** The rule of evidence or doctrine of law which precludes a person from denying the truth of some statement formerly made by him, or the existence of facts which he has by words or conduct led others to believe in. (Bird 1990:137)

> **Tort:** A civil wrong for which the remedy is commonly a common law action for unliquidated damages, and which is not exclusively the breach of a contract, or the breach of a trust or other merely equitable obligation. (Bird 1990: 325)

In our two definitions, we can distinguish 'generic' from 'accidental' features of the types mentioned: the 'rule of evidence or doctrine of law' and 'civil wrong' are essential features of the respective types, while in the second example the adverb 'commonly' is a restrictive or 'accidental' feature of the definition.

Picking up on this distinction, the translator may find it useful to pursue the difference between 'intension' and 'extension'. 'Extension' may be broadly defined as the class of objects to which a sign or term refers, or, as the *Shorter Oxford Dictionary* (1978) puts it, "the range of a term as measured by the number of objects to which it applies". 'Intension', on the other hand, according to the same source, is equivalent to the sum of the attributes comprehended in the concept.

As an example of a typical legal definition by extension, i.e. the inclusive sort, we may take the following 'bill of lading' (*conocimiento de embarque, connaissement, Frachtbrief*):

> *Ships*: in this contract this term includes sailing-boats, freighters, vessels, etc.
> *Container* includes any container, trailer, transportable tank, flat or pellet or any similar article used to consolidate goods.

Likewise, in the United States the *The Racketeer Influenced and Corrupt Organization Act* or *RICO* defines 'enterprise' (Solan 1993:78) in accordance with what we have called 'extension':

> 'Enterprise' includes any individual, partnership, corporation, association, or other legal entity and any union or group of individuals associated in fact although not a legal entity.

A simple example of 'intension', on the other hand, is the common clause in transport contracts in which the term 'carriage' is defined. It usually runs like this:

> 'Carriage' means the whole of the operations and services undertaken by the Carrier in respect of the goods.

Another instance of definition by intension (i.e. by systematic identification of the particularizing features of a term) is the gloss provided early in the last century by the judge in *Pawsey v Scottish Union and National* (1907) on the important term 'proximate cause':

> Proximate cause means the active, efficient cause that sets in motion a train of events which brings about a result, without the intervention of any force started and working actively from a new and independent source.

And a third illustration of intension comes in *Dred Scott v. Sandford* (1857), when the US Supreme Court declared the words 'people' and 'citizens' to be synonymous:

> The words 'people' of the United States and 'citizens' are synonymous terms, and mean the same thing. They both describe the political body who, according to our republican institutions, form the sovereignty and who hold the power and conduct the government through their representatives. They are what we familiarly call the 'sovereign people', and every citizen is one of this people, and a constituent member of this sovereignty.

4. Lexical vagueness (II)
Denotation and connotation; register

The distinction we have just drawn between intensive and extensive definition is plainly applicable to any specialist language and to any attempt to use words precisely. Connotation and denotation, on the other hand, might be thought to arise more naturally in linguistic contexts concerned with evaluation and subjective description, such as literature, historiography, and the so-called 'fuzzy' social sciences like sociology, psychology, economics, journalism and so on. However, as we have said, the language of the law is made up of three basic types of vocabulary: technical, semi-technical and non-technical. Of these, the technical type is, by definition, the least pervious to subjective suggestion and therefore the least open to connotative meaning, while the other types are correspondingly more prone to connotative meaning the closer they approximate non-technical or everyday speech.

Not infrequently words that are, or appear to be, technically transparent in one language turn out to be connotatively rich in another, with the result that the literal translation of concepts that are practically neutral in the source system may be semantically charged in the target code. For example, the Spanish legal term *tráfico jurídico* cannot be translated into English as 'legal traffic', partly because the phrase would be unclear in English but also because the word 'traffic', unless it refers to motor vehicles on the roads or on city streets, usually has pejorative associations with shady or illegal activity. We would therefore probably have to resort to an expansion like 'the documents that facilitate legitimate business transactions'. The point is that translators cannot expect to avoid the connotative traps of language just because they are dealing with legal texts.

For the sake of illustration, we shall briefly consider a few groups of terms that call for a certain amount of ingenuity on the part of the translator because of their different connotations and/or different register or degree of formality.

Fight, combat, oppose, resist, withstand, contest, contend and argue

All these terms may be described as hyponyms of the hyperonym 'defend', and in legal contexts they are associated with the idea of defending one's rights or position against the attack or the encroachment of one's adversaries. The first five (from 'fight' to 'withstand') are most commonly found in figurative usage aimed at stressing the idea that the parties concerned are regarded – or choose to depict themselves – as being victimized or as struggling heroically against unfair odds. Headlines in the tabloids about 'court battles' favour such terms, especially the monosyllabic 'fight' (e.g. 'British Mum to Fight Custody Order'). But there is nothing to prevent a lawyer from using the same expression (though perhaps replacing the 'mum' with 'Ms X' or 'we') or *The Guardian* or *The Telegraph* from coming up with a very similar headline, possibly preferring 'oppose' or 'resist' to 'fight' and certainly changing 'mum' to 'woman'. The last term, 'withstand', normally connotes a concerted and drawn-out strategy, but it and the other four have rhetorical connotations which make them unsuitable for use in formal proceedings, where 'contest', 'contend' and 'argue' are far more usual. For instance, phrases like 'a contested action' (*un contencioso*) or 'the prosecution contends/argues that...' (*la fiscalía sostiene/ argumenta que*) are standard in litigation. However, it is worth pointing out that the Spanish cognates of 'combat', 'oppose' and 'resist' (*combatir, oponer, resistir*) *are* habitually used in the formal context of 'defence', and are regarded as technically superior to *defensa*, which normally translates as 'defence counsel', 'defence team' or 'defendant'. This ought to be a reminder to translators that even in the case of cognates, and even when they are not false, what is connotation in one language proves to be denotation in another.

Gap and loophole

These terms share the sense of 'blank, deficiency, omission, ambiguity'. However, of the two, 'gap' is more commonly used of something missing, a space which ought to be filled, i.e. it conveys the idea of an unfortunate oversight, whereas 'loophole', which is in any case slightly more informal in register, normally connotes an omission which can be exploited to someone's advantage (*una laguna/escapatoria legal, lacune/échappatoire, Gesetzeslücke*). The choice of one or the other therefore depends very much on the specific context and on the pragmatic intention – law-abiding or devious – of the speaker. For example, a parliamentary commission may be given the task of 'plugging the gaps in current legislation', whereas a lawyer may adopt the tactic of 'exploiting a loophole in the current law'.

Breach, infringement, violation, contravention, transgression

The sense shared by the words in this group is the breaking of a law, a dereliction of duty or the failure to comply with an order. In legal contexts, the last term, 'transgression', may be discounted since it belongs more properly to breach of moral or religious codes. Of the others, it is more difficult to predict which will best fit a given context, but a useful rule-of-thumb for translators is that 'violation' often connotes deliberate law-breaking, 'breach' is most frequently found in civil law contexts concerning contracts, promises and other private or voluntary agreements, while 'infringement' is often the failure to abide by local bye-laws (*ordenanzas municipales, arrêtés municipaux, Gemeindeverordnungen, städtische Verordnungen*) or the accepted rules and regulations of trade, professional associations, governing bodies, etc. This leaves 'contravention' as perhaps the most neutral term, i.e. the one with the fewest definite connotations, but any such suggestion must be tentative.

In the foregoing analysis, we have occasionally referred to the 'register' of particular words, but something more should be said of this feature of modern semantics. In the first place, no translator can afford to ignore the importance of tone in the lexical and syntactic treatment of texts. Subtle though the adjustment sometimes is, matching the style of utterance is a crucial part of the process of naturalization, and translators should no more neglect communicative courtesy in their versions of texts than they would underestimate the importance of good (or bad) manners in social life. However, this should not be taken as a recommendation that translators go out of their way to make their versions of legal texts especially stiff and solemn in the hope that they will somehow sound more 'legal'. 'Matching' the tone means respecting it and imitating it as closely as may be by the appropriate linguistic means, i.e. through target-language construction and vocabulary. And this, in its turn, means taking account of recent changes in legal and judicial style.

Unquestionably, the dominant register of legal writing is formal, even highly formal. But the effects of the 'Plain English Campaign' are palpable, particularly at the level of vocabulary. Gone are the days when judges, whether out of genuine patrician ignorance or feigned unfamiliarity with the language of the low, would lean across to counsel and demand to have the witness's or the accused's street patois 'translated' into an English they could understand. It is not just at the higher (i.e. more archaic) level of vocabulary that this phenomenon is noticeable (e.g. the replacement of 'plaintiff' by 'claimant' or of 'affidavit' by 'sworn statement' or 'statement of truth'), but at the intermediate and lower levels too. This is nowhere more apparent than in the terminology used in commercial cases involving complex financial dealings, with the wholesale incorporation of formerly arcane terms belonging to the money trade, such as 'put' and 'call options', 'hedging' or 'insider trading'. (It is worth noting, incidentally, that the more colourful part of contemporary financial jargon has its origins in the gambling-dens of New York, Chicago and London and the shadier side of the racecourses of the English-speaking world.)

Law dictionaries and textbooks list and explain colloquial terms like 'sus [law]' – the law that until recently allowed the police to arrest loiterers on suspicion of intent to commit a crime – or 'gazumping' – the illegal practice by which the vendor of property artificially boosts the selling price by withdrawing from the transaction after the prospective purchaser has made an offer. As the examples show, it is not always possible for a translator to find terms that exactly match the register of the original, but any plausible version must at least begin by recognizing the switch of register for what it is.

5. Lexical vagueness (III)
Polysemy and the importance of context

We remarked earlier, in discussing legal vocabulary, that it is often the intermediate or semi-technical group that gives the translator most trouble because of the potential semantic range of the terms. For example, the word 'appropriate' as a verb belongs to this semi-technical group, but as an adjective it belongs to the third group (everyday or non-technical vocabulary). In its group two, or verbal, sense it means 'allocate, earmark, set aside', though in certain contexts there can be an implication of arbitrariness. As an adjective, it is not strictly speaking a legal term, though it is frequently found in legal texts, where it has its usual meaning of 'right, suitable, fitting'. A very large number of words found in legal or administrative texts exhibit this same tendency to shift from one category to the other. The word 'call', for instance, has at least 15 distinguishable senses in technical documents of this type. Unsurprisingly, the lesson is that mechanical, word-for-word translation is almost bound to fail, but this does not mean that the translator is thrown back entirely on intuition or guesswork. The internal coherence of both the source and the target text will always provide clues and most potential ambiguities can be cleared up by a combination of scrupulous attention to context and reliance on the better dictionaries. By far the greatest number of lexical errors in translation are caused by failure to notice, or adequately to deal with, terms that are not symmetrically ambiguous in the two languages and require to be dealt with via synonymy. Here are a few examples:

(a)   appropriate [vb.[1]] (*destinar, asignar [fondos], affecter à, bereitstellen*): Appropriate funds to pay for the new machinery
appropriate [vb.[2]] (*apropiarse arbitrariamente, s'approprier, sich aneignen*): Irregularly appropriate funds to one's own use
appropriate [adj.] (*apropiado, qui convient, entsprechend*): Make the appropriate order as to costs

(b)   condemn (*condenar, condamner, verurteilen*): Condemn a prisoner to death
condemn (*declarar ruinoso o no apto, déclarer inhabitable, für unbewohnbar erklären*): The building was condemned as unsafe
condemn (*censurar, reprobar, condamner, missbilligen*): This interpretation of the statute was condemned by later judges.

(c)   commission [n.[1]] (*encargo, cometido, mandat, Beauftragung*): Act within one's commission
commission [n.[2]] (*comisión, porcentaje, commission, Provision*): Work for a basic salary plus commission
commission [n.[3]] (*comisión, comité, commission, Kommission,* as in the EU): Submit a proposal to the commission
commission [vb.[1]] (*encargar, commander, in Auftrag geben*): A report was commissioned by the Home Secretary
commission [vb.[2]] (*poner en servicio activo, mettre en service, in Dienst stellen,*): A ship commissioned by the Ministry of Defence

(d)   service [n.[1]] (*servicio, services, Dienst*): A contract for services
service [n.[2]] (*notificación, assignation, Zustellung*): Acknowledge service of a writ
service [vb.] (*poner a punto, faire réviser, warten*): Have one's car serviced.

To close this section, let us briefly expand on the notion of context. Virtually any word or phrase has a potentially enormous range of meanings unless the sense is limited by a context. It is context, therefore, that enables us to resolve lexical ambiguity. Context may conveniently be brought under three heads. In the first place, there is what the pragmatists call the 'context of utterance', i.e. the immediate physical and temporal environment in which the communication takes place. This may be oral or written, there may be one or more recipients and oral communication may take place whether or not the recipient is in the physical presence of the speaker and whether or not the two are contemporaries (e.g. through films, videos or tape-recordings). Second, context may mean the immediate verbal environment in which the utterance is situated, i.e. the words or sentences that precede and follow it in the same text. This type of context is sometimes called the 'co-text' to distinguish it from the other senses of the term. The third sense is extralinguistic and consists of the habits, expectations and conventions characteristic of the society concerned, which in our case means the world of lawyers and the law, with its customs, its practice, its assumptions, its values and its procedural routines. These are learned by the usual cognitive processes of study, observation, training and interaction – in a word, by experience.

For the translator of written texts, the second type of context, i.e. co-text, is far and away the most immediate and important; indeed, there is not likely to be much opportunity for observation of the other two classes of context for the translator working in isolation. However, it is clearly impossible even for this kind of translator to ignore the extralinguistic context, and in fact the more that is known about it, the better the translation is likely to be. Finally, court interpreters are an obvious instance of translators for whom the here and now of debate, exchange and body language will be crucial pointers to the intended sense of terms that might be indecipherable without the light thrown on them by direct observation. We shall return in Chapter 7 to the translation problems raised by polysemy in legal vocabulary.

6. Lexical vagueness (IV). Homonymy

It is helpful to distinguish between homonyms and polysemous terms. A polysemous term is a single word that has acquired a number of distinct meanings, as we saw in the previous section with examples like 'commission' or 'service'. On the other hand, two words are said to be homonyms when they have identical forms but different meanings because they are derived from different roots. Examples that affect legal vocabulary include the words 'conviction' (the act of convicting) and 'construction' (in the sense of interpretation).[2] These

---

[2] Strictly speaking, both senses of 'conviction' and both senses of 'construction' could be

nouns are associated, respectively, with the verbs 'convict' and 'construe', rather than with their near phonetic neighbours 'convince' and 'construct'. The distinction is easily illustrated: 'Counsel for the defence used all his powers of *conviction*' as against 'The *conviction* was appealed from before the Court of Appeal'; and 'The House of Lords ruled against this *construction* of the statute' as against 'The *construction* was considered dangerous and had to be dismantled'. In the first case 'conviction' is synonymous with 'finding or verdict of guilty' and its antonym is 'acquittal'; in the second case the synonym and antonym are, respectively, 'persuasion' and (partially) 'uncertainty', 'doubt' or 'mistrust'. Similarly in the other example, the respective synonyms and antonyms are 'interpretation' and 'misconstruction or 'misinterpretation' in the first sentence, and 'structure' or 'building' and 'ruin, 'wreck' or 'destruction' in the second. We shall return to the term 'constructive' below.

7. Vagueness in legal lexical units (V) Synonyms, hyperonyms and hyponyms

In ideal conditions, translators of legal texts would have access to bilingual thesauri or dictionaries of synonyms and antonyms, cross-referenced to the major concepts of the legal systems concerned. Life would undoubtedly be much easier if we had easy access to linguistic tools that dealt systematically with the whole troublesome area of synonymy. We would like instant clarification of the nuances of meaning and usage needed to deal, for example, with the bewildering variety of terms for 'revoke', such as 'cancel', 'annul', 'quash', 'strike out', 'recall', 'reverse', 'dismiss', 'overrule', 'set aside', 'vary' or 'restore', all of which are in current use to refer to the courts' decisions concerning disputes on which they adjudicate.

Unfortunately, nothing of the kind is available at present, or likely to be forthcoming. As far as the present authors are aware, there is no such book in existence even for a single language, let alone in bilingual or multilingual format. All legal translators can therefore do is build up their own glossaries piecemeal and text by plodding text. After all, if comparative jurisprudence itself is still a minority discipline, one could hardly expect comparative forensic linguistics to have moved much beyond the 'problems of legal translation' stage, which is where we are right now.

Within this very limited perspective, what can be said is that when we speak

---

said to derive from a single Latin root in each case. However, in each case English has derived two different verbs ('convince' and 'convict' on the one hand and 'construct' and 'construe' on the other) from a single Latin original. The nouns are therefore best regarded as homonyms since they are associated directly with distinct verbs.

of the synonymity of terms allowed to belong partly or primarily to the field of law, we are usually talking of approximate or partial synonyms and not of interchangeable terms. A simple example of this is provided by the words 'legal', 'lawful' and 'statutory', all of which come under the more general sense of that which is 'right' or 'just'. All three terms imply that the act or issue in question is in accordance with the law, or permitted by it, but it is relatively easy to distinguish 'statutory' from the other two, since it refers exclusively to what is prescribed or tolerated by a written law, usually an Act or a ministerial Order. The other two are wider in scope, since they may be taken to refer to that area of the law that derives from long-established custom, and this may, in its turn, imply that the right in question has been determined in the decided cases. In many cases it does not seem to make much difference whether we say that a thing is 'lawful' or that it is 'legal'. However, set phrases like 'lawful wedded wife' (*legítima esposa, épouse légitime, rechtmässig angetraute Frau*) or 'be about one's lawful business', as against 'legal penalty', 'legal adviser' or 'legal rules' (*legal, marcado por la ley, juridique, judiciaire, juristisch*) perhaps provide us with a clue and allow us to suggest that 'legal' means 'directly concerned with or emanating from the law', whereas 'lawful' suggests something which is 'in general conformity with law, or not opposed to it'. The first, in other words, is more specific and the second more general.

Sometimes the translator's problem is that the source text contains phrases that are themselves made up of close synonyms, e.g. 'final and conclusive', 'false and untrue', 'null and void', which smack of tautology or linguistic overkill. A well-known instance is the first page of British passports, in which 'Her Britannic Majesty's First Minister' does not just request, but "requests and requires" the foreign authorities to allow the holder to pass "without let or hindrance". What should the translator do here? Do we translate literally and disregard logic in languages which may be less tolerant of redundancy than English appears to be? In the first phrase of the passport, do we run the risk of offending the foreign authorities by a translation that in all likelihood will sound like a veiled threat, with the polite 'requests' followed by the aggressive 'requires', so that the whole sounds like an official equivalent of 'whether you like it or not'? Perhaps the best solution is to replace the repetition, where target-language style seems to require modulation, with some form of adverbial or prepositional emphasis, e.g. *nulo a todos los efectos, nul et non avenu* or *null und nichtig* for 'null and void', *absolutamente falso, absolument faux* or *fasch und unwahr* for 'false and untrue', *ruega encarecidamente* or *nachdrücklich Bitten* for 'requests and requires', and so on. Rhetoric, after all, has its place in legal language, and it cannot be right for phrases that sound solemn and impressive in the original to be travestied by weak or ridiculous target-language versions.

In any case, few linguists and hardly any translators would accept that there is any such thing as a full synonym. The phrase 'null and void' is commonly used in attributive contexts ('the contract is null and void') but cases based on avoidance are never argued as though 'null' and 'void' were separate concepts; judicial discussion in such cases always centres on whether or not the agreement under discussion is *void* as a matter of law. This tells us there is no legal difference between the terms and that we are therefore entitled to translate them in any way compatible with target-language conventions. As for 'let and hindrance', the linguistic fact is that for many years 'hindrance' has been an everyday term meaning 'nuisance', 'drawback' or 'inconvenience', while 'let' in the same sense is now unknown outside of the rules of tennis, where it means that the first service has struck the 'obstacle' or net, and therefore has to be repeated.

The examples we have examined belong to the areas of semi-technical and non-technical vocabulary since strictly speaking technical terms have no exact synonyms. In translating technical words we normally select a term that is functionally equivalent, e.g. court (*tribunal, cour, Gericht*), judge (*juez, juge, Richter*), 'trial' (*juicio, procès, Gerichtsverfahren*), 'bail' (*fianza, caution, Sicherheitsleistung, Kaution*), but in more difficult cases, when a technical term is system-specific and therefore has no true synonym and no exact equivalent, a helpful technique is to make use of the *definiens* or hyperonym of the original. 'Tort' for example is a special kind of 'wrong', and so the target-language equivalent of 'wrong' (*agravio, ilícito, dommage, unerlaubte Handlung*) is an obvious candidate for selection. Where necessary, further definition or description can be added for greater accuracy (e.g. *agravio extracontractual, ilícito civil extracontractual, acte dommageable, rechtswidrige Handlung, die schadenersatzpflichtig macht*).

8.   Vagueness in legal lexical units (VI). Antonyms

Antonyms can be useful to the translator in emergencies, following the old rhetorical device of naming a thing by denying its opposite. For example, in criminal law, punishments that do not involve imprisonment are called 'non-custodial sentences'. As one would expect, group-three or everyday words present fewest problems to the translator, e.g. 'implicit/explicit', 'total/partial', and so on. Group-one terms should also prove straightforward, as in 'convict/acquit' (*condenar/ absolver, déclarer coupable/acquitter, verurteilen/freisprechen*) or 'plaintiff/defendant' (*demandante/demandado, Kläger/Angeklagte, plaignant/accusé* in Canada, although French also has *intimé* for the defendant in an appeal court, and *prévenu* in a criminal court). Once again, it is group-two or mixed terms that may prove most elusive, as is illustrated by the terms 'actual/constructive'.

These are genuine legal antonyms, since 'constructive' is habitually used in English legal contexts in opposition to 'actual'. The immediate difficulty for the translator is to distinguish this sense of the adjective (derived from the verb 'construe', i.e. interpret, understand, translate) from the common but non-legal sense of the same word (derived from the verb 'construct', i.e. build, frame). In legal parlance, the term means 'implied, analogous to, tantamount to, assumed or taken to be, tacitly presumed, virtual, understood as, as good as, arising from the operation of deduction, assumed for legal purposes, equivalent to all intents and purposes, so understood in law though not in fact', and so on. For instance, according to the doctrine of *constructive notice* people are assumed to be aware of facts that they can reasonably be expected to be aware of, whether or not the facts have actually been brought to their attention. Similarly, in the case of *constructive dismissal*, an employee may not have been actually dismissed by the firm, but the firm's conduct is taken as being equivalent to – construed as – dismissal. In cases such as this the employee may walk out on the firm or resign on the ground that the employer is in breach of contract. The employee may, for instance, have been unexpectedly demoted, or have suffered a cut in wages, or feel discriminated against, e.g. in cases of alleged sexual harassment. An employee alleging such *constructive* breach of contract by the firm is entitled to bring an action before an Industrial Tribunal claiming unfair dismissal, even if they walked out rather than being sacked. If the claim is successful, the employee will be awarded compensation for *constructive dismissal*, which we might translate as *despido sobrentendido, inferido, indirecto, licenciement implicite, Verhalten des Arbeitgebers, das als Kündigung auszulegen ist.*

Another example of this peculiar sense of the term 'constructive' occurs in the phrase 'constructive total loss', which is used in insurance. The term is applied to an insurance write-off, for instance of a car or a ship that has been involved in an accident (*épave, wirtschaftlicher/fingierter Totalschaden*). What is meant is that the damage is so severe that the cost of repairing the property exceeds its true value at the time of the accident. Spanish insurers have for many years used the literal equivalent *pérdida total constructiva* and this mistranslation has now been installed as the official one, readily understood by people in the business. But it is an instructive instance of the true sense of the Spanish word that many of the insurers who use it continue to be aware that it is related to the word *construir*, meaning 'build'. They explain the odd usage of the term by a fanciful etymology, assuming that the whole phrase means that the loss in value is so heavy that it involves 'rebuilding' the damaged vehicle or insured property, i.e. replacing it. An alternative to this anglicism would be *siniestro total analógico* or *siniestro total equivalente*.

9. Vagueness in legal lexical units (VII)
False cognates or 'false friends'

The last example in the previous section leads us naturally to a brief discussion of the issue of false cognates, or 'false friends'. These are extremely frequent in legal translation, especially with group-one terms that require complete accuracy. A typical instance is 'case', which is often wrongly translated in Spanish as *caso*. It is not that *caso* is always wrong; by and large, it can be said that when the English word is used to mean 'the particular facts of the case', *caso* is an acceptable equivalent (e.g. if a judge tells the jury that the case is a difficult or complicated one). But in expressions like 'the case against Smith' (the facts and arguments), 'the Johnstone case' (trial), 'the decided cases' (*la jurispru-dencia aplicable, jurisprudence applicable,* perhaps *die entschiedenen Fälle*), 'the prosecution rests its case' (its presentation), 'the defence case' (arguments made by the defence) and many others, the translator cannot mechanically repeat the meaningless cognate *caso*.

Even apparently simple words can be deceptive. 'Arrest', for instance, is not the same as *arrestar* or *arresto* when, as is usually the case, it is the police who are doing the arresting (*detener, detención, arrêter, arrestation, festnehmen, Festnahme*), and 'magistrate' is not equivalent to *magistrado*, since the former is the lowest-ranking criminal judge, and often a layperson, while the latter is a senior member of the judiciary and has reached this position through a combination of examination and lengthy experience.

Some cognates have meanings that partially overlap in two different languages, so that the terms will sometimes translate each other and sometimes not. For instance, 'sequestrate' and *secuestrar* are equivalent if what is seized is property, goods or an edition of a newspaper, but when a person is abducted and a ransom demand made the term is 'kidnap'. Similarly, a prohibition on the sale of arms or on trade generally is correctly called 'embargo' in both English and Spanish, while the temporary seizure or confiscation of goods or property for non-payment or in compliance with a court order has a variety of names in English ('seizure', 'confiscation', 'freezing order', 'Mareva injunction', 'distraint', 'attachment', etc.), but 'embargo' is not among them.

Likewise, 'article' can be *artículo, article or Artikel* in everyday use, and sometimes also as the technical name for the main subdivision of a statute, e.g. when we are referring to a ministerial order or a law drafted by the European Parliament, but in British Acts of Parliament this same subdivision is known as a 'section' (*artículo*). Speaking of Parliament, the 'legislature' is the law-making body (*cuerpo legislativo*) itself rather than the period for which its mandate lasts; the latter is called the 'life of the Parliament' (*legislatura*). 'Property' is the thing owned or capable of being owned (*propiedad*), but the fact of owning it or right to own it is 'ownership' (*propiedad, titularidad, dominio*). And 'prejudicial' (*perjudicial*) means 'causing prejudice, harmful, detrimental' whereas the Spanish cognate *prejudicial* means 'preceding judgement or trial', i.e. 'preliminary [matter or ruling]'.

The list of false friends is a very long one, but perhaps enough has been said to drive the point home. Translators cannot be too careful where cognates are concerned and legal vocabulary is a potential minefield for the unwary. The only advice we can offer is to trust nothing, to suspect everything, to check all terms in reliable dictionaries and to develop a close familiarity with the language of the law by constant and careful reading in both languages.

10. Figurative language: metaphors and buried metaphors

It is often, though quite erroneously, thought that specialist vocabularies like those of science, the law or technical disciplines are largely free of figurative elements, and indeed that the more precise the subject, the less room there is for discourse clothed in the garb of metaphor. Part of this is prejudice, of course, and derives from the popular misconception that figurative language is embroidery and mere decoration, quite unsuited to the plain speaking and hard facts of science. But it is a view that simply does not stand up to scrutiny, since all language is an inextricable mixture of figurative and non-figurative elements, even though speakers are not always aware of the fact. When we say, for example, that we have 'grasped' an idea or an explanation, we are using a metaphor for the mental process, and the common words 'understand' and 'comprehend' are also based on metaphors ('standing beneath' a concept, or 'capturing' it with the mind), though nobody is conscious of these images when using the words. These are what are called 'buried metaphors' and language is full of them, whether scientists and jurists like it or not.

Contemporary spectrometrists, for instance, talk blithely of 'coherent light' and 'rocking constants' and they are invariably surprised to be told that these are striking and rather beautiful metaphors. And the eighteenth-century jurist Lord Mansfield had clearly forgotten the origins of the words 'law' and 'legal' when he gave vent to his frustration and remarked that metaphors were deceptive and should be avoided in legal language. The Latin word *lex*, from which our modern word 'legal' is derived, originally meant a 'bundle of tied sticks', so that conceptually the old Roman lawyers were using a figure of speech to express the idea of something 'binding'. Similarly, the English word 'law' comes from a root meaning 'layer', which suggests that the original idea of the law was of something stratified or hierarchically arranged.

More recently, judge Benjamin Cardozzo has recognized the importance of metaphorical terms in legal language and, while warning against the overuse of figurative terminology, has given such usage his blessing. So, too, the Yale jurist Wesley Hohfield, at the beginning of the twentieth century, commented on perfectly sound and clearly comprehensible figurative expressions that have long been part of legal diction. These include phrases like 'This ruling is *on all fours with* the recent decision of the High Court' (in complete agreement with), or 'covenants *running with the land*' (are parallel to [ownership of] the land). In classic legal lexical units like 'the *burden* of proof' (*la carga de la prueba, la charge de la preuve, Beweislast*) or *corpus delicti* (the body of the facts that constitute an offence), the metaphorical sense of the terms is plain for all to see. As a recent commentator has said, there can be no doubting the pedigree of legal metaphors 'where liens *float*, corporations *reside*, minds *hold* meetings, and promises *run* with the land' (Cruz-Martínez 1999:303).

Cruz could have gone further and reminded readers that the word 'lien' is, or was, itself a metaphor (literally a 'bond' or 'tie'). Similarly, when a person 'discharges' (*cumple, remplit, erfüllt*) their contractual duties, the image conveyed by the term is that of unloading or laying down a burden. Or when a contract, promise or trust is described as 'bare', 'nude' or 'naked', we are looking at a literal translation of the metaphorical Latin phrase '*nudum pactum*', and what is meant is that the promise is unsupported by any consideration (*contraprestación, causa contractual, contrepartie, Gegenleistung*).

In fact, there are hundreds of metaphors, buried and unburied, in the language of the law. But this does not mean that the legal translator has a sort of poetic licence in dealing with them. Given the traditional and eminently conservative nature of legal phraseology, it is quite likely that the same or similar figurative usages will be found in many different languages. Whenever this is not the case, perhaps the wisest course is for the translator to choose the plainest possible rendering rather than run the risk of fanciful or highly coloured expressions at odds with the generally formal and even solemn tone of this type of text.

11. Syntactic ambiguity

Some of the terms we looked at in the earlier sections on homonyms and polysymy (e.g. 'consideration', 'commission' and 'conviction') may be regarded as special types of false cognates. But it is worth mentioning that some false friends are syntactic. To take a real-life example, the use of the present perfect tense in the sentence 'I *have been* his sole agent for twenty years' obviously implies that the speaker still occupies that position. However, the literal Spanish translation (*He sido...*) was understood to mean 'I was...[until recently]', when clearly what was wanted was *Soy su agente desde hace 20 años* (similarly, *Je suis... depuis...*, and *Ich bin... seit...*).

The previous example concerns structural ambiguity *between* languages, but of course syntactic ambiguity more usually poses a problem inside a single language, and so becomes a problem of translation only if the translator has to decide which of two or more possible senses is the one intended. Ambiguity can be quite literally a matter of life and death, as in one infamous English case, which has recently been made the subject of a film. This 1950s case involved the murder of a policeman during a shootout with one of two young men who were carrying out a robbery when the police arrived on the scene. The older of the two men, who was unarmed, surrendered but his accomplice, who was armed with a pistol, continued to resist arrest. During the exchange of fire, the police several times urged him to give himself up and to hand over the pistol, and according to police evidence given at the trial, the man who was in police custody called out 'Let him have it, Chris!' seconds before the gunman shot and killed an officer. Unfortunately for the elder defendant, the police maintained that the meaning of these words was not 'Hand over the gun,' as the accused claimed, but 'Shoot him' (i.e. 'Let him have the punishment he deserves'). The jury believed the police version and the man was hanged as an accomplice to murder. He has recently been pardoned after the case was reopened, but though there were other factors involved in the decision to rule that there had been a miscarriage of justice (*error judicial, erreur judiciaire, Justizirrtum*), it is difficult to escape the conclusion that it was the accused's unfortunate choice of words that hanged him. Obviously no translator would relish that sort of responsibility.

Fortunately, not all syntactic ambiguities have such devastating consequences. Some of the most commonplace involve simple-looking constructions with the conjunctions 'and' and 'or', as anyone who has ever studied basic formal logic knows. Take, for instance, the following sentence:

> Whenever any body of persons having legal authority to determine questions affecting the rights of subjects, *and having* the duty to act judicially, act in excess of their legal authority, they are subject to the controlling jurisdiction of the King's Bench Division exercised in these writs. (*R v Electricity Cors, ex parte London Electricity Joint Committee Co.* [1920])

The question here is whether the phrase 'and having the duty to act judicially' is to be understood as implying a further limiting condition (i.e. 'and *also* having the duty') or as expressing a consequence of the previous one (i.e. 'and *hence* having the duty'). The simple answer is that we do not know, since logic and grammar allow either interpretation. So much so, indeed, that for many years the courts held that the intended sense was the first one, until the issue reached the House of Lords, where it was decided that the true construction was the second one.

Since the ambiguity is inherent in the syntactic structure of the sentence, any translation that reproduces this is bound to be correct, in the sense that it will be equally ambiguous, and for the same reason. And that, of course, is what translators must do in cases of this kind, since it is no part of their business to decide between alternatives that split the judiciary and which are owing, ultimately, to

slack drafting. However, it is an uncomfortable position to be in since no translator likes to produce sloppy versions of apparently authoritative originals

As for 'or' clauses, most people in this computerized age are aware that
there are two 'ors': the inclusive and the exclusive. One implies 'either p or q,
not excepting both p and q', and the other means 'either p or q, but not both'.
Similar difficulties can crop up with words like 'other' and 'another', where it
may be unclear if the additional elements referred to are of the same or of a
different kind to the first (e.g. 'cheques, credit notes or *other instruments*').
Sometimes the ambiguity will not arise because the context and its logical implications will clarify the sense. For example, if two tennis players reach the
final of a championship, the statement 'either A or B will take the trophy' must
mean one or the other but not both. But in many cases the meaning will be
indeterminable in purely linguistic terms. If this happens in a legal text and it is
impossible to be sure of the intention of its drafter, all the courts can do is to
apply one or other of the judicial rules of construction we described earlier.
Once again, the translator can only reproduce the literal sense of the source text
and leave any question of interpretation to the parties involved or, if they cannot agree, to the courts.

3. Some Pointers to the English Legal System

1. Introduction. The translator and the legal background

In Chapter 1 we remarked that a working knowledge of the main features of the English legal system is a prerequisite for the translator of legal English texts. No doubt this will sound like a truism to many readers, but anyone who has even a slight acquaintance with the vast market in semi-professional translation, or who has ever had the opportunity to examine documents translated in connection with everyday transactions like contracts, deeds of sale, wills or notarised instruments, is aware of how seldom the proper combination of linguistic skill and background knowledge is in fact found. Trained lawyers who translate need a minimum of linguistic awareness, which the preceding chapters were in part intended to provide. This and the following chapter are intended primarily for their opposite numbers, i.e. translators or linguists who have little or no grounding in English law or who, for practical and professional reasons, need to brush up on the main concepts of that field. In this chapter we shall thus look briefly at the major sources of Anglo-American law, outline the structure and functions of the court system, and clarify the roles of the various classes of judges and lawyers who operate within the system. The chapter following this is devoted to discussion of proceedings and procedure in the civil, criminal and administrative courts and tribunals and to analysis of a number of key terms from the point of view of the legal translator.

There is a considerable disparity between the Anglo-American system of law and the systems in place in the so-called 'civil law countries'. It would be a mistake to underestimate the linguistic difficulties this situation causes translators. However, translators moving between the two systems do not, in most cases, face the dilemma of absolute terminological asymmetry. The arrangements are different, but the concepts, and the words in which those concepts are expressed, can usually be found and matched, so long as one knows where to look, and provided one is prepared to make the usual allowances for terms that, in any given language pair, can never be entirely coextensive. Satisfactory approximation must be the translator's goal in cases where a certain amount of semantic shortfall or overlapping is inevitable. Gaps will sometimes have to be plugged and rudimentary bridges occasionally erected. Indeed, one of the strategic challenges of this type of translation is the continual need for systematic comparison and patient selection and discarding. But, given a satisfactory grasp of the underlying legal systems, the translator's headaches will, as usual, be chiefly linguistic.

The 'civil law' or 'Continental law' system we have just mentioned is also known as 'codified law' because the major sources of its legal norms and rules are organized codes or collections. These are normally divided into a civil code, a penal code, an administrative code, a code of commercial law, and a written constitution that stands above them all as a 'law of laws' setting out the basic rights and principles from which all the rest are held to flow. Against this formidable systematization stands the pragmatic organization of the English common law system. It is partly based on the ancient rules of precedent or case-law (*derecho jurisprudencial, derecho casuístico, droit jurisprudentiel, Fallrecht*), i.e. the principle that the rules and judgements adopted by the higher courts in decided cases are binding in certain circumstances on lower courts hearing actions based on similar facts. However, the dividing line between the two systems is becoming increasingly indistinct through growing contact between them as a result of, for instance, the role of the United Kingdom as a Member State of the European Union, the prominence of the United States in international organizations, and the flood of trade between the English-speaking countries (including key players like Canada, Australia, New Zealand and South Africa) and the rest of the world.

It is worth adding that although US federal law originated from the same English sources as all the others, it tends towards a greater systematization and codification. Since 1925 it has been in the form of the United States Code. This Code brings together all the relevant statutes under fifty heads or 'titles', and it is supplemented annually by new additions and recodified and updated every six years.

2.   The translator and the sources of English law

Consider the references made in the following texts:

(a)   If there was at one time a supposed rule that the doctrine of *Donoghue v Stevenson* did not apply to realty, there is no doubt under modern authority that a builder of defective premises may be liable in negligence to persons who thereby suffer injury: see *Gallagher v J McDowell Ltd*, per Lord MacDermott CJ, a case of personal injury. Similar decisions have been given in regard to architects (*Clayton v Woodward & Sons Builders Ltd, Clay v A.J. Crump & Sons Ltd*). *Gallagher*'s case expressly leaves open the question whether the immunity against action of builder-owners established by older authorities (e.g. *Bottomley v Bannister*) still survives. (Lord Wilberforce, in *Anns v London Borough of Merton*, House of Lords, [1977] 2 All ER 492)

(b)   *Held*—(i) A simple contract can in Equity vary a deed (i.e. a lease), though it had not done so here because the simple contract was not supported by consideration. (ii) As the agreement for the reduction of rent had been acted upon by the defendants, the plaintiffs were estopped in Equity from claiming the full rent from 1941 until early 1945, when the flats were fully let. After that time they were entitled to do so because the second agreement was only operative during the continuance of the conditions which gave rise to it. To this extent, the limited claim of the receiver succeeded. If the receiver had sued for the balance of rent from 1941, he would have failed. (*Central London Property Trust Ltd v High Trees House Ltd [1947]*; quoted Keenan 1963/1989:589)

(c)   The council relied on section 111(1) of the Local Government Act 1972. Section 111(1) provided that a local authority should have power to do "anything . . . which is calculated to facilitate, or is conducive or incidental to, the discharge of any of their functions." It was common ground that section 111(1) was wide enough to empower the council to take part in pre-application consultation, since such activity was calculated to facilitate or was conducive or incidental to the discharge of its planning functions under section 29 of the 1971 Act.

Without going into the detail of the issues, it can be seen at a glance that text (a) contains references to earlier cases, text (b) several times mentions rules of equity, and text (c) refers to sections of a particular Act. These, as we have said, are the three principal sources of English law – case-law, equity and statute law – and we shall now look at each of them in turn.

(a) Common law

The concept of common law goes back to medieval times, when judicial principles that were found to be shared by lawgivers in many regions of England gradually gained universal recognition in the whole country. But the expression as used in the English-speaking countries does not connote a system of laws that is merely inherited from the (possibly somewhat primitive) usages of their ancestors. The dominant idea is rather that of a set of *shared* rules, as is clear from the definition given in the *Oxford English Dictionary*: "The unwritten law of England, administered by the King's courts, which purports to be derived from ancient and universal usage".

No doubt venerable translations of 'common law' as the Spanish *derecho consuetudinario* or the French *droit coutumier* will not be easily displaced. Yet they are misleading since they stress the idea of 'custom', thus suggesting a system of laws that are quaint, peculiar and local rather than a set of *unwritten* rules of universal application. It is also true that *all* modern systems of law take account of traditional social practice and the decisions of the higher courts in determining how the law is to be applied to a given case. There is therefore no very convincing reason why the English system alone should be described as *consuetudinario* or *coutumier* when what is really conveyed by the term 'common law' is that the courts' decisions are based on *commonly* or *universally* accepted principles. It seems more satisfactory, for these reasons, to call it *derecho común*, while German may have some reason to accept *das Common Law* when referring to the British system.

The common law originally developed through the courts' decisions in cases involving property, personal injuries (*daños personales, préjudices, Körperverletzungen*), contracts and some of the earliest identified torts such as trespass (i.e. to pass beyond) (*invasión de la propiedad, violation de propriété, Besitz stören*) or interference with goods (*tráfico no autorizado con los bienes de terceros, retención indebida, atteinte illégale aux biens*). The custom arose of regarding the judgements of decided cases as authoritative and, eventually, as binding in later similar cases. Thus precedent was born, and the influence of the judges on the development of case law was so great that it is sometimes called 'judge-made law'. Even today the main principles applied to the laws of contract and tort derive essentially from common-law decisions sanctioned by long custom.

(b)   Equity

In modern legal texts, this word is unlikely to be used in the original etymological sense of 'fairness' or '(natural) justice', so that literal translations based on the Latin *aequitas* (*equidad, équité*) are not recommended. As one modern commentator puts it, whatever may have been the case originally, equity "is certainly no longer a court of conscience" (Keenan 1989:9). As a term of English law it is applied to certain concepts, principles and remedies (*soluciones judiciales, recours, Rechtsbehelfe*) that were formerly excluded by the common law but were gradually recognized, developed and administered in the Middle Ages by the Lord Chancellor in his role as 'keeper of the king's conscience'. Originally the principles concerned were related to property rights in the context of the possession and ownership of land deriving from the feudal system; the common law recognized only legal rights and would not entertain claims based on beneficial rights (*derechos usufructuarios, d'usufruit, Nutzungsrecht*) such as uses and trusts (*fideicomisos, fidéicommis, bis an die Grenzen des Eigenturms erweitertes Nutzungsrecht*).

Equity therefore grew up as a means of tempering the excessive rigour of the common law with a series of distinct principles based on natural justice. By the end of the nineteenth century, common-law and equitable jurisdiction had become merged through the creation of the High Court of Justice, whose Chancery Division took over a great deal of the business of the old Chancellor's Court, or Court of Chancery. In the changeover, the old rule survived which held that in the event of a conflict between common law and equity, equity was to prevail. This is the true basis of the modern distinction between the two sources of legal principle. Simplifying greatly, the upshot is that the courts at their discretion may grant or withhold (refuse to give) equitable remedies. However, it should be remembered that this is a discretion as to whether or not equity is to be applied, not a discretion as to how it should be applied. The rules of equity are now as fixed and definite as those of common law or statute.

Nevertheless, this allows the translator to view equity as a set of discretionary rules or remedies. Accordingly, in appropriate circumstances proceedings can be brought or remedies applied for under equitable principles, though there are special rules determining parties' rights to do so. For example, there is a basic rule that the normal remedy for breaches of civil law rights is damages (*daños y perjuicios, dommages-intérêts, Schadensersatz*) – the common-law remedy – and that no other remedy is available if, in the opinion of the court, an award of damages would be adequate. However, if the plaintiff can establish that the defendant's behaviour represents a permanent or continuing threat to their rights, they may be entitled to ask the court for an injunction (*medidas cautelares, injonction, einsweilige Verfügung*), which is an equitable remedy.[1] Translators should bear in mind that the English principle embraces both precautionary and discretionary principles.

Note that precedent works as much in equity as in common law. This means a judicial decision is not given merely on the basis of what a judge thinks fair and right in the circumstances but also on what has been viewed as reasonable and lawful in past decisions based on similar facts. Similar principles apply to legal relationships like trusts and to causes of action arising out of equitable estoppel[2].

---

[1] Etymologically speaking, the word 'injunction' simply means 'order' and is related to the verb 'enjoin' meaning 'impose, prescribe; order; prohibit'. Like its Latin counterpart, the term applies both to orders to do and to refrain from doing, which are commonly distinguished by the respective expansions 'mandatory injunction' and 'prohibitory injunction'.

[2] The concept of 'estoppel' is often very close to the doctrine of *actos propios* familiar to Spanish lawyers (in the sense that one is 'estopped' or prevented from a particular course of conduct by one's previous behaviour, or one's 'own acts'). In other cases, such as 'estoppel by record', the idea is akin to that of *res judicata*. However, many Spanish lawyers are reluctant to use these vernacular phrases as translations of the English term. They argue that the scope of the English doctrine is far wider and technically so highly developed that it has no true equivalent in any other language. The English word is often used untranslated in law textbooks and academic writing in many countries.

(c)   Statute law

The third and by far the most important source of English law is statute (*legislación, textes de loi, kodifiziertes Gesetz*), i.e. the written laws or legislation drafted and passed by Parliament. The principal written laws are known as Acts of Parliament (or 'Acts of Congress' in the US), though there is also supplementary and delegated legislation like ministerial orders (*órdenes ministeriales, ordres, Verordnungen*), local bye-laws (*ordenanzas, arrêtés municipaux, Gemeindeverordnungen*), and so on. Statute law is the highest source of law, and is binding on everyone, including judges. Judges must apply the law; they cannot change it. In fact, they themselves often remark in their decisions and rulings that the making of exceptions to rigid rules is legislative, not judicial work. But clearly their opinions are authoritative and after a number of judges in the higher courts have drawn attention in their judgements to weaknesses, complications or contradictions in the law, it is not uncommon for Parliament to heed their indirect advice and introduce new legislation to clear up difficulties. Moreover, there are a number of statutes that have been specifically designed to modernize and codify areas of the common law, for example the construction that is to be put on certain terms frequently used in contracts or specifying what types of behaviour give rise to actions in tort. If such statutes were not passed from time to time, the judges would not always be saying the same as the legislators, there would be confusion and uncertainty about some areas of the law and it would be impossible for the law to be adapted to suit the changing circumstances of modern life. For similar reasons, Parliament occasionally passes laws to amend (*modificar, amender, ändern*) earlier Acts or to repeal (*derogar, abroger, aufheben*) them wholly or in part.

3.   The branches of English law. Jurisdiction and the court structure

Many countries with legal systems based on the Continental or Napoleonic code of law recognize four distinct jurisdictions: civil law, criminal law, administrative law and employment law (or 'labor law', as the Americans say). By contrast, the English system, though it recognizes these distinct branches or areas of the law, distinguishes essentially between two jurisdictions: the civil and the criminal. A great deal of the business conducted by the administrative and employment courts in many European countries is handled, under the British system, by a set of lower courts or quasi-judicial bodies known collectively as 'administrative tribunals'. We shall deal more thoroughly with them in Chapter 4. As we shall see a little later on, the High Court has an inherent supervisory jurisdiction over the activity of these tribunals as well as exercising a fully developed administrative function of its own in cases of conflict between the governors and the governed.

The tables provided in this section and the next one are intended to show at a glance the relative positions of the English civil and criminal courts in the hierarchy, but the relationship between them has been greatly simplified. In particular, no attempt has been made here to explain the complex mechanisms by which particular cases are assigned to particular courts, nor is any indication given as to which court is competent in appeal cases. Students interested in these matters should consult any of the standard law textbooks listed in the bibliography (Barnard 1985, 1988; Blackstone 1999).

In civil matters, the general rule is that proceedings commence at first instance in the court that is competent bearing in mind the nature and complexity of the claim and the amount involved. The administrative tribunals are dealt with more fully in Chapter 4. As for the magistrates' courts, we shall see a little later that they are mainly concerned with criminal cases, though they have a limited civil jurisdiction in such matters as adoption and licensing. Otherwise, civil proceedings not involving these tribunals usually start in the county courts or, more rarely, in the High Court. Finally, both the Civil Division of the Court of Appeal and the House of Lords are exclusively concerned with appeals. The House of Lords, as the 'court of last resort', deals only with issues referred to it by the lower courts on 'matters of law of general public importance', which are certified as such by the referring court and posed in the form of questions to be answered 'yes' or 'no' by the 'Law Lords' (*magistrados de la Cámara Alta, juges siégeant à la Chambre des Lords, der letzten richterlichen Instanz beim Oberhaus, Richter des House of Lords*).

Clearly, a key question for translators is whether the names of these English courts should be translated and, if so, how. As in many issues raised by translating, there are two schools of thought. The conservative modern view, which likes to present itself as progressive but is really extremely ancient, is that no element in a text for translation capable of being regarded as a proper noun or as a culturally bound unit should be translated, or, to put it in the somewhat pretentious terms favoured by this school, the appropriate 'technique of translation' in such cases is reproduction (i.e. non-translation). This is, for instance, often the practice of the Translation Service of the European Commission. Until quite recent times it led to the anomaly whereby the 'R' of '*Regina*' (= 'Queen') in the names of cases before the European Court of Justice at Strasbourg was solemnly transcribed into Spanish as '*Regina*', thus giving the casual reader the impression that some otherwise unidentified female of that name was continually involved in litigation with very senior institutions of the community. (The German newspaper habit of referring to the same august personage in her more personal manifestations as '*Die Queen*' seems hardly less absurd.) However, the institution has the weight of apparent authority, and translators ought at least to consider this option.

One alternative is to adapt the names by analogy, much as happens when the British 'Secretary of State for the Home Office', or 'Home Secretary', is referred to in some European languages as the 'Minister of the Interior', or the Chancellor of the Exchequer is called the 'Minister for Finance', or the Inland Revenue service is translated as the 'British Tax Authority'. In our view, so long as excessive literalism is avoided and the resulting translations do not conflict with the actual names of courts in the target-language system, these adapted forms will often be more acceptable than opaque formulations like 'The Divisional Court of the Queen's Bench Division of the High Court of Justice'.

If these suggestions are not deemed appropriate, the translator has no option but to describe the courts and court officers not by analogy with their opposite numbers (*colegas homólogos, homologues, Pendants*) in the target system, but purely in terms of function, e.g. 'the appropriate court', 'the relevant jurisdiction', 'the competent judge', and so on. While this may work occasionally as an alternative to repetition, it seems too clumsy to be used as a standard method.

ENGLISH CIVIL LAW COURTS

HOUSE OF LORDS

COURT OF APPEAL
(CIVIL DIVISION)

HIGH COURT OF JUSTICE

Queen's Bench Division	Chancery Division	Family Division
Divisional Court	Divisional Court	Divisional Court
COUNTY COURTS		MAGISTRATES' COURTS

ADMINISTRATIVE
TRIBUNALS

The following is a summary of the business dealt with by the civil courts:

County Court

In England and Wales, there is at least one of these in virtually every county, so the name of the court coincides with the administrative divisions of the regions.[3]

---

[3] In Scotland, the essential division is rather different. The court of first instance for both civil and criminal cases is the Sheriff Court; the second-instance court is the High Court for criminal appeals and the Court of Session for civil appeals or complex civil actions. The Court of Session is divided into an Outer House and an Inner House, the latter having a First and Second Division. Further appeal is to the House of Lords. In appeals involving matters

However, to translate the English 'county' as a Spanish *provincia* should not be pushed too far, since in Spain the *Audiencia Provincial* is a second-instance court, whereas county court business is normally first-instance and cases are heard by a single judge sitting alone. By law, all divorce cases must begin in the county courts, though contested divorce proceedings may be referred to the High Court. Otherwise the actions heard here concern civil disputes over land, tort, contract and other claims not exceeding a stated maximum, which is always subject to variation.

The High Court

As the table shows, this court, which together with the Crown Court, Court of Appeal and House of Lords constitutes the 'Supreme Court of Judicature', is divided into three 'Divisions'. The Queen's Bench Division (or 'QBD', known as 'King's Bench' when the reigning sovereign is male) has the widest jurisdiction of the three, including appellate jurisdiction in some criminal cases and inherent supervisory jurisdiction over the inferior courts and the administrative acts of the government and local corporations through the system of 'judicial review' (*revisión judicial, control judicial o administrativo, contrôle judiciaire, gerichtliche Überprüfung*).

Judicial review is the means by which the High Court exercises its inherent jurisdiction of supervision of the acts and proceedings of the lower courts, tribunals and public bodies with judicial or quasi-judicial functions. It is not properly speaking a form of appeal but rather provides a remedy for any party who complains that the lower court or administrative body is acting in a manner that is incompatible with basic rights or natural justice. The issue must be one of public law (*derecho público, droit public, Öffentlichesrecht*), which includes but is not confined to administrative action. Essentially the applicant (*recurrente, suplicante, requérent, Antragsteller*) will allege that the offending body has either acted *ultra vires* or has unlawfully declined to exercise its jurisdiction, or that its act or failure to act involves an error of law on the face of the record. Judicial review is also available where the applicant wishes to challenge (*impugnar, contester, anfechten*) the validity of arrest (*detención, arrestation, Arrest*) or detention (*retención, détention, Festnahme*) especially if he or she is threatened with deportation or extradition. In that case the application comes under the rules of *habeas corpus*; otherwise, the applicant will seek one or other of the so-called prerogative orders.[4]

---

commenced under Scots law, at least one member of the House of Lords bench must be a Scottish judge, given that the underlying system is different.

[4] These are the so-called 'prerogative orders' by which the High Court discharges its inherent supervisory functions. *Mandamus* orders a lower court to exercise jurisdiction or perform some similar legal function when it is failing to do so; *certiorari* orders the inferior court to

The original jurisdiction of the Queen's Bench Division (QBD) primarily involves major claims or complex proceedings in tort and contract. This is the most general division of the three that make up the High Court, which explains why it has the largest number of judges of all the divisions. It also contains a specialist jurisdiction in the Admiralty Court, which deals with issues arising out of maritime law, such as collisions at sea, damage to cargo, or salvage.

The Chancery Division specializes in actions involving land, property, contentious probate and trusts. Through its highly specialized Commercial Court it also has exclusive control over matters involving company law (*derecho mercantil, droit des sociétés, Gesellschafstrecht*), which hears cases concerning winding-up (*disoluciones mercantiles, Liquidation*) and bankruptcy (*quiebra, faillite, Konkurs*), banking, insurance and financial matters. A further area of specialization within this division is the field of patents, copyright and intellectual and industrial property generally.

The third branch of the High Court is the Family Division, responsible for matters relating to defended divorces, problematic adoptions not solved by the magistrates' courts or the county courts, the custody and wardship of minors and non-contentious probate.

As the table shows, each division of the High Court has its own 'Divisional Court' to deal with matters referred to it both by the competent division and by relevant inferior courts. For purposes of translation, the only important issue here is that the term 'divisional' implies 'appeal' (perhaps *apelación, recours, Rechtsmittel*), and this must be catered for in the version chosen. In general, translators of legal texts should bear in mind that rights of appeal are very wide-ranging and that English invariably uses the word 'appeal', whereas many Latin languages have alternative terms based on cognates of 'recourse' (*recurso, recours*). The result is that the target-language cognate of 'appeal' may not always be the correct term; the choice of word will depend on the nature of the appellant's claim, the stage of the trial reached, and similar factors. (Spanish for instance has a rich array of types of *recurso*, the *recurso de apelación* being only one of about a dozen.)

The Court of Appeal (Civil Division)

In the light of what we have just said, translators should be aware that the Court

---

remit the record (*autos, fe de lo actuado*) to the High Court following a well-grounded complaint (*queja motivada o bien fundamentada*) of error of law, acting *ultra vires* (*excederse en el uso de sus atribuciones o actuar en exceso de la jurisdicción*), etc; and *prohibition* orders the lower court to refrain from acting in excess of its jurisdiction or oppressively, unlawfully, etc. The order of prohibition is intended to prevent the injustice from happening, and so it is available where the court is satisfied that the applicant would have had a right to an order of *certiorari* if the act had been carried out.

of Appeal has no original jurisdiction and is a purely appellate court, but it is by no means the only source of judgements on appeal in the United Kingdom. As a very rough guide, readers may assume that the natural order of court precedence is that set out in the accompanying tables, and that appeal as a rule is from the court giving judgement to the one next above it in the hierarchy. But there are many exceptions, most of which have no bearing on how proceedings should be translated, so we shall not concern ourselves with them here. It is much more important practically for translators to realize that the same court has two separate jurisdictions, clearly indicated by their names: the Civil Division and the Criminal Division.

Hearings in the Court of the Appeal, like appeal hearings in general, are based on the assumption that the facts as found by the trial court are correct. This is because, as a principle of law, and of common sense, the judge (or jury) who had the advantage of seeing and hearing the witnesses and the evidence was in a much better position to determine their veracity than a tribunal that only hears the evidence at second-hand and possibly months or years later, when memory may be inaccurate and physical proof may have perished. Proceedings therefore go ahead on the basis of what is called 'notional re-hearing' (a revision of the case, virtually a new trial based on the previous one) where the main points taken are matters of law. There are three judges on the bench and decisions can be unanimous or by a majority. In keeping with the British tradition, the three judges deliver their opinions in order of seniority, but all must speak, even if it is only to concur with the judgement of their colleagues. Contrast this with the Spanish system, where one judge, not necessarily the most senior, is designated as rapporteur (*ponente, juge rapporteur, Berichterstatter*) and the others only deliver a separate judgement if they express a dissenting opinion.

The House of Lords

The first point to be made here is that the House of Lords, as the highest court in the land and the court of last resort, must be carefully distinguished from the upper house or chamber (*cámara superior, Chambre haute, Oberhaus*) in the British parliamentary system. When the House sits as a court of law, only the handful of professional judges are involved. In fact, by one of those odd twists or eccentricities for which the British are famous, when a court of the House sits, it normally does so in an unimposing committee room and the judges, usually five in number, wear ordinary civilian clothing rather than the solemn robes and wigs that characterize their colleagues in the lower courts. This is so even when they enter the debating chamber to deliver their opinions.

It is also worth stressing that the judges are not chosen from the people who happen to be members of the House of Lords, but rather are distinguished career judges promoted to the House in order to be members of the very select group of senior judges appointed members of the 'Judicial Committee of the House of Lords'. They are the equivalent of the constitutional court of those countries that have a written constitution (which appears to mean every parliamentary democracy except the United Kingdom) and combine these functions with those of supreme court judges of appeal elsewhere. They are popularly known as the 'Law Lords', but translations of this expression which could suggest that they are 'lords' who happen to be judges or lawyers should be resisted as inaccurate. As we have said, it is the other way round.

The House of Lords exclusively hears appeals on matters of law, always with leave and solely in answer to certified questions concerning matters of law of general public importance. Until the 1960s the House's decisions were binding on the House itself and on all inferior courts, and so the only way it could depart from (*desvincularse de, s'éloigner de, abweichen von*) its own precedents was by 'distinguishing' cases deemed to have been wrongly or dubiously decided. Nowadays, after an uncomfortable precedent has been distinguished by several differently formed committees, it can be disapproved by a later committee considering a case in which one of the parties has referred it to the disputed judgement.

4.   The English Criminal Courts

The major distinction between Anglo-American criminal law and that of the 'civil-law' or 'Roman-law' countries is that the former is generally recognized as being adversarial rather than inquisitorial. The Crown (or the State, or the People) takes the place of the plaintiff, rather than an 'examining magistrate' (*juez instructor, juge d'instruction, Untersuchungsrichter*) taking the lead in testing the evidence (*pruebas, preuves, Beweismaterial*) or pressing charges against an accused person. It is true that in England the Director of Public Prosecutions (DPP), in Scotland the Procurator-Fiscal and in the US the District Attorney (DA) make a decision like that of the Continental *Ministerio Fiscal, Parquet* or *Staatsanwaltschaft* as to whether an accused person should stand trial. It is also true that, in England, all criminal prosecution must begin with a brief hearing at the magistrates' court (approx. *juzgado de guardia, tribunal de police, erstinstanzliches Gericht für Strafsachen niederer Ordnung*), which decide whether an accused person should be freed or stand trial. Lastly, as we will see below, the magistrates also decide whether a charge relates to a summary offence, an indictable offence or an offence triable either way, and thus, indirectly, whether or not trial by jury is an option. Whatever happens, there is no true parallelism between proceedings under the two systems, so that all translators can do is to record more or less literally what the documents say without trying to force them to lie down with one another.

ENGLISH CRIMINAL COURTS

HOUSE OF LORDS

COURT OF APPEAL
(CRIMINAL DIVISION

HIGH COURT OF JUSTICE

Divisional Court

Queen's Bench Division

CROWN COURT

MAGISTRATES' COURTS

Above the magistrates' courts is the Crown Court, which may be regarded as the quintessential criminal court under the English system. It is here that jury trial is typically found, though there are also jurors in coroners' courts – courts convened when a death occurs unexpectedly in a public place, and which have to decide whether the victim died 'by misadventure' (*por accidente, accidental, accidentelle, Unglücksfall*), 'by his own hand' (suicide) or by homicide at the hand of 'a person or persons unknown'. The essential outlines of proceedings before the Crown Court are discussed in Chapter 4.

From the point of view of procedure, everything that has been said earlier about the Court of Appeal (Civil Division) is true of the Criminal Division; and as court of last resort, the House of Lords performs the same function in criminal as in civil cases.

5. The vocabulary of litigation

In all modern democratic states, private disputes that reach the courts in the form of litigation come down to confrontations or contests between two sides, with the judges acting as umpires and applying the rules of the contest between the disputants.

Unsurprisingly, the standard vocabulary of litigation is strongly suggestive of this antagonistic focus and is made up to a very considerable extent of antithetical terms stressing the central ideas of partisanship, battle, conflict and opposition. Inevitably, the outcome of a 'courtroom battle' is a judicial decision declaring a winner and a loser. There can be no drawn matches at law, and if the parties cannot reach an out-of-court settlement (*arreglo o acuerdo extrajudicial, à l'amiable, außergerichtlicher Vergleich*), there is no alternative to a judgement determining the success of one party and the failure of the other. As we shall see, even the decisions themselves break down into opposing semantic fields subsumed under the basic antonyms of 'upholding' (*estimar, confirmer, bestätigen*) and 'dismissing' or 'repelling' (*desestimar, rejeter, abweisen*) the arguments presented by each side, i.e. judgements for the plaintiff and against the defendant (*fallos condenatorios, décisions de condamnation, Verurteilungen*), and vice versa (*fallos absolutorios, décisions absolutoires, Freispruche*).

Before we attempt to provide an outline of the linguistics of litigation, we might examine the logic of the translations provided for the English terms in that last sentence. Unlike the Latin languages, modern English does not use 'absolve' as a legal term at all, and 'condemn', which normally has moral or religious connotations, is only used in law to indicate the punishment imposed on an accused person convicted of a serious crime, e.g. 'condemn to death or to life impisonment'. In all modern systems of law the case is brought by the plaintiffs and so the onus is on them to prove their assertions and make out their claim. Therefore if the claim succeeds in law, the plaintiff is entitled to judgement, and if it fails, there must be judgement for the defendant. In the Latin languages, following the lead of Roman law, this is expressed by saying that the judgement either 'condemns' or 'absolves' the defendant, but, logically, since the defendant has not brought the action, the plaintiff is neither 'absolved' nor 'condemned'. In other words, the terms describing the nature of the decision follow from the relative positions of the parties: a *fallo condenatorio* is one which favours the plaintiff and 'condemns' the defendant, and, contrariwise, a *fallo absolutorio* is a decision in favour of the defendant, who is 'absolved' of the plaintiff's claim. English, more bluntly, talks of 'judgement for the plaintiff' or 'judgement for the defendant'.

It is equally crucial for translators to remember that, if there is an appeal, the appellant (*recurrente, appelant, [Berufungs]Kläger*), logically, will be the party who has lost at first instance, or at least the party who is dissatisfied with the result, while the winner will be the 'respondent' (*parte recurrida, défendeur, Beklagter*). However, since either the plaintiff or the defendant can win or lose at first instance, translators should be careful not to confuse the identities of appellant and respondent, even if their roles appear to be reversed. In reported cases, English courts sometimes retain the dual reference in phrases like 'the plaintiff (here the respondent)', but they do not always remember the plight of the ordinary reader struggling to keep up with the logic of forensic analysis. Nor do their Spanish colleagues, who often refer to the appellant as the *demandante*, even if they are referring to the party who was originally the *demandado*. It is thus essential that translators keep their eye on the ball, so to speak.

Finally, as should be obvious, either side can win the appeal, since the court above (*tribunal ad quem, oberes Gericht*) may agree or disagree with the decision of the court below (*tribunal a quo, unteres Gericht*). If the decision favours the appellant, we say that the appeal has been 'allowed' or 'upheld' and if the respondent wins, we say that the appeal has been 'dismissed'. Once again, translators should be careful to distinguish between 'granting leave to appeal' (allowing the appeal to go to court) or 'refusing leave to appeal' (not allowing it to proceed), and allowing or dismissing it at the end of proceedings. In the first case, all the court is saying is that in the circumstances and in law the applicant is or is not entitled to lodge the appeal; in the second case, we are talking about the appeal court's final decision on the matter.

Litigation, as we have said, is a legal contest between two parties: the plaintiff or claimant and the defendant. The action (or 'proceedings') is begun by the plaintiff, who brings (or 'files') a claim (*demanda, reclamación, réclamation, Rechtsanspruch*) against the defendant, usually by issuing a writ (*notificación de emplazamiento, assignation, Klageschrift*). The defendant can then do one of three things:

(1)   admit (*admitir, reconnaître, zulassen*) the claim and settle (*satisfacer la pretensión del demandante, satisfaire à la prétension du demandeur, einen Schaden regulieren*);
(2)   do nothing; or
(3)   deny the claim and file a defence (*contestar a la demanda, résister à la prétension du demandeur, eine Forderung anmelden*).

If the claim is admitted (1), the matter is at an end and there is no need for trial. If the defendant fails to file a reply (2) within the time allowed (usually 14 days), the plaintiff is entitled to move for a default judgement (*sentencia en rebeldía, non-comparution, Versäumnisurteil*) and, if necessary, to request the court to commence enforcement proceedings, i.e. to take steps to force the defendant to settle the claim. These steps include court orders for the seizure (*embargo, saisie, Beschlagnahme*) of a debtor's property, the freezing (*bloqueo, congelación o embargo preventivo, blocage, Sperre*) of their assets (*bienes, propiedades, biens, Besitzvermögen*), the attachment (*intervención, retenue, Pfändung*) of their salary and bank account, or the judicial sale of some or all of their goods. However, if a defence is filed (3), we have the beginning of the classic civil action and trial, i.e. the contest we referred to earlier. Let us now examine the main concepts and the principle features of the vocabulary of claim, defence and judgement.

The starting-point for proceedings before the courts, as we have said, is the writ or document in which the plaintiff is required to show cause why the action has been brought. This is not the same as proof (*prueba, demostración, preuve,*

Beweis), which belongs to a much later stage of proceedings. It is a mixed state-ment of fact and law which, if proved, would entitle the complainant to the remedy sought (*petitum, pretensión, recours, Rechtsbehelf*). In other words, it is an allegation that an act or acts of the defendant named in the writ has de-prived the plaintiff of a right recognized by the law, or has unlawfully injured him, his dependants or his property.

The cause of action (*fundamento de la demanda, motif d'action en justice, Klagegrund*), then, is the fact or act complained of; and the right of action (approx. *legitimación, droit d'agir en justice, Klagerecht*) derives from some recognized law or legal principle allegedly breached by the defendant's act. In this general context, it does not matter whether the right is general – e.g. the right to health and safety at work, or to proper standards of quality in manufac-turing, or to freedom from nuisance caused by noise, pollution, and so on – or particular – e.g. the right to expect that a contract will be honoured, or that our neighbours will not block our view or our light by building a wall where they shouldn't. Nor does it matter whether the right contended for springs from stat-ute or from common law. So long as there is a reasonable basis for the complaint in both fact and law, or *prima facie* case (sufficient elements at first sight), the action will be allowed to proceed and the defendant will have to contest it.

The defendant can answer the complaint in a number of ways. The simplest is denial pure and simple, which is called 'traverse' (*contradicción o negación simple, contestation, Leugnen*), e.g. when the defendant says 'I do not owe X £1000 or any other sum'. This is a sufficient defence because of the basic rule that the 'burden of proof' (*carga de la prueba, charge de la prueve, Beweislast*) is borne by the party making the assertion or bringing the charge. The outcome of the case will then depend entirely on the evidence, and the onus is on the plaintiff to prove 'on a balance of probabilities' that the defendant is 'liable' (*responsable, haftbar*) for the harm (*daño, perjuicio, Schaden*) to their rights. Incidentally, 'guilt' and 'innocence' belong exclusively to criminal law. In pri-vate or civil law cases, what has to be proved is the 'liability' of the defendant, who is not 'accused' of anything. This means that it is up to the plaintiff to show through evidence that the defendant is bound to compensate him or her for some private injury (*perjuicio, préjudice, dommage, Verletzung, Schaden*) caused by the defendant's act.

However, there are often more sophisticated defences, such as a challenge to this particular plaintiff's right to bring this particular action; or a defence allegation that the action is out of time or 'statute-barred'; or that there has been a mistake in identity and the defendant is not the person identified in the writ; or that the defendant is the person named, but the act complained of was carried out by someone else; or that the defendant is not legally responsible because of their age or position or mental condition; or that the claim is defeated by a prior or stronger right of the defendant.

This latter position may lead to what is called a 'counterclaim' (*reconvención, contrademanda, demande reconventionnelle, Gegenforderung*) by the defence. For example, if A sues B for a debt of £5,000, B can counterclaim by alleging that A previously owed him £3,000. Depending on the tactics used by each side, B could go on to agree to settle the debt to A so long as A agrees to pay the amount outstanding to B; in other words, B could use the suit to offset the old debt against the new.

6. Common terms in litigations

So far we have seen that the defence can contest the suit by denying either the right of action, or the cause of action, or both. Obviously, there are innumerable ways in which this can be done and, as judges are never tired of repeating, every case will depend on its own merits and on its own peculiar facts. From the translator's point of view, what matters is to become familiar with the words that are likely to be used in connection with the generality of lawsuits, and that is the aim of the following list of terms, each illustrated in relation to the aims of the parties:

Answer (*contestar, responder, répondre, antworten, contestación, refutación, Antwort*)
As explained earlier, this is the defendant's way of meeting the claim. But in a phrase like 'The judge found that the defence had provided a complete answer to the claim', the sense is that the defence is successful and the action is defeated or refuted. (In the traditional sense; see 'reject'.)

Argument (*argumento, debate, argument, Argument*)
Like 'submission' and 'contention', this term refers to exchanges between the two parties in the course of proceedings, especially oral debate before the court during hearings (*vistas, audiencias, audiences, auditions, Hearings*), e.g. 'The Court of Appeal heard argument on points of law from both counsel'. Basically, then, the word has the sense it normally has in logic and in everyday civilized discussion, without any suggestion of heated exchange. Nor does it connote deviousness, craft or cunning. The Spanish term *argüir* (to point to a conclusion) should therefore be treated with extreme caution.

Cause (*causa, fundamento, cause, Ursache*)
In very formal contexts, this word is equivalent to 'case' or 'action', e.g. 'To plead a cause in contract'. When the word has its more ordinary sense of 'reason', we have seen that there is a technical distinction between 'cause of action' (*fundamento de la demanda, motif d'action en*

justice, Klagegrund) and 'right of action' (*fundamentos de derecho, legitimación, droit d'agir en justice, Klagerecht*). In a court calendar, the cases awaiting judgement or called for immediate hearing are called the 'cause list' (*relación de las vistas, rôle d'audience, Terminliste*).

Claim (*pretensión, reclamación, reivindicación, revendication, Rechts-anspruch*)
Essentially, the basis of the plaintiff's case, but also used for counterproposals put forward by the defence. The common usage is, e.g. 'The plaintiff's claim was upheld'.

Contention (*tesis, argumento, assertion, Behauptung*)
Particular argument or point of view put forward by one side or the other during argument or pleadings with the aim of convincing the judge or jury. Translators should note that, since judges are not parties to the suit and their decisions are final, judicial 'argument' is regarded as a combination of logic and legal principle leading to a finding (*resolución, conclusion, Festellung*). It is therefore not called 'contention', since its purpose is not to convince, but to decide. The verb is 'to contend' (*sostener, mantener, soutenir, behaupten*). Both the noun 'contest' and the adjective 'contentious' are related to this strongly argumentative term. Example: 'The defence strongly contended that the case was statute-barred.'

Counterclaim (*reconvención, demande reconventionnelle, Gegenfor-derung*)
See explanation in the previous section. As a verb the term means to enter a counterclaim.

Injury (*lesión, daño, perjuicio, préjudice, dommage, Schaden, Verletzung*)
In law it is not just people's bodies that can be injured; their rights can suffer injury too. Where necessary, the physical sense is distinguished from the moral by adding the adjective 'personal' (*daños personales*), e.g. 'In tort, damages are usually only awarded for personal injuries or damage to property'. Close synonyms are 'harm' and 'damage'. Translators should note that as nouns in this sense both 'harm' and 'damage' are uncountable, e.g. 'His rights suffered harm', 'Her goods suffered damage'. 'Damages' (*daños [y perjuicios], dommages-intérêts, Schaden*) in the plural has an entirely different meaning: it is the compensation paid to the successful plaintiff for injury to or interference with their rights.

Lawsuit (*pleito, litigio, procès, Prozess*)
A civil action or proceeding. See also 'suit'.

Pleadings (*alegaciones, escritos de pretensiones o de posiciones, con-clusions, Plädieren*)
Formal written statements provided by each side, setting out the facts on which they propose to base their case at trial. They develop or refine on the bare statements made in the original statements of claim and defence, e.g. 'In modern law, pleadings may be amended even after close of plead-ings'. The verb is 'to plead' (*declarar, alegar, plaider, plädieren*).

Probable cause (*indicios racionales de criminalidad, base de la impu-tabilidad, preuves, vermutlicher Grund*)
Term commonly used in US criminal law to indicate the need for some *prima facie* evidence of wrongdoing before a suspect can be arrested and charged, e.g. 'The judge ordered the arrested man to be released without charge as the DA's office had failed to show probable cause'.

Put forward (*exponer, presentar, sostener, défendre, vorbringen*)
Very similar to 'argue', 'propose' or 'submit', e.g. 'The arguments put forward by counsel for the defence'.

Reject (*rechazar, desestimar, negar, denegar, inadmitir, rejeter, zurückweisen*)
The choice of the appropriate word in translation will depend very much on who is doing the 'rejecting'. There is a world of difference, of course, between rejection of an argument by the opposition (*adversario, parte contraria, partie adverse, Gegenpartei*) and rejection by the court, which is fatal. A little like the use of 'refute' in a similar sense: traditionalists hold it means 'to disprove unanswerably by logical argument', as in mod-ern Spanish and other Latin languages, and somewhat casual moderns believe the verb to be synonymous with 'deny'. When judges 'reject' an argument, they regard it as 'refuted' in the traditional sense; counsel, on the other hand, continually attempt to 'reject' the arguments put forward by the other side.

Submission (*tesis, argumento, intervención, alocución, présentation, Vorlage*)
Often synonymous with 'contention', this word is also used for speeches or statements made orally by counsel in open court, e.g. to the jury at the conclusion of the trial. The verb is 'to submit' (*defender la tesis de que, argumentar, mantener, sostener,* perhaps *suggérer, proposer, vorlegen*). Example: 'After counsel's final submissions, the judge gives directions to the jury.'

Suit (*pleito, litigio, action, Prozess*)
A civil action or proceeding. The related verb is 'to sue' (*demandar, poursuivre, klagen*). In addition to its basic sense, this word is found in the phrase 'at the suit of', meaning 'on the motion of, at the request of',

e.g. 'The hearing was held in chambers at the suit of the defendant'. In some old cases, the action itself is designated 'X at the suit of Y' (sometimes abbreviated to 'X a.t.s. Y'), where X is the defendant and Y the plaintiff. Nowadays, of course, the adversarial nature of the proceedings is indicated by the use of 'v' (for 'versus') between the names of plaintiff and defendant, e.g. 'Green v Brown'.

Title to sue (*derecho a entablar demanda, legitimación, titre d'attaquer en justice, Klagerecht*)
Equivalent to 'right of action', e.g. 'Only parties to a contract have title to sue for breach of the agreement'.

Wrong (*injusticia, mal, perjuicio, acto ilícito, conducta antijurídica, faute civile, Unrecht*)
In legal language as well as in everyday speech, 'wrong' is the opposite of 'right'. More specifically it is any unlawful act that causes loss or harm to another or to society as a whole. There are many near-synonyms for 'wrong' that are used in specific legal collocations, e.g. 'breach' (*incumplimiento, quebrantamiento, infraction, vulneración, manquement, rupture, Bruch*), 'infringement' (*infracción, contravención, infraction, contravention, [Rechts-]Verletzung*), 'infraction' (*infracción, infraction, Verletzung*), 'contravention' (*infracción, contravención, infraction, contravention, Zuwiderhandlung*) and 'violation' (*violación, vulneración, infraction, Verstoß*). However, though there is inevitably a strong note of moral indignation present when litigants air their grievances (*agravios, quejas, griefs, Beschwerde*) in court, morals have very little to do with the law. General words for moral wrongdoing like 'transgression' or 'misdeed' are therefore not legal terms in English.

7.   The language of judges

Since the purpose of legal proceedings is most often to adjudicate between parties and to determine and uphold rights by means of authoritative rulings, it is hardly surprising that two very productive semantic fields in the context of the law are those of positive and negative decisions. Legal relationships commonly depend on the existence of duties and obligations, which may be of two types: either public and general (e.g. the duty to pay one's taxes or not to harm one's neighbour) or private and voluntary (e.g. contracts, guarantees, negative stipulations or binding promises [*pactos o promesas vinculantes, qui engagent, verbindlich*]). In criminal cases the law specifically prohibits certain kinds of conduct and prescribes particular punishments for those who commit the forbidden acts. On the other hand, when the plaintiff in a civil action bases their claim on the defendant's failure to perform a specified duty, or alternatively alleges that some act of the defendant infringes one or more of their rights, the purpose of the action is to obtain relief or compensation through an appropriate court order (*orden judicial, auto, ordre du tribunal, Gerichtsbescluss*).

In their pleadings, both sides attempt to persuade the court to disregard the other parties' arguments, and the losing side is entitled to appeal (*recurrir, faire appel, ein Rechtsmittel einlegen*) against the judgement or any part of it, whether final or interlocutory. Courts may therefore be asked to make orders allowing or disallowing the rights pleaded for. Though 'order', 'judgement', 'verdict', 'ruling' and 'decision' are the general terms describing judicial determinations, there are a wide variety of partially synonymous verbs in common technical use to specify the nature of the decision made. Translators need to be alive to the particular context, since the English expression selected is normally a matter of usage or collocation rather than strict semantics.

Once the parties have argued their respective cases and made their final submissions, the court gives its decision on both facts and law. This decision may be final, disposing of the central issue between the parties, in which case it is said to be judgement 'on the merits' (*sobre el fondo de la cuestión, jugement sur le fond, in der Sache selbst, nach materiellem Recht*), or it may be a preliminary ruling (*resolución sobre un incidente previo, jugement préalable, Vorabentscheidung*). But even in the latter case, it may effectively put an end to the action if, for instance, it is in the form of an order striking out the claim as disclosing no cause of action. The judge may deliver the judgement orally at the conclusion of the case, or reserve judgement (i.e. take time to consider the case before giving a judgement).

The basic terms in which this decision is expressed are 'judgement for the plaintiff' (*fallo condenatorio, décision de condamnation, Urteil im Sinne des Klägers*) and 'judgement for the defendant' (*fallo absolutorio, décision absolutoire, ein Urteil im Sinne des Beklägters*), or more simply, 'this action succeeds' or 'this action fails'. However, as there are numerous technical terms for particular decisions, translators may find it helpful to check the following list of the most common ones. For convenience of reference, we have laid them out in two groups: the positive terms upholding and giving effect to the arguments of one of the parties, and the negative terms dismissing the contentions of the losing side.

8. The terms used in favourable judicial decisions

Accept (*acoger, dar validez o crédito a, admettre, annehmen*)
Not really a technical term, but often needs refinement in translation, e.g. 'The judge said he could not accept that part of the plaintiff's argument'.

Affirm (*ratificar, confirmar, confirmer, bestätigen*)
Often found with its usual meaning of 'state, declare', but in technical

use preferred to 'confirm' or 'ratify' to indicate that an appeal has failed and the jury's verdict or the trial judge's decision is correct, e.g. 'The appeal was dismissed and the sentence affirmed'.

Allow (*estimar, attribuer, accorder, erlauben*)
Verb used when the appeal court decides in favour of the appellant, thus reversing the earlier decision, e.g. 'For the reasons I have given, I would allow this appeal'. Translators should be careful to distinguish between 'allow' and 'give leave'. If an appeal is *allowed*, the appellant has won; if *leave to appeal* is granted all that is meant is that the court recognizes that the appellant has an arguable case and that the appeal should therefore be heard.

Apply the proviso
A difficult term to translate due to the very particular implication of the term '*the* proviso'. The proviso (*condición, salvedad, condition, Klausel*) involved here is the proposition that a superior court of appeal can decline to interfere with the verdict of a jury or the sentence passed by the trial judge, even if the judge has misdirected the jury or erred in law, *provided that* no actual miscarriage of justice has ensued. This means that the appeal is technically successful but that the judgement stands.

Approve (*aprobar, ratificar, confirmar, confirmer, ratifier, billigen*)
Said of the decision of an appellate court when it confirms the judgement of the court below, e.g. 'By a majority, the Court of Appeal approved the decision of the trial judge'.

Award (*conceder, adjudicar, accorder, zubilligen; laudo, indemnización, indemnisation, Zubilligung*)
As a verb, commonly found in the part of the judgement in which the amount of damages is specified, or custody is given to one or other of the spouses in a divorce case, e.g. 'The plaintiff was awarded £5,000 in damages' or 'The wife was awarded custody of the children'. Sometimes the translator may find it more natural to express this idea from the point of view of the loser; for example, the first of the two illustrations above could be translated *El tribunal condenó al demandado a pagar una indemnización de 5.000 libras* (The court ordered the defendant to pay damages of 5,000 pounds). As a noun, 'award' means the amount of the damages allowed by the court and also the compensation ordered after arbitration.

Entitle (*dar derecho, donner droit, berechtigen*)
Widely used in legal texts in both active and passive constructions, especially 'be entitled to' (*tener derecho a, avoir droit à, berechtig sein zu*). Both counsel and judges are commonly heard to say that a plaintiff

is, or is not, 'entitled to succeed', e.g. 'If the plaintiff can prove her injuries were caused by consuming the defendant's product, she is entitled to succeed'.

Find [for/against] (*fallar, resolver, pronunciar sentencia [a favor o en contra de], rendre un verdict [en faveur de/contre], zu jds Gunsten entscheiden*)

Courts exist to determine the facts and the applicable law, which together constitute the 'findings' (*fallo, conclusion, Festellungen*). Therefore, to 'find for the plaintiff' is to give judgement for them. 'Findings' are also the conclusions reached by the author of a report or public enquiry. Similar to 'rule' and 'hold'.

Give [or grant] leave: See 'allow'.

Give judgement for

Phrase explained earlier. It will be remembered that it is used to announce the winner and can apply to either party, e.g. 'Judgement was given for the defendant'.

Good (*válido, responsable, fiable, de fiar, de solvencia, de confianza, conforme, valable, gültig*)

Simple and effective term used to mean that a contract, for instance, is valid, e.g. 'The court ruled that the agreement made orally in the presence of witnesses was good in law'. Also said of a reliable trader or company, e.g. 'The firm was described as 'respectably constituted and normally considered good for its normal business engagements'.

Grant (*otorgar, conceder, acoger la pretensión de una de las partes o acceder a su solicitud, accorder, zubilligen*)

Give, allow, accede to a request, e.g. 'The court granted an extension to allow the defendant to prepare his case'. See 'leave'.

Hold (*resolver, fallar, conclure, entscheiden*)

Classic term describing the act of a judge or court in announcing their decisions. In law reports the past participle 'held' is often found printed in capitals at the very end and followed by a brief statement of the final result, e.g. 'HELD: Judgement for the plaintiff'. The term can also be coupled with adjectives such as 'liable' and 'innocent', as in 'The defendant was held liable for the plaintiff's losses' or 'innocent of any wrongdoing'. However, the word is also used subjectively by counsel in arguing their cases, and it is then equivalent to 'maintain', 'argue', 'claim', etc., rather than 'find', e.g. 'We hold that there is no basis for this claim'. Translators should take care to bring out this nuance in their versions, since the pragmatic assumption is that lawyers argue and urge their clients' claims more or less vehemently, whereas judges dispassionately 'find' and objectively apply the law. In announcing their decisions, therefore, judges do not 'claim', or 'maintain', or 'argue', but simply 'state' or 'find', which is what 'hold' means in that context. See also 'find' and 'rule'.

Make out (*demostrar fehacientemente, justifier une plainte, nachweisen*) Said of the successful litigant, who achieves their aim by proving their case by argument and evidence, e.g. 'The plaintiffs have not made out their case, so there must be judgement for the defendant'. Also used with the particular fact or issue as object or as subject of a passive sentence, e.g. 'Liability / malice is clearly made out'.

Rule (*emitir un fallo, statuer, entscheiden*) Like 'find', 'rule' refers to judicial decisions, but in this case exclusively on a point or points of law. The noun is 'ruling', e.g. 'The case went to the House of Lords for a ruling on the scope of the law'.

Sanction (*sanción, sancionar, autorisation, autoriser, Sanktion, sanktionieren*) An ambiguous word in English and many other languages, since it is related both to 'approval' and to 'punishment'. In this context, it is the positive senses that concern us, e.g. 'The court ruled that the legal principle invoked by the defence had the sanction of tradition and case-law'.

Satisfy (*convencer, convaincre, überzeugen*) A formal rather than a technical term meaning 'convince, assure beyond reasonable doubt', e.g. 'The jury was satisfied the accused had not intended to kill the victim'.

Succeed (*triunfar, prosperar, déclarer admissible, Erfolg haben*) This ordinary-looking word is often used by judges as a terser alternative to 'give judgement for the plaintiff' or 'allow an appeal'. The usual phrase is simply 'This claim succeeds', but in many languages it is unlikely that literal versions will prove acceptable. Translators may well have to adjust their versions to meet language-specific requirements of style and register (e.g. *Procede estimar el presente recurso, nuestro fallo ha de ser favorable a las pretensiones del demandante [o ha de ser condenatorio],* etc.). The opposite, naturally enough, is 'fail'.

Sustain (*admitir, aceptar, admettre, accorder, als rechtsgültig anerkennen*) Used principally in the phrase 'Objection sustained' (or just 'Sustained') pronounced by the judge when counsel for one side objects to the illegal tactics, like leading questions, being used by the other side during examination of witnesses. If the judge deems that the question is fair, the phrase is 'Objection overruled' (or 'Overruled').

Uphold (*estimar, confirmar, confirmer, bestätigen*)
A common alternative to 'allow', e.g. 'The decision was upheld on appeal'. In legal contexts the term is not uncommonly used in its everyday sense of 'defend, support' (*defender, apoyar, faire respecter, unterstützen*), as in 'It is the duty of the courts to uphold the law'.

Warrant (*justificar, autorizar, justifier, rechtfertigen*)
As a noun, this can mean an authorization or certificate, as in 'an arrest warrant' (*orden de detención o de búsqueda y captura, mandat d'arrêt, Haftbefehl*). And in commercial use it means 'guarantee'. But in judicial use, and in formal contexts generally, it has the meanings indicated above, e.g. 'The judge remarked that nothing in English law warranted the claims made in the plaintiff's pleadings'.

9. The terms used in unfavourable judicial decisions

Annul (*anular, extinguir, annuler, abroger, annullieren, für nichtig erklären*)
This verb is used chiefly with the noun 'marriage'. Both in Canon Law and in lay contexts, it is a means of declaring that the marriage never existed, i.e. it was 'null' or 'a nullity' (*nulo, nul, nichtig*) from the beginning due to some formal impediment. Less frequently the term is found with 'bankruptcy order' in the same sense. In very formal contexts, the term applies to a resolution canceling delegated legislation, and it is also used in a similar way by the Court of Justice of the European Communities. However, it is not the best term where a contract is being referred to. In that case, it is usual to say that the contract is null, or is null and void (*nul et non avenu, null und nichtig*), or is a (complete) nullity. Compare this with the use of 'avoid'.

Avoid (*anular, rescindir, annuler, aufheben*)
The legal sense of this verb is quite distinct from the everyday one. In law it means 'to make or declare void' and is applied to the act of one of the parties to a contract by which they declare their decision to treat the agreement as non-existent or to consider themselves no longer bound by it. It should be noticed that a contract cannot be avoided for breach (*incumplimiento, manquement, Bruch*) but only where the agreement was reached on the basis of misrepresentation or undue influence by one of the parties. In such a case the contract is said to be *voidable* but not *void*. A *void* contract is one that never existed in law, usually because one or both of the contracting parties was mistaken as to its terms or because the subject-matter itself did not exist at the time the agreement was made.

The distinction between a *void* contract and one that is merely *voidable* is therefore very important. In the latter case the party wishing to avoid the contract must do so before any goods exchanged under the original agreement have been sold on to third parties; otherwise, they will be irrecoverable. The act of avoiding a contract in these circumstances may also be called *rescission*, *setting aside* or *repudiation*. However, translators should take care with the term 'rescission'. (See *rescind.*)

Cancel (*cancelar*, *dejar sin efecto*, *lever*, *révoquer*, *aufheben*)
In many ways this is the most general word in the group and is in everyday use in its etymological sense e.g. 'cancel an appointment / a reservation / an order'. It is most often found in legal contexts when a court order is issued nullifying the effect of some document.

Dismiss (*desestimar*, *denegar*, *rejeter*, *abweisen*, *entlassen*)
This is essentially the act of a court when it rejects a claim, an action, an application or an appeal or, in criminal law, a charge. Dismissal is the final judgement of a court and always means that there is judgement for the defendant or the respondent / appellee. The dismissal of an appeal follows full argument, but in civil proceedings at first instance the order is very often given at the interlocutory stage when the court decides that the plaintiff's action cannot succeed in law or that there is no proper basis for the claim. A claim may also be dismissed 'for want of prosecution'. Criminal proceedings may be dismissed if in the judge's opinion there is no *prima facie* basis for trying the accused on the offence charged. The court will also formally dismiss the case against the accused and acquit him or her if the prosecution at trial drop (or withdraw) the charges for lack of evidence or for any other reason.

Overrule (*rechazar*, *revocar*, *anular*, *annuler*, *rejeter*, *aufheben*)
A higher court or instance may overrule the decision of a lower one on a matter of law. The word is also used in the sense of 'dismiss' when the judge rules against an objection raised by counsel (*abogado*, *avocat*, *Rechtsanwalt*) for either side to the tactics or method used by counsel for the other side during examination or cross-examination of witnesses. Here, the phrase is 'Objection overruled' (*denegada la protesta*, *objection rejetée*, *Einspruch abgeleht!*) and the opposite is 'Objection sustained' (*se acepta la protesta*, *objection retenue*, perhaps *Einspruch stattgegeben*).

Overturn (*anular*, *revocar*, *casar*, *faire annuler*, *casser*, *aufheben*)
One of several words ('reverse' and 'quash' are the other common equivalents) for the act of a court of appeal when it reaches a decision opposite to that given by the lower court, or trial court. An example is 'The judgement was overturned on appeal to the House of Lords'.

Quash (*anular, revocar, casar, annuler, aufheben*)
Equivalent to 'reverse', 'overturn' or 'set aside'. It is most often used in criminal appeals when the verdict or sentence of the trial court is over-ruled. As a result, the usual object of the verb is 'conviction' or 'sentence', e.g. 'The convictions were quashed by the Court of Appeal on the ground that they were "unsafe and unsatisfactory"'. It is worth stressing that the quashing of the original sentence is not necessarily favourable to the per-son convicted. For example, it is not uncommon for the appeal to be brought by the Crown on the ground that the sentence is too lenient (*leve, léger, milde*). In this event the appeal is known as 'the Attorney Gener-al's reference', and if the original sentence is quashed, the result will be that a more severe penalty is imposed.

Repeal (*derogar, revocar, abroger, aufheben*)
Term meaning to revoke a statute or Act of Parliament (i.e. a written law), which are the usual objects of the verb or subjects of equivalent passive sentences, e.g. 'The Act was repealed by a narrow majority'. The word seems never to be used with reference to decisions, verdicts or judgements.

Repel (*desestimar, revocar, denegar, anular, casar, abroger, zurück-weisen*)
A Scots Law term equivalent to 'quash', 'overrule', 'overturn', 'reverse', 'dismiss', etc., e.g. 'The court repelled the defender's reclaiming motion'.[5]

Repudiate (*negarse a reconocer, refuser d'honorer, nicht anerkennen*)
In contract law, an alternative expression to **avoid** or **set aside**. It is most commonly used in connection with contracts made by minors (minors *can* make valid contracts in certain cases, contrary to popular belief), e.g. 'The father repudiated the contract on his daughter's behalf on the ground that she was clearly not entitled to purchase goods to the value of £2000'. The term 'repudiation' is also sometimes used to refer to words or acts of a party to a contract which plainly signify that he or she has no intention of fulfilling his side of an agreement; in this sense it is equivalent to 'antici-patory breach' of contract (*aviso o anticipo de incumplimiento de contrato, rupture anticipée de contrat, antizipierter Vertragsbruch*), which may mean that the contract is regarded as void or voidable.

Rescind (*rescindir, resolver, abrogar, résilier, anéantir, abroger, für ungultig erklären*)
Properly speaking, rescission is the act of setting aside, repudiating or, more formally, 'abrogating' a voidable contract, usually on the ground

---

[5] Other Scots Law terms that should be noted here are 'defender' rather than 'defendant' (just as 'pursuer' is used instead of the English term 'plaintiff') and 'reclaiming motion' rather than 'appeal'.

of misrepresentation, whether innocent (*errónea o inadvertida, dol spontané*, perhaps *nicht betrügerisch*) or fraudulent (*fraudulenta, frauduleux, dol provoqué, betrügerisch*), e.g. 'The buyer brought an action for recission when tests showed that the cloth described in the contract as 'pure cotton' contained 20% synthetic fibres'. The term is often inaccurately used when the party injured by the other party's breach (*incumplimiento, manquement, Vertragsbruch*) treats the contract as discharged. However, strictly speaking, in cases of this kind, it is the breach which brings the contract to an end (or 'discharges' it) rather than any retaliatory act of the injured party. An even more misleading use of the term is met with every other day in the newspapers when, for instance, we read that a football star is threatening to 'rescind' his contract unless his club pays him a substantial increase in wages. Legally if the player carries out this threat he will be in breach of contract. Rescission in the proper sense is actually the injured party's remedy or their defence. It provides a remedy if the injured party brings an action to have the contract set aside on the ground that it was induced by misrepresentation; and it is a defence if the action is brought by the other party to enforce the contract. In any event, the party intending to rescind must clearly indicate to the other party, either by actual communication or by publicly evidenced words or acts, an intention to treat the contract as discharged. Moreover, rescission will only be allowed if *restitutio in integrum* is possible, i.e. if goods bought and sold under the original contract can be restored to their original owners. Where the goods have passed into the hands of third parties (*terceros, tiers, Dritter*), rescission is no longer possible, since it is aimed at restoring the parties to the positions they were in before the contract was agreed. It is worth noticing in passing that this restoring of the parties to their original positions is the usual purpose of damages awarded in tort rather than of damages awarded in contract; in the latter case, the aim is to place the parties in the position they would have been in if the contract had been performed as agreed. The reason for this apparent anomaly is that rescission in a formal action in the civil courts is an equitable remedy, as is its conceptual opposite, 'specific performance'. The normal common-law remedy in all such cases is the award of damages, so that rescission is the exception rather than the rule.

Reverse (*revocar, resolver a favor de la parte contraria, annuler*, perhaps *kassieren*)
This term describes the act of a court of appeal when it completely overturns (reverses the orientation of) the judgement of the trial court and gives a decision in favour of the side which lost in the court below, e.g. 'The House of Lords allowed the appeal, thus reversing the judgement of the trial court'.

Set aside (*desestimar, anular, invalidar, annuler, abroger, aufheben*)
The legal sense of this phrase is to cancel or make void, which is simply

a formal application of its ordinary meaning. Thus, we talk about setting aside a judgement, an order, a decision, or a contract.

Stay (*archivar, sobreseer, suspender, surseoir à, aussetzen*)
Term used both as transitive verb and as noun, in the sense of an order halting or suspending proceedings before a court. Stay of action or of proceedings (*archivo de las actuaciones, sursis, Ruhen des Verfahrens*) may be ordered if the court regards the claim as frivolous (*temeraria, pas sérieux, unbedeutend*) or the plaintiff's conduct as unreasonable, e.g. 'The court stayed proceedings when the plaintiff in a personal injuries action refused to submit to a medical examination'. Another common use of the term is in the phrase 'stay of execution', when a judgement debtor is granted an extension to pay the successful litigant and thus avoid enforcement action.

Strike out (*denegar, anular / desestimar [in limine], inadmitir, declarar no haber lugar a, annoncer l'extinction d'une action, déclarer un non-lieu, ausstreichen*).
The everyday English sense of this expression, equivalent to 'cross out' or 'cancel' some mistaken or unwanted portion of a written text, is not very far away from its legal meaning. In law it means the decision of a court to cancel, dismiss or reject a course of action sought, or an application made, by a litigant. It refers most particularly to the dismissal of an action (*acción, demanda, poursuite, Klage*) or claim (*pretension, prétension, réclamation, requête du demandeur, Anspruch*) at an early stage (*in limine*) or at an interlocutory stage (*fase interlocutoria, incidente de un proceso, phase interlocutoire, Zwischensstadium*) of a proceeding or appeal. The translator will therefore want to distinguish it from partial synonyms like 'quash', 'set aside', 'reverse', and so on, which are unfailingly related to previous court orders or decisions. An example is 'The court struck out the claim on the ground that it disclosed no cause of action'. 'Striking out' is therefore a judicial matter, although many practising lawyers do not seem to be aware that the expression is a term of art.

Upset (*revocar, alterar, modificar, anular, enmendar, desaprobar, renverser, modifier, révoquer, umstoßen*)
In legal use, this term is semantically close to 'overturn' or 'vary'. It is found in connection with some order of a higher court interfering with or modifying an order, or part of an order, issued by a lower court, e.g. 'It is unusual for the High Court to upset the discretion of a Registrar'.

Vary (*revocar una sentencia [sustituyéndola por otra], modifier, réduire, abändern*).
This is one of those self-evident terms whose legal sense is not substantially different from its everyday meaning. When a court of appeal *varies*

a judgement, it alters it without departing entirely from the decision of the trial court. In a sense, therefore, a decision of this kind confirms the view of the lower court, in that the judgement is still for the same party, though the award or punishment is necessarily different, e.g. 'The Court of Appeal, in varying the Crown Court's judgement, reduced the verdict of murder to one of manslaughter'.

4. Civil and Criminal Proceedings Administrative Tribunals

1. Introduction

The purpose of this chapter is to complete the outline of the Anglo-American legal system begun in the previous chapter. In the first part of this block, we have examined the sources of English law and explained the court structure and the roles played within it by judges, prosecutors, barristers and solicitors. It is time now to look in detail at proceedings (*juicios, procedimientos, procès, poursuites, Gerichtsverfahren*) in the criminal and civil courts and the administrative tribunals. We shall also explore a number of related technical terms ('process', 'proceedings', 'procedure', etc) which, in our experience, legal translators can find difficult to distinguish from one another. In many sections of this chapter we have been at pains to stress the new terminology used in the 1998 Civil Procedural Rules, which have been in place since 26 April 1999 and which replace the earlier sets of rules contained in publications like *The White Book*, *The Green Book* and other judicial guides to procedure.

2. Civil proceedings

The civil courts, which usually means the county courts and the High Court of Justice, hear cases (*entienden en, entendent, ahören, verhandeln*) brought by persons who claim to have suffered some wrong, harm or injury. These wrongs may be of different kinds, e.g. personal injury (*daños personales, dommage à la personne, Personenschaden, Körperverletzung*), loss of or damage to property (*pérdidas o daños materiales, perte ou détérioration de biens matériels, Sachschaden*), damage to reputation (*daños morales o perjuicio causado a la imagen, atteinte à la notoriété, Schädigung des Rufes*) or to rights (*vulneración de derechos, atteinte aux droits,* perhaps *Verletzung der [bürgerlichen] Rechte*). The injured party (*el perjudicado, la partie lésée, der/die Geschädigte*) who brings the action is called the plaintiff or claimant (*demandante, actor, plaignant, Kläger*) and their adversary is the defendant (*demandado, intimé, Beklagte*). Depending on the nature of the claim and of the rights alleged to have been infringed, proceedings may follow different procedural rules based on either common law or statutory principles. Thus cases involving contract or tort are based on common law rules, including equitable principles, whereas matters concerning traffic accidents or accidents at work will be heard in accordance with the law as laid down in the relevant statute.

Since the notion of tort and the relevant legal rules are unique to the English system, any translation into another language is necessarily conceptual and approximate. Moreover, whatever translation is chosen (e.g. *agravio, ilícito civil extracontractual, préjudice, Delikt*) will always be a one-way adaptation; in other words, the translation of these terms back into English can almost never be 'tort', since the source language will not possess a separate set of procedural rules or principles distinguishing one kind of *agravio, préjudice or Delikt* from another. As a result, the appropriate English translation of the foreign term is likely to be along the lines of 'non-contractual civil wrong', 'civil wrong or liability outside the scope of contract', etc. In any case, it is quite likely that the name of the specific tort concerned will be much easier to translate, since there are a very limited number of torts and the type of injury concerned will be familiar enough to lawyers trained in other systems. Thus, for example, the major tort of negligence easily translates as *negligencia, négligence* or perhaps *Fahrlässigkeit*; defamation is *difamación, diffamation* or *Diffamierung*; nuisance might be *daños causados por objetos peligrosos, nuisance* or *Belästigung*.

Apart from tort and breach of contract, civil cases often turn on disputes concerning property rights, successions or contentious probate proceedings, divorce suits, unfair dismissal actions, or disputes over industrial or intellectual property, amongst many others. In some of these matters, e.g. divorce proceedings, the claimant is sometimes called the 'petitioner' and the defendant the 'respondent'. In such cases the translation may be unaffected; Spanish still calls the parties *demandante* (or *actor*) and *demandado*, French has *demandeur* and *défendeur*, German *Kläger* and *Beklagte*. These terms may also hold at the appeal stage, where English prefers 'appellant' (*recurrente, appelant* and *Beschwerdeführer[in]* are the available alternatives).

In all civil proceedings, the plaintiff seeks a remedy (*compensación, indemnización, recours, Rechtsbehelf*). The usual remedy is damages (*daños y perjuicios, dommages-intérêts, Schadensersatz*) and in fact there is a rule that no other remedy will be allowed if the court considers that damages is 'an adequate remedy', i.e. that the payment of damages by the defendant to the plaintiff is sufficient to redress the latter for the injury caused 'so far as money can do it'. Other forms of remedy are relief – which sometimes involves the exemption from a charge (*carga, frais, Gebühr*), duty (*deber, devoir, Pflicht*) or liability (*obligación* o *responsabilidad, responsabilité, Verantwortlichkeit*) – and the granting of an injunction (*adopción de una medida cautelar, injonction, einstweilige Verfügung*). Injunctions are best understood as temporary court orders issued to one of the parties, usually the defendant, to do or refrain from doing something in the meantime until the court has reached a final judgement in the matter. Examples include an order to a newspaper not to publish material complained about or an instruction to a spouse during divorce proceedings to stay away from the matrimonial home until the matter is settled. Yet another type of remedy is the 'account of profit', which involves the evaluation and restitution of advantages that have been obtained unjustly. This is used in some commercial and intellectual property cases to force the offending party to re-store to the rightful owners any profits made from unlawful trade in goods or marks, and it is an alternative to damages.

So far we have been discussing the rules, laws and norms that regulate private and business relations between persons or commercial firms (i.e. 'legal persons'). This kind of law is called 'substantive law' (*derecho sustantivo, droit matériel, droit substantiel, materielles Recht*). But there is a judicial counterpart of this called 'procedural law' or 'adjective law' (*derecho adjetivo o procesal, droit procédural, formelles Recht*) which is the name for the set of rules or norms binding courts in their handling of matters brought before them. Clearly the aim of these rules is to ensure that all proceedings before the courts are dealt with efficiently, fairly, openly, consistently and without undue delays, or in other words with 'due process of law' (*con las debidas garantías procesales, procédure en bonne due forme, ordnungsgemäßes Verfahren*).

2.1 The new 'Civil Procedure Rules'

Another way of putting the distinction mentioned in the previous paragraph would be to say that English law uses the term 'proceeding[s]' to refer to the particular type of matter involved in a case and the term 'procedure' to describe the judicial method or machinery used to adjudicate and determine it. Prior to 26 April 1999 there were two main sets of procedural rules: on the one hand, the Rules of the Supreme Court applicable to matters heard before the High Court of Justice, the Civil Division of the Court of Appeal and the House of Lords; and on the other, the County Court Rules applicable to these civil courts of first instance. However, with effect from 26 April 1999 the new 'Civil Procedure Rules 1998' have replaced both earlier sets of rules.[1]

Naturally enough, the translator of legal English will have to be aware of these changes and bear them in mind in all future cases. But given the overwhelming amount of material from previous cases and the training of contemporary lawyers, it is likely that we are some way short of a complete overhaul of linguistic usage in the legal sphere. Contemporary translators, in other words, will have to be up to speed with current terminology, but this will in no way exonerate them from responsibility for adequate knowledge of older texts. Thus, the translator should be aware that the term 'Order' has become 'Part' in the new Civil Procedure Rules (CPR), which are accompanied by a set of Practice Directions (norms for correct practice), numbered in paragraphs and cross-referenced to the relevant Rules (e.g. 'PD 29, para. 6' means 'paragraph 6 of the Practice Direction to Rule 29'). Moreover, the older rules have been

---

[1] The Rules of the Supreme Court and the County Court Rules are contained in two books familiarly known as *The White Book* and *The Green Book*.

recodified as schedules (appendices) to the new rules. Hence, the 'Rules of the Supreme Court' (RSC) are now Schedule 1 and the 'County Court Rules' (CCR) are Schedule 2. A combination of these elements gives us the following typical CPR formulation:

> CPR Part 15, Defence and Reply
> RSC Order 53, Application for Judicial Review
> CCR Order 16, Transfer of Proceedings.

2.2 The overriding objective

Nevertheless, it is true that a new approach to the linguistics of the law has developed out of this reformulation of the procedural rules in English civil law. This has involved four chief principles of restructuring, whereby the rules have been simplified, modernized, reorganized and unified, in line with the overriding objective: 'All cases should be dealt with justly' in order to ensure that all the parties are on an equal footing, to save expense, to deal with the case in a way which is proportionate to the amount of money involved, to ensure that the case is dealt with expeditiously and fairly, and to allot to it an appropriate share of the court's resources. Here are the four chief principles:

1. Simplification
The attempt at a systematic overhaul of legal English aimed at reducing the technicalities to coherent expression within the understanding of a majority of competent speakers not especially trained to the law and its subtleties. (This in response to the 'Plain English Campaign' in Britain and the US in the 1980s and 1990s).

2. Information Technology (IT)
The determination to make use, for the benefit of the majority and in the interests of greater openness and efficiency, of the latest information technology, notably computers and the Internet.

3. Case Management
The desire to speed up and streamline proceedings by placing matters from an early stage in the hands of procedural judges, with a view to ensuring that parties manage each stage competently and that proceedings move along at a satisfactory rate.

4. Tracking
The need to allocate each case to the proper procedural track. This has involved actually creating the 'tracks', based fundamentally on the amount involved and the complexity of the issues between the parties.

Let us take each of these new features in turn and examine briefly its consequences for the translator of legal texts.

(a) The simplification of legal language

The chief means used to ensure that the language of the courts is comprehensible to the average user of the English language are the leaflets which are made available to the prospective litigant (*litigante, plaideur, demandeur, Prozeßpartei*) at the enquiry desks of the courts and at other public outlets. These leaflets outline in ordinary language the essential procedures (*trámites, procédures, Verfahren*) for commencing an action and go on to describe the nature and basis of a claim, the likely stages that will follow, the matter of representation, how costs are incurred and distributed, how tracking may affect the issue and how long a litigant may expect to wait for judgement, as well as questions involving witnesses, statements and so on. Apart from this, a few classic legal terms deemed to make unfair demands on the understanding of the average person have been replaced with others thought to be more generally accessible. Thus, 'claimant' replaces 'plaintiff', as we have said; and 'pleadings' is ousted by 'statements of case' (*alegaciones, plaidoirie, Darlegung des Standpunktes*). (We should point out that this simplification can occasionally lead to momentary confusion, since the older forms provided the plaintiff – now the 'claimant', i.e. the person who is making a 'claim' – with an opportunity to make a 'statement of claim'. This should not be confused with the present 'particulars of claim', which is what a Spanish lawyer would probably call *escrito de pretensiones*, or *Klagebegründung* in German). Similarly, the Latin word *affidavit* (*declaración jurada, écrit sous serment, Affidavit, eidesstattliche Versicherung*) is now replaced with the expression 'statement of truth', and the term 'leave' (*permiso, autorización, autorisation, Erlaubnis*) has given way to the word 'permission', as when a party makes an application or takes some procedural step 'with the permission of the court'.

(b) The use of new technology

The new rules of procedure actively encourage the use of IT and electronic means of communication generally. Thus, some procedural hearings may be conducted by telephone and judges' instructions to the parties may be sent out via the Internet. The same means may be used for the more routine stages of filing or exchange of documents, as well as for the purposes of automation of the bureaucratic process at certain trigger dates, chasing up the parties, sending out reminders, and so on.

(c) Procedural judges

With a view to circumventing the delaying tactics and gamesmanship formerly indulged in by the parties, the new rules of procedure have increased the power of the judges and given them a much more proactive role rather than the reactive one that was characteristic of the Masters who, under the old dispensation, intervened only at the request of the parties. The new procedural judges (judges operative at preliminary stages) are empowered to act on their own initiative and may adjourn proceedings (*aplazar, suspendre, die Verhandlung vertagen*), stay them (*suspender, archivar, surseoir, die Verhandlung aussetzen*), consolidate actions (*acumular procesos/causas, accumuler, Klagen miteinander verbinden*), strike out statements of case (*desestimar los escritos de pretensiones, rayer, ausstreichen*) as showing no cause of action (*por falta de legitimación, sans motif déterminé, ohne Klagegrund*) or as being an abuse of the process of the court, and hold interlocutory hearings by telephone. They may also impose sanctions on the party who fails to comply with the time limits (*plazos, délais, Frist*) or alternatively relieve that party from sanctions if they deem there is good cause. Further, they may order a litigant whose arguments appear flimsy or shadowy to pay a sum of money into court as security for costs.[2]

2.3 Unification of procedure

One of the major innovations of the Civil Procedure Rules is the unification of the procedures for commencement of all civil law claims. This involves a radical restructuring of the earlier system, though not its complete abandonment. Gone are the old rules distinguishing between actions begun in the High Court and those commenced in the County Courts.[3] In their place there is now a single system based on service of a claim form by the claimant on the defendant. Judicially, the matter effectively begins when proceedings are served by means of this form, which must be accompanied by another form containing the particulars of claim. In this statement, the claimant sets out the facts relied on, details the nature and object of the claim, and states the remedy sought, as well as the relevant legal grounds. The claim should also be accompanied by the response pack, which contains three forms: one for acknowledgement of service (*acuse de recibo, accusé de réception, Bestätigung der Zustellung der Klageschrift*), one for admission of the claim and one for defence of the claim.

Should the defendant fail to acknowledge service within 21 days, the claimant is entitled to seek default judgement from the court. If, on the other hand,

---

[2] This is common practice when the party is a foreigner or habitually resides abroad, and it is then translatable as *arraigo en juicio*.

[3] Before the Woolf Reforms, actions commenced in the High Court were begun by the plaintiff serving a writ of summons on the defendant. In the over 300 County Courts, on the other hand, the action began with a request for summons. For the plaintiff's legal advisers the first issue to decide was which court to address. Normally the basis for this decision was the value of the claim, the County Court being chosen when the sum involved was relatively small, since judgements tend to be swifter in these courts than in the High Court, costs are lower, and lawyers' fees as taxed by the court are considerably cheaper.

the defendant fills in and returns the admission form, he or she is obviously admitting at least some part of the claim. Thirdly, the return of a defence form signals the defendant's intention to contest (*impugnar, contester, attaquer,* perhaps *anfechten*) the action. Various types of defence can be set up, the chief ones being the following:

Traverse (*contradicción o impugnación simple, contestation, leugnen*)
Here the defendant simply denies the facts alleged in the plaintiff's claim. This is sufficient, since it is a principle of all litigation, civil and criminal, that the burden of proof (*carga de la prueba, la charge de la preuve, Beweislast*) rests on the party pressing a claim or levelling an accusation against the other party.

Confession and avoidance (*reconocimiento de los hechos y presentación de otros de distinto valor jurídico, reconnaître et exciper, Gegenvorbringen ohne Bestreitung des Klageanspruchs*)
In this case the defendant admits the literal truth of the fact or facts alleged by the claimant but adds others which, if true, would effectively defeat the claim.

Objection in point of law (*excepción dilatoria, exception dilatoire, Bestreiten der Schlüssigkeit der Klage*)
Though the general rule is that the defendant is not required to raise issues of law at the reply stage, there are tactically sound reasons for doing so when the point is so fundamental that a successful defence of it would dispose of the whole issue. The defendant may therefore move for the point to be tried as a preliminary issue. In extreme cases the defence may even apply for the claim to be struck out on the grounds that it discloses no cause of action, is frivolous or vexatious, or is an abuse of the process of the court.

Counterclaim, cross-claim or cross-action (*reconvención, contrademanda o contrarreclamación, demande reconventionelle, Gegenanspruch*)
Strictly speaking a counterclaim is not a defence, though the cross-claim called 'set-off' is. In the latter case both the original claim and the set-off must be monetary and they must be related; the defendant does not deny the plaintiff's claim but sets off against it (as a 'counter-weight') a prior claim of his own, possibly deriving from a different transaction or set of facts. In effect, the defence in such a case is asking the court to make an order on the difference between the two claims. A counterclaim, on the other hand, need not be monetary and need not arise out of the same subject-matter as the original claim. It can be regarded as virtually a new claim in which the roles of claimant and defendant are reversed, but with the advantage to the defendant that he or she can apply for stay of execution (*suspensión de la ejecución, sursis, Einstellung*

der Zwangsvollstreckung) of any judgement favourable to the plaintiff
on the original action until judgement is given on the counterclaim.

2.4. Allocation to track

Once the defence position is known, the procedural judge provides both parties
with allocation questionnaires, which they must complete and return, thus allowing the case to be assigned to one or other of the procedural tracks in
accordance with the amount involved and the judge's view of the complexity of
the issues involved. The tracks are:

The small claims track
This is the appropriate track for ordinary claims not exceeding £5,000,
with procedural rules of such simplicity that it ought to be possible for
litigants to conduct the cases themselves without the need for lawyers.
(One of the leading principles of the new procedural environment is to
give all members of society much greater access to justice. Indeed, *Access to Justice* was the title of the report – 'The Woolf Report' – published
by the Rules Committee, under the chairmanship of Lord Woolf, which
drafted the new Procedural Rules).

The fast track
This is the track used for claims valued at between £5,000 and £15,000
and for those involving non-monetary claims, e.g. claims seeking an injunction (*medidas cautelares, injonction, einstweilige Verfügung*) or
specific performance of a contract (execution of the contract to the letter) when the plaintiff alleges breach of contract. By and large, this track
will take over, simplify and speed up those cases that, under the old dispensation, came under the County Court structure. With regard to the
time frame in fast-track cases, it is predicted that matters that formally
took 83 weeks to reach trial in the County Court will now go through in
38 weeks – less than half the time. Typical matters for fast-track allocation include claims based on professional negligence, fatal accidents,
contentious probate, fraud[4], undue influence (*prevaricación, tráfico de
influencia, abuso de poder*[5]*, intimidation, traffic d'influence, abus de*

---

[4] The individual or company bringing an action for fraud will do so before the civil courts,
since their aim will be to recover the sum lost quite independently of any criminal action on
the matter, which will, of course, be the responsibility of the Crown Prosecution Service or
CPS. Technically under Spanish law this kind of action is regarded as inherently criminal
and is termed *querella*, thus distinguishing it from an ordinary civil action. Fraud in English
law is both a crime and a tort, so that the injured party's remedy is an action for fraud.
[5] Here again a certain asymmetry should be noted. The terms *prevaricación* and *tráfico de
influencia* are appropriate in Spanish law only if the defendant is a civil servant (*funciona-
rio*). Under English law, this would be a fact for the court to consider in evidence in order to

pouvoir, ungebührliche Beeinflussung), defamation and claims against the police or those based on allegations of malicious prosecution.

The multitrack

This is the appropriate track for cases valued at over £15,000 and/or deemed to be unusually complex. In general, cases involve commercial and business law, company law and so-called specialist proceedings, including arbitration (*arbitraje, arbitrage, Schiedsverfahren*), Admiralty proceedings (maritime law) and intellectual and industrial property. Many of these matters eventually entail hearings of some degree of complexity in the High Court. The same is true of other multitrack issues such as judicial review[6] and the technical legal construction of documents like wills, title deeds, leases and other instruments by which land and other property pass from one owner to another. The Chancery Division of the High Court has jurisdiction over these complex issues regarding property, while the Queen's Bench Division, with its dual civil and criminal jurisdiction, hears all issues concerning judicial review and has the exclusive right to issue the prerogative orders of *certiorari, mandamus* and prohibition. It is also the court that rules on applications for *habeas corpus*.[7]

Provision is made under the new rules for the procedural judges to encourage the parties to avoid the risks, expense and loss of time involved in litigation by seeking some other means of settling their differences. Such out-of-court settlements were also possible under the old rules and they are now referred to collectively as 'Alternative Dispute Resolution' or 'ADR'. However, in the opinion of many experienced lawyers it is unlikely that parties, once they have decided to embark on proceedings, will be easily persuaded to give in to pressures from the courts or from their own lawyers, since this might well involve them in heavy financial loss. It is probable that many will prefer to press on with their claim or defence and run the risk of a trial of the action. For the moment, there are few differences to the actual mode of proceedings except that the courts have a duty to ensure that trials in fast-track cases will not last longer than one day. Courts are also under a duty to prevent time-wasting, for example by refusing to grant extensions to the time limits for each stage or to allow each side to use more than one expert witness (*perito, témoin expert, sachverständiger Zeuge*) except in very unusual circumstances.

---

determine the nature of the authority, trust or power supposed to have been breached, and not in itself a matter of law, save in exceptional cases.

[6] See section 3 (b) in chapter three.

[7] This ancient rule for the protection of the individual's basic right to freedom allows the High Court to intervene in cases of alleged false arrest or false imprisonment; if the police, the CPS or the Home Secretary fail to justify holding the suspect, the court can order immediate release.

In civil cases, the public hearing is called the 'trial', though it is sometimes known as the 'trial proper' because of the long-standing colloquial tradition of using the word 'trial' for the whole of proceedings from service of the initial writ to final judgement. The procedure is externally very similar to that of the criminal trial, described in detail in section 4.3. Because of their importance as examples of oral legal genres, the roles of the judge, or judges, and of counsel for both parties are dealt with separately and in detail in sections 7 and 8 of Chapter 5.

Again, there is little formal difference between these genres in civil and criminal cases, except that in civil proceedings jury trial is the exception rather than the rule and at first instance the decision on both facts and law is usually made by a single judge sitting alone. However, in defamation cases there is a jury, who not only deliver the verdict but also decide on the amount of the damages if the verdict is for the plaintiff. In the absence of a jury, counsel will not normally be given the right to make a final speech; the judge's decision will be based on the arguments submitted in the pleadings and in open court and on the evidence led.

However, one very important conceptual difference between civil and criminal trial is the standard of proof required. Given the jeopardy (risk, danger) in which an accused person stands – loss of life or liberty, a heavy fine and social disgrace – the standard of proof in criminal cases is higher than in civil trial. For a verdict of guilty to be recorded, the prosecution must prove the accused's guilt 'beyond reasonable doubt', but in civil cases the standard required is the lower one of proof 'on a balance of probabilities'.

3.   Right of action, cause of action. Some basic terms

The phrase 'right of action'[8] refers to the basis of a claim made by a plaintiff in bringing a matter before the courts and consists in an assertion that he or she has suffered an injury to some legal right alleged to exist. As we have seen, the rights alleged to have been infringed may be purely private or individual, in which case they may give rise to a civil action, or public and general, in which case they may give rise to a criminal action, depending on the type of behaviour complained of. In either case, the first step is for the complainant to establish that the right existed and has been infringed. If the matter is criminal, it is in a sense more straightforward, since all criminal conduct is 'automatically' wrong, i.e. it takes some concrete form such as theft, physical attack, rape, and so on, defined as unlawful by some statute. In these cases, of course, the victim will still have to prove the assertion in a court of law, and in the English-speaking countries generally it is the state or the Crown who prosecute (*persiguen*

---

[8] See section five in chapter three.

judicialmente, poursuivent en justice, strafrechtlich verfolgen) all wrongdoing of this kind. But the right of action derives from the commission of the offence itself.

In civil law matters, on the other hand, the right of action is potentially more difficult to establish, since the plaintiff first has to show that they had a particular or individual right to begin with, that this right has been infringed (*infringido, lesionado, enfreint, verletzt*) by the defendant and that the defendant did not have some equal or prior right to do what has been complained of. Given this added difficulty, and the expense and protractedness of litigation, plaintiffs often prefer to test the strength of their right, or cause, of action by submitting a preliminary issue to the court for decision. If the court confirms that the facts of the case show a cause of action, one of two things may happen: the matter may proceed to trial or the defendant may decide to settle out of court.

From the point of view of the translator, the most important point is to distinguish between the different names given to the issue at different stages. Thus, at the initial or theoretical stage, lawyers will usually refer to an 'action', 'cause of action' or 'right of action', by which they mean the legal basis on which they contemplate proceeding in the matter. Once this stage is past, it is more usual to find the term 'case' being used, though of course this is the most common word of all in English to refer to any matter involving two parties and their lawyers, whatever the stage reached. (As a result, it is perhaps one of the words that translators out of English should earmark for special treatment, since its is unlikely that the basic paronym will in all cases be the most appropriate term.)

In formal references to the matters pending between two parties, the term usually found is 'suit' or 'lawsuit', the latter being more common in US than in British usage. Thus, translators will have to deal with phrases like 'parties to the suit' or 'at the suit of X' in lawyers' writings, as well as similar references in judgements, official law reports, textbooks, etc.

Once an 'action' has become a 'case' in the minds of the people pursuing it, it becomes particularly difficult to predict when they will use the term to refer to the legal issue in hand, or to the correct way of handling it, or to the factual and legal issues they will actually rely on in court, or to the facts they or the court will ultimately centre on, or to the successive decisions or final judgement which that or a higher court will deliver. This means that 'case' is a word that legal translators should treat with the greatest care, but it does not mean that the obvious cognate or paronym should be avoided if it is the natural term. In Spanish translation, for example, 'case' can always be translated as *caso* if it is the special facts or general issue under consideration that are referred to, as when judges refer to *el caso de autos* (i.e. 'the case at issue, the instant case') or even make comments like *como en el caso presente* (i.e. 'as in [the facts of] the present case').

At its widest, the phrase 'probable cause', which is more common in US usage, refers to the general basis on which an action is pursued, and may therefore be regarded as equivalent to 'cause or right of action'. However, it seems to be used principally in criminal cases, whereas the term 'cause of action', at least in British usage, is almost entirely confined to civil matters, as when a preliminary issue is dismissed 'as disclosing no cause of action' (*por falta de legitimación, aucun motif d'action en justice*, perhaps *ohne Klagegrund*). Similarly, the terms 'suit' and 'lawsuit' (*demanda, poursuite en justice, Klage*) normally connote a civil law case rather than criminal proceedings (*proceso penal, juicio criminal, procédure criminelle devant une juridiction pénale, Strafprozeß*).

The final group of terms we shall consider here, 'process, proceedings and procedure', can be confusing to translators because they are similar in form and all derive from the same root, but their meanings are quite distinct.

In legal use, the word 'process' can refer to different things. As an uncountable noun, it means generally all the documents served (*notificados, assignés, zugestellt*) by one party on the other through the medium of the court and thus forming the origins of the court record. But it can also have its everyday meaning of an organized and methodical arrangement by which a particular matter is brought to the attention of the relevant authority and effectively dealt with, as when we speak of 'due process of law' (*las normas procesales, los trámites legales previstos, par voies légales, ordnungsgemäßes Verfahren*). Thirdly, it is found in the expression 'abuse of the process of the court' (*quebrantamiento de las normas procesales, abus de procédure, Miß-brauch des Prozeßverfahrens des Gerichts*), where the sense is that one party is misusing some rule of procedure or of trial which it is the court's duty to supervise and uphold. A very common type of 'abuse of the process of the court' is unreasonable delay in prosecuting an accused for alleged offences, which may have the effect of prejudicing his defence or depriving him of the right to a fair trial.

The two remaining terms, 'proceedings' and 'procedure', are at first slightly more difficult to distinguish from one another. A rule of thumb the translator may find helpful is to look on 'proceedings' as answering the question '*What* happens?' and to regard 'procedure' as answering the question '*How* does it happen?' Thus, 'proceedings' is often partially synonymous with 'action', 'case' or 'suit', whereas 'procedure' is a partial synonym for 'rules, legal norms or requirements'. The following examples should help clarify usage:

(a)   The plaintiff <u>served process</u> on the defendant within seven days (*notificación de la demanda*).

(b)   The Divisional Court ruled that the decision to charge the accused six years after the events referred to in the information was an <u>abuse of the process</u> of the court (*abuso de derecho, conducta temeraria contraria a las normas de enjuiciamiento*).

(c)   When her attempt to settle the dispute amicably failed, she <u>brought pro-ceedings</u> against her neighbour (*presentó una demanda*).

(d)   The judge <u>stayed proceedings</u> when the key prosecution witness failed to appear (*declaró el sobreseimiento de la causa*).

(e)   The jury was ordered to withdraw while the judge discussed <u>procedural issues</u> with counsel (*cuestiones procesales o de procedimiento*).

(f)   Practice directions for judges periodically supplement and update the <u>rules of procedure</u> (*normas del derecho adjetivo, leyes de enjuiciamiento, derecho procesal*).

4.   Criminal proceedings

There are three major features of the English system of classification and treatment of crimes that are likely to cause initial difficulty to the legal translator working between the English and one or other of the Continental or civil law systems. In the first place, the English criminal law is not organized into a single, coherent body or code as is the case in many other countries. Although English judges and legal practitioners sometimes refer to the 'penal code', they are really talking about an extremely diffuse arrangement of independent laws or statutes, which are constantly being modified and updated, often through a complicated process of piecemeal insertions and cross-references. Secondly, English law no longer distinguishes by name between serious and minor or relatively minor crimes. However, although the distinction between felony (*delito grave, délit grave, Verbrechen*) and misdemeanour (*falta, infraction mineure, Vergehen*) has been obsolete for many years, it is a matter of common sense that all crimes are not equally serious, nor are they all dealt with in the same way by the courts. And thirdly, the English or common law system is unique in that the prosecution of crime is not the responsibility of the courts or the judiciary but is left in the hands of state or administrative prosecutors who are ultimately answerable to the government of the day. This means, for example, that in the English system of criminal justice there is no true counterpart of the 'examining magistrate' (*juez instructor, juge d'instruction, Untersuchungsrichter*) or the inquisitorial procedures associated with that figure.

As a result of these peculiar features of the English system, all crimes are now habitually referred to as 'offences' in the statutes creating and defining them. The nature of each individual offence is set out, often at great length and with a profusion of technical detail, in the numbered sections and subsections of the Act (*ley, loi, Gesetz*) concerned, and the Act itself carries a descriptive title, which is referred to by name by the police officers who arrest or charge a suspect and by the parties and the courts during criminal litigation. Thus, we find, for example, the Road Traffic Act 1991, the Theft Act 1968 or the Sexual

Offences (Amendment) Act 1976. Likewise the rules of criminal procedure are scattered over a large number of statutes, which are continually being amended and updated, such as the Magistrates' Courts Act or the Prosecution of Offences Act.

4.1 Arrest and charge

We said above that in contemporary English legal usage there are no specific terms distinguishing between more and less serious crimes. However, the distinction does, of course, exist; it is seen clearly in the sentences imposed following a verdict of guilty and in the court and mode of trial. All criminal proceedings begin in the magistrates' court and it is there that the decision on the appropriate mode of trial is made. But before a person can be taken before the magistrates he or she must first be arrested and charged, and this is done in one of two ways:

* by summary arrest (*detención sin mandamiento judicial, arrestation sommaire,* perhaps *Festnahme ohne Haftbefehl*)
* by arrest with a warrant (*detención con mandamiento judicial, orden de búsqueda y captura, arrestation avec mandat d'arrêt,* perhaps *Festnahme mit Haftbefehl*).

Given that the police have wide powers of arrest, and that by far the majority of suspects are charged with arrestable offences, the former is by far the more common. However, if they have reason to suspect that a person has committed or is about to commit an offence, the police can lay an information in writing on oath (*bajo juramento, serment, unter Eid*) before a magistrate and obtain a warrant for the arrest of the suspect. A person should be told that he or she is under arrest and the arresting officer must caution him or her (*advertirle, se porter caution, warnen*) as to their right to remain silent. This caution, which is called a 'Miranda warning' in the US, is to be as administered in the following words (or words as close to them as possible): 'You do not have to say anything. But it may harm your defence if you do not mention, when questioned, something which you later rely on in court. Anything you do say may be given in evidence.' Traditionally an arrested person had an absolute right to remain silent, but a recent change in the relevant British law now means that the prosecution and the courts are entitled to draw adverse inferences from an accused's exercise of that right, both after charging and in court. The person will then be taken to the police station (*comisaría, commissariat, Polizeirevier*) to be interviewed (*interrogada, interrogé,* perhaps *ausgefragt*). If the police believe they have enough evidence, they must charge the prisoner; otherwise he or she must be released, though of course the same person may well be rearrested later on the same charge or charges if further evidence is uncovered.

4.2 Types of offence

When an accused person is brought before (*comparece ante, comparaître devant, vor Gericht erscheinen*) the magistrates, what happens next will depend on the nature of the offence charged. All offences are now set out in statutes, though some originally arose at common law, and they fall into three categories: summary offences (*delitos menos graves o faltas, infractions mineures, délits mineurs, summarisch verfolgbare Straftaten, die ohne Mitwirkung von Geschworenen abgeurteilt wird*), indictable offences (*delitos graves o muy graves, crimes, délits graves, Straftaten, die auf Grund eines Mitwirkung von Geschworenen abgeurteilt werden kann*) and offences triable either way (*delitos intermedios, délits intermédiaires,* perhaps *Zwischenstraftaten*). In our translations into Spanish and French here we have followed the Continental habit of identifying the offences by their degrees of seriousness, but what English law actually does is to distinguish them by the mode of trial appropriate to each. If the statute creating the offence does not specify that it is either summary or triable either way then the assumption is that it is indictable. In practical terms, therefore, offences are identified as being one of the following:

> **Summary offences.** This means lesser crimes, such as motoring offences, fit for trial by the magistrates summarily (approx. *en juicio verbal, sommairement, summarisch*), i.e. before the magistrates themselves without a jury.

> **Indictable offences.** These are serious or very serious crimes (e.g. murder, rape or armed robbery), which must be tried before judge and jury at the Crown Court, following a formal indictment (*acta de acusación, accusation formelle, formelle Anklageschrift*) prepared by a representative of the Crown Prosecution Service or CPS. In Britain as in all modern countries, crime is always prosecuted in the name of the state (in Britain, the Crown) because of the public nature of the law infringed and the public interest in punishing crime and seeing that justice is done. This explains the name of the quintessential criminal court (the Crown Court) and the habit of referring to the prosecutor as 'Crown counsel' (*el fiscal,* perhaps *procureur de la République, Staatsanwalt*) and of calling prosecution witnesses 'witnesses for the Crown'. In the same way, criminal cases are headed, for example, 'R v Jones', where the 'R' means either *Rex* or *Regina* depending on whether the reigning monarch is king or queen. In either case the heading is read aloud or referred to orally as **'the Crown or the Queen against** Jones', not '**R versus** Jones'.[9]

> **Offences triable either way.** These are intermediate offences, like theft or common assault, which, depending on the seriousness of the facts

[9] Likewise, in civil cases headings like *Green v Brown* are read out or referred to orally as 'Green **and** Brown', not 'Green **versus** Brown'.

alleged, may be deemed more suitable for trial by the magistrates or by the Crown Court. However, at present, even if the magistrates feel that they are competent to try one of these offences, the accused is entitled to insist on trial at the Crown Court if he or she prefers a jury trial, as is often the case. There is nothing the magistrates can do to prevent this except warn the accused of the Crown Court's greater power of sentencing in the event of a verdict of guilty.

In any event, whether or not an accused person has a right to choose the court and mode of trial, criminal proceedings, as we have said, will always begin at the magistrates' court. If the offence is summary and the accused pleads guilty, the magistrates may sentence him or her there and then, though this is unusual. (In cases of minor motoring offences an accused may plead guilty by post.) If they decide not to do so, this will normally be because they need more time to look into the prisoner's background and previous criminal record, if any. If the accused is not sentenced, the magistrates must decide whether to grant bail or to remand (i.e. to order a return to prison until the case is decided). If, on the other hand, a person accused of a summary offence pleads not guilty to the charge, a date will be fixed for the trial and a decision taken on bail. It should be noticed, incidentally, that the police may also grant bail – police bail – to a person arrested and freed pending further enquiries.

Where an accused appears before the magistrates charged with an indictable offence, the proceedings take the form of a preliminary enquiry (*diligencias preliminares, enquête préliminaire, gerichtliche Voruntersuchung*). Since the magistrates in this situation are regarded as 'examining justices' rather than judges, this is theoretically close to the Continental notion of the *instrucción*, though it should not be forgotten that the court is not acting inquisitorially but is really testing the prosecution evidence to see whether there is a *prima facie* case for trial at the Crown Court. If they decide there is they move on immediately to the stage known as 'committal proceedings', whereby the accused is indicted for trial at the Crown Court. Committal may be on bail (*auto de procesamiento y orden de libertad bajo fianza, mise en liberté sous caution, Freilassung gegen Kaution*) or in custody (*auto de procesamiento y orden de ingreso en prisión, garde à vue, in Haft*). If the justices think the evidence is insufficient, they may either reduce the charge or discharge (release) the accused.

Though 'either way' offences seem the most complicated, proceedings in these cases are really a half-way house between the two situations we have just discussed. After the magistrates have heard the charge and listened to the outline of the prosecution case, it is up to them to decide whether they are competent to try the matter. As we have seen, this will depend partly on the gravity of the particular charge and the facts alleged by the prosecution, but it should also be borne in mind that the magistrates have limited powers of sentence (a maximum of six months' imprisonment and/or a £5,000 fine on any one charge, and a maximum of one year's imprisonment on two or more charges taken together). If they come to the conclusion that the accused, if found guilty, would deserve a more severe sentence than they have power to impose, they must send him or her for trial at the Crown Court. (It is also possible, for the same reason, for them to send the accused to the Crown Court for sentencing after finding them guilty following summary trial, and persons accused of either way offences must be told of this possibility if they opt for summary trial.) Thus, in either-way cases the magistrates may decide to send an accused to the Crown Court or the accused may choose this option against the opinion of the magistrates, but an accused cannot insist on a summary trial if the magistrates believe the matter is too serious for them to try it.

During all these pre-trial proceedings, reporting restrictions (*el secreto sumarial, restrictions imposées aux médias, Ausschluss der Öffentlichkeit*) may be imposed or raised at the court's discretion. If the court is of the view that an accused could suffer particular prejudice from being tried locally (e.g. in some cases of sexual offences or where the accused is a prominent figure in local affairs), it has a further discretion to order the trial to take place at some other court in a different locality.

4.3 The trial

For the translator, the very marked formal differences between summary trial and trial on indictment are probably less important than the procedural differences between civil and criminal trials, which in turn depend on the purpose for which proceedings are brought in each case and the legal consequences of the final outcome. In general, civil trials determine the rights of individuals or juristic persons who disagree on some issue of private law. The trial normally ends with a judgement for the plaintiff or for the defendant and commonly, when the plaintiff is successful, with the award of damages. It should be noticed that English law does not 'condemn' or 'absolve' the defendant, since there is no question in civil matters of guilt or innocence. Instead the purpose of the trial is to decide whether or not the defendant is liable (responsible) for the loss, injury or infringement alleged by the plaintiff. The damages or any other remedy granted to the plaintiff should not be viewed as a punishment of the defendant but as a duty imposed on him or her to compensate or relieve or redress the plaintiff for the wrong suffered.

In criminal cases, on the other hand, it is society as a whole, through the prosecutor, that is represented as a matter of public interest, on the view that criminal acts endanger or destroy general principles and standards of conduct, morals and public safety laid down in statutes concerned with public law. For this reason those accused of criminal offences face punishment if found guilty. In criminal trials the two sides are the prosecution and the defence. In the traditionally adversarial context of British law, the judge takes no part in litigation but is there simply to apply the law, to decide the contest and to see that justice is done. In summary trials the magistrates decide on both facts and law, whereas in trial by jury in the Crown Court, the jury are the 'triers of fact' while the judge is responsible for questions of law, including the conduct of the trial, the admissibility of evidence and the applying of the verdict, which means discharging (releasing) the accused if the verdict is one of acquittal (*fallo absolutorio, acquittement, Freispruch*) or not guilty (*inocente, innocent, unschuldig*) and the passing of sentence (*imposición de la pena, prononcer la sentence, rendre le verdict, das Strafurteil fallen*) on the accused if the verdict is one of guilty.

Because of the potentially disastrous consequences personally, socially and financially of a guilty verdict for an accused, the standard of proof required is higher in criminal than in civil law. The classic formula for criminal cases is that the judge or jury must be 'satisfied beyond a reasonable doubt' of the guilt of the accused before they can reach a verdict of guilty; otherwise they must acquit. What this means is that since reasonable human beings can seldom be 100% sure about anything, perfect certainty is an inappropriate standard, but a jury should convict if they decide, after careful consideration of the evidence, that even making allowances for the possibility of human error it is very likely that the accused is guilty. What the expression 'beyond a reasonable doubt' does not mean is 'beyond any doubt' (*sin duda alguna, sans doute aucun, ohne die geringsten Zweifel*); literal translations often seem to give this erroneous suggestion of something approaching absolute certainty. Nor does the phrase imply, at the other extreme, that it is sufficient if the jury believe, on the whole, that the accused is 'more likely than not' to be guilty. This, in fact, is the rather lower civil standard of proof, which is usually described as 'proof on the balance of probabilities'. Reverting once again to percentages, what this means is that in extreme cases a balance of 51% against 49% is sufficient. This may seem a risky standard, but it should be borne in mind that in criminal trials the jury is being told that there are actually three possibilities, which in plain English would be equivalent to 'yes', 'no' and 'I'm not sure'. They must acquit in both the latter cases. In civil judgements, on the other hand, there are only two possibilities, and judges can never find that they are equally divided between the two conflicting claims (or, if they are, they must not say so!).

In civil trials, there is one exceptional case where the judge sits with a jury. This is in the trial of actions for defamation, in which the rule is that the jury finds on the facts and, if they find for the plaintiff, they also fix the amount of the damages.

Criminal trial is based on the presumption of innocence, i.e. the accused is deemed innocent until proved guilty. As a result, the prosecution bears the burden of proof or the '*onus probandi*', just as the plaintiff does in a civil trial. However, in both civil and criminal trials, the burden of proof may be reversed if the defendant alleges some special fact or circumstance that requires to be proved separately, e.g. in criminal law, the special defences of insanity or automatism (involuntary behaviour). Otherwise, it is up to the prosecution to establish both the *actus reus* (*conducta delictiva, comportement délictueux, robjektive Tatbestand, strafbare Handlung*) and the *mens rea* (*dolo, intention délictueuse, subjektive Tatbestand, verbrecherische Absicht*) against the prisoner. After counsel for the prosecution has set out the facts and outlined the witness statements on which the Crown case is based, counsel for the defence may submit (argue) that 'there is no case to answer' (i.e. the existence of a wrongdoing has not been established). If the court allows this submission, the matter is at an end and the accused is acquitted. Otherwise, the issue is then tried by each side calling witnesses and leading evidence. The case for the Crown is presented first, followed by the defence's submissions. Each witness is examined first by the side calling him or her in what is called examination-in-chief; next comes cross-examination by the other side; and finally, if necessary, comes re-examination, aimed at rebutting (refuting) evidence that has arisen in cross-examination.[10]

5. Administrative, Industrial and Domestic Tribunals

Most Continental systems of law distinguish four separate jurisdictions, or independent areas of the law, each with its own court structure and rules of procedure. These are the civil courts, the criminal courts, the administrative courts, and the courts with jurisdiction in social and family matters such as contentious divorce and custody matters or employment tribunals. Here the first problem for the translator, as so often when dealing with the language of the law, is the asymmetry of the underlying legal systems. In the British and US courts generally, cases belonging to the last two types are distributed between administrative, industrial and domestic tribunals, at the lower end of the scale, and special Divisions (*Salas, Chambres, Kammern*) of the higher civil courts at the upper end. In a sense, then, the law of the English-speaking countries is essentially divided into civil or private law and criminal or public law. Moreover, in Britain, which has no written constitution, there is no exact equivalent of the Constitutional Court found in so many countries. Instead, the High Court has inherent jurisdiction in important matters of public law

---

[10] See sections 7 and 8 in chapter five for a more detailed account of the oral legal genres called the examination of witnesses, the counsels' closing speeches, and the judge's summing up and charge to the jury.

concerning fundamental rights[11], while the House of Lords, as the 'court of last resort', is charged with delivering final authoritative statements about the correct interpretation and application of the law in appeals referred to it and certified as containing points of law of general public importance.

In Britain, there is now a wide variety of tribunals, many of them equipped with their own system of appeal. Not all of them are administrative in nature and not all of them are public courts of law, so the comparison with the Continental system of Administrative Law as an independent jurisdiction should not be pressed too hard. But as the name 'tribunals' suggests, they exist to adjudicate on disputes in the administrative, industrial or professional spheres. There is usually some appeal structure that will enable people aggrieved (*perjudicados, partie lésée, Belastete*) by the tribunal's decision to have their cases reconsidered and, if necessary, brought within the jurisdiction of the ordinary courts, commonly the county courts, the Queen's Bench Division of the High Court (judicial review) or the Court of Appeal. When there are important disputes about jurisdiction, it is even possible for such matters to reach the House of Lords, though this is naturally very rare.

The number of such tribunals is not fixed by law, and there can be as many as are deemed necessary for the conduct of administrative, social and professional affairs. Most of them are created by statute, and because of this they are sometimes referred to collectively as 'statutory tribunals'. The justification for their number and diversity is their speed, cheapness and efficiency: matters before them are heard quickly and relatively informally, and in cases of exceptional complexity there is provision for recourse to the higher civil courts. It is worth adding that these courts came into being for historical and social reasons after the Second World War. They developed during the 1950s, i.e. at the time of the creation of the Welfare State under the Labour administration. Since then, under both Conservative and Labour governments, they have continued to expand and diversify in an attempt to meet the new needs of an increasingly complex industrial society.

Some administrative tribunals, especially those that are administrative in the strict sense of adjudicating on disputes between government and governed, are courts of record (i.e. they keep a permanent record of their sessions) and are amenable in the usual way to the control and discipline of the ordinary courts. Examples include the Social Security Tribunal or the Lands Tribunal. These courts deal with complaints from people dissatisfied with the decisions of the ministerial department or local authority concerned. They have a permanent

---

[11] As we have already seen, in England the High Court exercises this jurisdiction through the system of 'judicial review', which enables it to control the acts of the Administration. However, in the US, which does have a written constitution, any state or federal court is entitled to pronounce upon the constitutional or unconstitutional nature of legislative matters relied on before it.

chair, who is usually a person who has held high judicial office or a barrister or solicitor of at least seven years' standing, and normally two other members, who are professional people with the appropriate experience and expertise. Sessions are public, oral and informal and the complainant is often unrepresented, but the decision is written and reasoned. There is also further right of appeal to the ordinary courts.

The Industrial Tribunal is similar in structure and working method, though its field of competence concerns claims arising from industrial or commercial disputes, such as unfair dismissal, redundancy, employment contracts, equal pay, sex discrimination or sexual harassment in the workplace. Naturally enough, to ensure fairness and guarantee a balanced outcome, the non-judicial experts who sit with the chair on the panel are drawn from both sides of industry, i.e. employers and employees. Below the Tribunal there is a body called the Advisory, Conciliation and Arbitration Service[12], or ACAS, whose name tells its own story. It is only if the parties cannot settle their differences through arbitration that the matter will go forward to the Tribunal.

The reader may be wondering why cases dealt with by this court come under the heading of 'administrative law' and, of course, the reader will be right to wonder. There is little we could call 'administrative' in any real sense about these matters, since government bodies, whether central or local, need not be involved in disputes between management and workers. All that can be said is that there is a habit of referring to these tribunals generally as 'administrative', possibly because there is a perception that they are closer to the everyday problems of the ordinary citizen than the somewhat remote 'courts of law'. Probably, too, there is a consensus that the good offices (*buenos oficios, bons offices, gute Dienste*) of the Administration can contribute usefully to social harmony, which is why the tribunals were set up in the first place. In any event, some British lawyers believe that a separate jurisdiction of administrative law under a specific Division of the High Court is long overdue (Keenan 1963/1989:94).

To complete the picture, something should be said of the related group of 'domestic tribunals'. These are essentially the governing boards or disciplinary committees of professional bodies or associations (*colegios profesionales, associations professionnelles, Berufsverbände*) or trade boards or guilds (*gremios, corps de métiers, Innungen*) with a restricted membership. Some of these tribunals are statutory whilst others are regulated on contractual principles. Two types may be distinguished: professional associations such as the General Medical Council, the Law Society or the Architects' Registration Council; and trade associations such as the Security and Investments Board that supervises the Stock Exchange, the Milk Marketing Board or the many commercial guilds and boards that oversee particular sectors of trade, industry and agriculture. Once again,

---

[12] In the US, the Mediation and Conciliation Service.

the translator faced with these terms should take account of the nature of the association (statutory or otherwise) and its powers (purely disciplinary or regulatory) in deciding on the most suitable equivalent. Clearly, statutory bodies are ultimately answerable to the higher courts, so that they are tribunals in the stricter sense. But even in the case of the contract associations, parties aggrieved by their decisions are entitled to apply for judicial review. The difference lies in the remedy they may seek. The prerogative orders of *mandamus, prohibition* and *certiorari*[13] are only available in cases involving public law, i.e. administrative law in the pure sense. By contrast, those seeking relief against an association to which they are contractually bound are entitled only to apply to the High Court for an *injunction* or for a *declaration* of their rights. The reason why they are entitled to even this redress is that otherwise the board or association would be regarded as attempting to oust (exclude) the jurisdiction of the courts, which is plainly unlawful.

Now that we have covered the overall structure of the so-called 'administrative' tribunals, it will be helpful if we look at some examples of the cases they deal with and how their procedure is implemented. Of all the tribunals we have mentioned it is probably the Industrial Tribunal, or 'Employment Tribunal', as it is also sometimes called, whose function and availability are most familiar to the ordinary citizen and, therefore, most representative for our purposes, so we shall base our illustrations on its proceedings. We have already outlined the type of case that is likely to come before the Tribunal, so we shall now concentrate on basic points of procedure. Readers are referred to section 2 in Chapter six, where the ordinary rules of contract are explained.

The parties will naturally be employer and employed and the ground or grounds of complaint will necessarily be contractual. Though the law assumes freedom of contract, there is an awareness that parties may not always be of equal bargaining power (i.e. they do not have the same power when negotiating the contract). The Tribunal thus gives the employee an opportunity to redress the balance when there is a *prima facie* appearance of unfairness between a stronger and a weaker party. This is at its most evident when the employee claims unfair dismissal or failure by the employer to implement terms of the employment contract involving pay, status or promotion. Regardless of what individual contracts may say, there are certain statutory rules that must be complied with, contained in laws such as the Industrial[14] Relations Act 1971[15], the

---

[13] See paragraph (b) in 2.1 (*The multitrack*) in this chapter.

[14] The word 'industrial' is commonly found in British usage in the sense of 'work-related', irrespective of the nature of the work. Thus, the translator will come across 'industrial accident' (*accidente laboral, accident du travail,* perhaps *Arbeitsunfall*), 'industrial action' (*medidas reivindicativas, grèves du travail, Arbeitskampfmassnahmen*), 'industrial arbitration' (*arbitraje laboral, arbitrage au conseil du prud'homme, Schlichtung bei Arbeitskonflikten*) or 'industrial dispute' (*conflicto laboral, conflit du travail, Arbeitskonflikt*). By contrast, the

Employment Protection Act 1978, and the Employment Act 1989. In the usual way, these statutes update some areas of the law and they repeal others that have become outdated. The general issues covered by these laws include such basic matters as retirement age, health and safety at work, paid holidays, sick pay, maternity leave, arrangements for trade union activities and workers' and employers' rights in the event of dismissal and redundancy.

In accordance with current legislation, employers, who in common law are vicariously responsible for any acts performed by their employees in the course of their employment, are required to provide their workers with itemized pay statements accompanying their salaries or wages. These pay slips must specify gross pay (*sueldo íntegro, solde de tout compte, Bruttolohn*), net pay (*salario líquido o neto, salaire net, Nettolohn*) and deductions (*retenciones, retenues, prélèvements, Abzüge*), the latter including social security payments, income tax and contributions to pension schemes.

This, then, is the legal background to any industrial dispute that may arise between employer and employee. As we have already pointed out, in case of dissatisfaction on either side (usually the worker) the rules provide for mediation by the Advisory, Conciliation and Arbitration Service. To ensure good faith by both sides and maximize the possibility of an amicable solution, the ACAS conciliation officer who arbitrates in the dispute gives an undertaking that no allegation made by either party will be made public or given in evidence if the conciliation fails and the matter proceeds to the Tribunal for a hearing. But within the same rules of confidentiality and relative informality, it is part of the officer's duty to indicate to the parties at each stage what, as a matter of experience, the likely outcome will be if the issue does go before the Tribunal.

Matters that do get this length tend to be allegations of irregularities involving redundancy, unfair dismissal, unfair promotion procedures, racial or sex discrimination, or sexual harassment. Time and again, in dealing with all such claims, the key term invoked by the tribunal is the word 'reasonable', and cases depend so much on their own facts that it is pointless to generalize here. Whatever the particular merits of each claim, there are four possible outcomes:

---

term 'corporate' is found in phrases referring to the firm or company as a legal entity or to a corporation's owners, managers and shareholders as distinct from its workforce. Common phrases therefore include 'corporate assets' (*activo social, actif social, Unternehmenswerte*), 'corporate body' (*ente social, personne morale, juristische Person*), 'corporate capital' (*capital social, capital social, Gesellschaftskapital*), 'corporate group' (*grupo de empresas, groupement d'entreprise, Unternehmensgruppe*), 'corporate logo' (*logo[tipo] social, logo d'entreprise, Firmenlogo*) or 'corporate name' (*denominación social, raison sociale*, perhaps *Sachfirma*). In US usage, 'labor' is found rather than 'industrial' in many instances, including 'labor law' instead of 'employment law'.

[15] In the US, the National Labor Relations Act (NLRA).

a)   The claim is dismissed and the employee is *forced to accept* the employer's decision;

b)   The claim is upheld (*se estima, confirmée, bestätigt*) and the employee is *reinstated* in his or her former post;

c)   The claim is upheld and the employee is *reengaged* on different terms;

d)   The claim is upheld wholly or in part and the employee receives a cash sum *in compensation*.

One final peculiarity of the system is worth commenting on. It sometimes happens that an employee opts to leave a job without actually being dismissed. For example, a man who feels he has been unfairly passed over for promotion, or a woman who feels she has been subjected to intolerable sexual harassment, may walk out of their jobs and still bring a claim for unfair dismissal. This is possible thanks to the concept of 'constructive dismissal' (*despido analógico, sobreentendido o inferido, conduite d'un employeur cherchant à provoquer la démission d'un employé,Verhalten des Arbeitgebers,das als Kündigung auszulegen ist*), i.e. the view that the firm's disregard for the employee's rights and dignity is equivalent or tantamount to dismissal.[16] The Department of Employment periodically issues guidelines on the objective liability of employers in cases of alleged discrimination in which firms fail to take effective action to protect the rights of vulnerable employees, and these guidelines are conscientiously applied by the Tribunal, along with the relevant statutes.

---

[16] See sections 2 and 8 in chapter two for the meanings of 'constructive' and 'construction'.

5. Genres in the Translation of Legal English (I)

1. Introduction: Legal genres in translation

A useful innovation in the theory and practice of specialized translation is the concept of *genre*, which has also found its way into contemporary textbooks on the teaching of English for specific purposes, following the examples of Swales (1990) and Bhatia (1993). By 'genre,' or 'text type', we mean each of the specific classes of texts characteristic of a given scientific community or professional group and distinguished from each other by certain features of vocabulary, form and style, which are wholly function-specific and conventional in nature. In the particular case of the language of the law, examples of genres include witness statements, statements of claim, contracts and judgements. The term 'text' is being used here in the wide sense to include written genres (e.g. contracts) and oral genres (e.g. a judge's charge to the jury). It is also possible to distinguish sub-genres such as divorce judgements, debt judgements, judgements in default, judgements on appeal, and so on.[1]

Given this broad definition of the term, it makes perfectly good sense to speak of 'genres' in everyday communication. For instance, anyone with a working knowledge of the appropriate conventions can tell at a glance whether a given text is a letter of condolence, a recipe or a piece of advertising copy. And relatively sophisticated speakers of a language will probably be able to determine, on the basis of the respect or otherwise shown for conventions, whether the genre is being used seriously, playfully or ironically, and possibly whether the genre is being invoked for real-world purposes or is being exploited for the purposes of fictional representation.

Texts belonging to a given genre display at least the following stylistic and formal features:

---

[1] We shall not make an issue here of the possible differences between 'genres' and 'sub-genres', though we are aware that some scholars do distinguish between the two on the basis of macrostructures and the treatment of such matters as politeness markers. However, the essential point for the present discussion is that the notion of the 'legal text' is insufficient and that the translator of texts appearing under this rubric will come up against a wide variety of writings, among which the following are likely to be represented: (1) statutes or sections drawn from the written law of a particular country; (2) wills; (3) contracts and similar agreements of a commercial nature; (4) court orders; (5) articles by lawyers for publication in learned journals; (6) notes by lawyers or experts in the law to be included in specialist publications; (7) textbooks by experts on the law of particular countries; (8) commentaries on general or specific points of law published in the media; (9) texts of any of the foregoing types taken from comments made in the media by jurists; (10) authoritative statements of the law of a particular state reproduced in the media; (11) articles on matters concerning the law published in the media by non-experts; (12) any fictional representation of the foregoing, etc.

(a)   A shared communicative function expressed by means of the same per-
        formative verb.[2] For example, all injunctions are in the form of orders
        that must be strictly complied with, whether they involve performing an
        act or refraining from a specific action; this peremptory nature of the
        order is thus built into the text in the form of a warning as to the conse-
        quences of non-compliance.

(b)   A similar macrostructure, i.e. format or organizational outline. For in-
        stance, all judgements are arranged into a minimum of three basic sections:
        facts as found, relevant law, and decision or ruling.

(c)   A similar discursive mode of developing the macrostructure (narrative,
        descriptive, imperative, optative) and similar discourse techniques aimed
        at satisfying the discourse expectations of the recipient or addressee.

(d)   A common lexical and syntactic arrangement of the material and a com-
        mon set of functional units and formal features, e.g. in statutes and other
        legislative texts, the abundant use of indefinite pronouns, passives and
        impersonal forms of the verb, 'shall' forms of the future to indicate legal
        obligation, extensive lists of categories or classes of persons and objects
        to whom or to which the law applies, and so on.

(e)   Common socio-pragmatic conventions, e.g. the hierarchical structure of
        the judiciary as reflected in the abbreviated titles of different judges, and
        the appropriate style of address ('my Lord', 'your Lordships', 'your Hon-
        our', 'your Worship', together with the highly conventional use of certain
        verbs or verb phrases in given contexts ('submit', 'put it to you', 'crave',
        'petition', 'pray', 'grant', 'give leave', 'restore [an injunction]', 'discharge
        [an injunction]', 'strike out', etc.).

This, then, is the general sense in which we are using the term 'genre' in this
book. We said earlier that there are written and oral sub-genres of a given genre,
but it is also possible to identify other subsets of the major text type found in
each of the areas into which the law can be subdivided (civil law, criminal law,
administrative law, employment law, European Union law, land law, property
law, etc.) and in the various activities in which legal practitioners are involved.
Since these activities are many and various, the resulting legal genres will be
equally diverse. The practitioners, who include judges, jurists, barristers, solicitors, legal draftsmen and clerks of the court, produce a large number of text
genres in which their aims, opinions, decisions, requests and conclusions are
expressed. These include Acts of Parliament, judgements, writs, injunctions, wills,

---

[2] See Chapter 1, section 6 (f).

contracts, law reports, submissions, pleadings, affidavits, arrest warrants, title deeds, subpoenas, legal textbooks and learned articles. We shall return to this group later on when we come to consider specific problems of legal translation.

The identification of genres is of great assistance to translators since it helps them focus on the particular needs and functions being catered for in a given original, and to look further and deeper into the nature of the particular texts they are dealing with. Genre identification allows translators to go beyond mere matters of lexical equivalence (polysymy, synonymity and related issues), syntactic equivalence (nominalization, passivity, modality, word order and similar considerations) or stylistic equivalence (solemnity, formality, figures of speech and other rhetorical devices, severity or asperity of tone in oral utterances, and so on). There is, of course, a sense in which a text cannot be translated at all unless the translator recognizes the genre to which it belongs. But what we are advocating here is a more systematic awareness of text typology. In fact, the translator who has taken the trouble to recognize the formal and stylistic conventions of a particular original has already done much to translate the text successfully.

2. The macrostructure of legal genres: university degrees and diplomas

Let us now look in more detail at some of the main formal and stylistic conventions of legal genres, remembering that by macrostructure we mean the dominant outline or organizational framework of a given genre, i.e. the layout of its constituent parts.

A good example of a highly conventional genre is the university degree or diploma. Because of the increasing mobility of university students and researchers, this is a kind of administrative text that professional translators regularly have to deal with. Analysis of the standard layout of English and Spanish examples shows a striking similarity of macrostructure, which may be brought under the following heads:

Identification of the issuing authorities:
English: The Board of Trustees of the University of X ...
Spanish: Juan Carlos I, Rey de España, y en su nombre el Rector de la Universidad de X ...

Academic justification for the award:
English: ... on the recommendation of the Senate of the University ...
Spanish: ... considerando que, conforme a las disposiciones y circunstancias prevenidas por la legislación vigente ...

Purpose of the certificate (expressed by a performative verb):
English: ... does hereby confer upon J.N. the degree of...
Spanish: ... expide el presente título de ...

Rights and privileges conferred by the award:
English: ... with all the rights and privileges appertaining thereto...
Spanish: ... que faculta al interesado para disfrutar los derechos que a este título otorgan las disposiciones vigentes ...

Place and date of issue:
English: Given at P., this twelfth day of June, nineteen hundred and eighty-eight.
Spanish: En L., a 12 de junio de mil novecientos noventa y ocho.

Signature:
English: The Chairman of the Board of Trustees.
Spanish: El Rector.

3. Certificates

Generally speaking, it is unusual for SL and TL versions of a text genre to display the degree of symmetry we have seen at work in the case of university degrees. Nevertheless, we cannot overstress the need for the translator to be thoroughly familiar with the macrostructure appropriate to a particular genre in a given language pair, since each text type is expected to conform rigidly to the usual conventions. Where the expected formats do not coincide, the translator will almost certainly have to massage the bones of the layout, so to speak, in order to bring the structure of the target version into conformity with expectations. In many situations, a certificate, for instance, must *look like* a certificate in order to be accepted as such, and a certain amount of structural tampering may be required to bring this about. In English, certificates are very often headed 'To whom it may concern' and commonly begin with some bald statement such as 'This is to certify that...', ending with the place, date and signature. The same elements are found in Spanish certificates, of course, but the order, at least in formal examples, is usually different. The traditional equivalent to 'to whom it may concern' is *Y para que conste en donde convenga* or *a los efectos oportunos*, a formula that appears at the end of the certificate rather than at the beginning. Moreover, whereas in English the person signing the certificate is identified at the end, above the signature, the place for this information in Spanish is at the very beginning, and the usual practice is for the issuer's rank and professional or official capacity to appear alongside the identification, e.g. *Dra. Margarita Lillo Martínez, Secretaria del Centro.*

Naturally enough, variation is possible. By ancient tradition, English certificates issued by private persons, or written statements made on oath by individuals, conventionally begin 'I, the undersigned, John Smith, hereby certify/hereby solemnly declare...'. Conversely, the recent proliferation of Spanish certificates beginning *A quien concierna* (literally, 'To whom it may concern...'), or words to that effect, is no doubt an interesting instance of the malleability of contemporary Spanish usage and the dominance of English as the standard model. But whatever the current fashion in the business world, we have never seen this formula used spontaneously in certificates issued by court clerks or administrative staff employed by official bodies. In both languages, the standard formats that the translator will normally come across in official documents are the ones described in the previous paragraph.

4. Statutes

Despite the fame of the English system of common law and the importance within it of judge-made law based on the rules of binding precedent, by far the greatest number of new laws introduced in Britain are the outcome of parliamentary decision. This legislative activity takes the form of statutes (*legislación*, and NOT *estatuto*s, which is a different thing). Statutes are either Acts of Parliament, which are passed by Parliament and come into force (*entran en vigor, entrent en vigueur, in Kraft treten*) on the date on which they are enacted (*promulgadas, promulguées,Gesetzeskraft erlangen*) by receiving the royal assent (*sanción real, assentiment de la reine, königliche Zustimmung*), or Orders (*órdenes ministeriales, arrêtés ministériels, Ministerialerlasse*), for which individual ministers and their departments are responsible. All Acts, before they become such, are presented to Parliament for debate, discussion and emendation in the form of bills (*proyectos de ley, projets de loi, Gesetzesvorlage*),[3] which at a still earlier stage started life as draft bills (*anteproyectos,* perhaps *avant-projets, Gesetzesentwurfe*). The macrostructure of a typical Act is made up of the following elements:

(a) The short title
This appears at the top of the page, below the royal seal, and is the name by which the Act is commonly known and cited, e.g. 'Road Traffic Act 1988', 'Law Reform (Miscellaneous Provisions) Act 1971'. The date, as one would expect, is the year in which the Act received the royal assent. An alternative system of reference is to omit the short title and cite instead the calendar year and the chapter number to which the Act was assigned in the Statute Book, optionally including the date of the session. Acts passed prior to 1963 are often

---

[3] The term 'bill' in some contexts is equivalent to 'law' (e.g. the Bill of Rights [*carta o declaración de derechos*]), and in others to the verdict or decision of a jury, as in the expression 'true bill' (*fallo o veredicto ratificado por los miembros de un jurado*).

cited by reference to the regnal year (the year of the monarch's reign), session and chapter.

(b) The long title

The long title should not be confused with the preamble, which is explained in the next section. It is in fact a formal and sometimes fairly elaborate description of the scope and purpose of the Act, invariably beginning with the words 'An Act ...' followed by some performative verb such as 'to amend...' or 'for codifying....'. An example of the briefer long title is 'An Act for codifying the law relating to the Sale of Goods'. An example of the more complex type is provided by the Hire-Purchase Act 1964, which reads as follows:

> An Act to amend the law relating to hire-purchase and credit-sale, and in relation thereto, to amend the enactments relating to the sale of goods; to make provision with respect to dispositions of motor vehicles which have been let or agreed to be sold by way of hire-purchase or conditional sale; to amend the Advertisements (Hire-Purchase) Act 1957; and for the purposes connected with the matters aforesaid.

Note that the long title forms an integral part of the law, since its serves as a contextual frame of reference that may be invoked as an instrument of interpretation and construction of the meaning to be attached to the legislator's words in the event of dispute.[4]

(c) The preamble

Not all contemporary statutes contain a preamble. Where there is one, it is normally very brief; its purpose is either to relate the law to the altered social, political or commercial conditions that, in Parliament's view, justify the introduction of new legislation, or simply to set out the facts or state of the law for which Parliament is intending to legislate. The usual formula is one or more 'whereas' clauses, or equivalent clauses of the 'in view of' or 'given that' type.

(d) The enacting words

This is an unvarying and highly solemn formula, couched in archaic English to increase its impressiveness (the complex mood of the impersonal verb – a mixture of optative and passive – the formal titles, the rhetorical repetition of prepositions to balance the phrases, the pairing of prepositions or prepositional phrases, the placing of the adjectives and participles after their nouns, and so on). The optative functions as a performative, giving legal force to the statute. Here is the hallowed formula:

---

[4] See chapter 1, section 8 for the notion of legal construction.

Be it Enacted by the Queen's most Excellent Majesty, by and with the advice of the Lords Spiritual and Temporal, and Commons, in this present Parliament assembled, and by the authority of the same, as follows...[5]

(e) The parts, articles and sections of statutes

Acts are divided into parts, sections, subsections, paragraphs and sub-paragraphs. Sections are indicated by a number, and subsections by a number in brackets; paragraphs are shown in lower-case letters between brackets and sub-paragraphs in lower-case Roman numerals, also between brackets. In citation, there is no space between numbers and brackets, so that sub-paragraph (iii) of paragraph (b) of subsection (2) of section 18 is printed 's 18(2)(b)(iii)', where 's' stands, of course, for 'section'. Given the precision of these references, the preposition used to direct attention to the exact location of the matter of law under discussion is usually 'at'. English statutes are extremely densely worded, partly as a result of the legislative habit of framing each subsection, and sometimes an entire section, as a single complex sentence built up from a dizzying number of subordinate and interpolated clauses and phrases, which are distributed over the paragraphs and sub-paragraphs. A good example of this complexity is seen in section 1 of the Further Education Act 1985:

1.   (1) For the purposes of this Act goods are supplied through a further education establishment if they result—

     (a)   from its educational activities;
     (b)   from the use of its facilities and the expertise of persons employed at it in the fields in which they are so employed;
     (c)   from ideas of a person employed at it, or of one of its students, arising out of its educational activities.

  (2) For the purposes of this Act services are supplied through such an establishment—

     (a) if they are provided by making available—
        (i)   its facilities;
        (ii)   the expertise of persons employed at it in the fields in which they are so employed;

     (b) if they result—
        (i) from its educational activities;
        (ii) from ideas such as are mentioned in subsection (1)(c) above.

---

[5] A similar formula is found in most US legislation, viz: 'Be it Enacted by the Senate and House of Representatives in Congress assembled and by the authority of the people of the State of ..., as follows...'.

It is not uncommon for one or more subsections of an Act to be devoted to clarification of the precise legal meaning to be attached to some of the terms used in it, or to contain one or more interpretative clauses. These clauses normally begin 'This Act shall be construed...' and are designed to aid construction of the scope and purpose of the statute as a whole or some particular part of it. For instance, section 2(10) of the Further Education Act 1985 defines two of the terms used in it as follows:

(10) In this section—

'rate fund' —

> (a) in relation to the Inner London Education Authority *means* any fund for which a precept is issued by the Greater London Council; and
> (b) in relation to any other local education authority, *means* the county fund or general rate fund; and

'year' *means* a period of twelve months ending with 31st March. [Emphasis added.]

(f) Schedules

Schedules are appendices containing miscellaneous information and clarification, such as prescribed forms to be used in connection with the Act for purposes of application, registration, information transfer, etc; detailed illustration of matters referred to in the body of the law, often in the form of tables, tariffs and so on; a list of repeals effected by the Act; a list of temporary or transitional provisions, and other data of a similar kind.

Note that when proposed legislation is progressing through Parliament in the form of Bills, the texts are technically broken down into clauses, sub-clauses and paragraphs rather than the subdivisions described above. However, since this is a mere convention, the translator who is (unusually, one would imagine) called upon to deal with a Bill is obviously free to select any suitable system of subdivision that makes sense in the target language. They may very well opt to use the same terms in translating both Bills and Acts.

5. Law reports

In modern Britain, as in all democratic countries, Parliament is responsible for creating the bulk of new laws, in the form of statutes or Acts which are binding on everyone, including the courts. However, although many countries accept that judicial decisions can, to a limited extent, be a source of new law by establishing settled precedents, the role of the superior courts in the British common law system is much more decisive in this regard. Under the doctrine of *stare decisis* (Latin = 'stand by the decided cases'), all equal or lower courts are bound by the decisions of the higher courts unless and until one of the higher courts departs from the precedent on proper legal grounds. This means that the common law courts have retained a genuine lawmaking function based on judicial construction of the legislator's intention and on judges' interpretations of general principles and doctrines of law. The rules and legal principles created by these precedents are called case-law or judge-made law to distinguish them from statute law.

Given this power of the higher courts, it is obviously very important for accurate records of court proceedings to be kept. Later judges and litigants must have full access to the facts of earlier cases of a similar kind and, especially, to the reasons given for reaching a particular decision. Legislation, as we have seen, is recorded in the statute book. Records of case-law, on the other hand, are to be found in publications called 'law reports', prepared by lawyers who specialize in this type of work. There are various bodies that provide this service. One is the Incorporated Council of Law Reporting, which has been in existence since 1865. But virtually the standard series nowadays is the collection known as the All England Law Reports (commonly abbreviated to 'All ER'), which enjoys great prestige in the profession and is regularly cited by lawyers, judges and commentators as the authoritative source of information about particular cases. Besides these semi-official reports, some of the 'quality newspapers' like *The Times, The Financial Times* and *The Independent* regularly publish much shorter reports on significant cases, and reference to these is not uncommon in legal texts. For the sake of brevity, we shall take our example from the pages of the *Financial Times*[6]. The text can be broken down into the following parts:

Introduction

The introductory section sets out the name of the case, the court at which the case was heard and the identity of the judge or judges responsible. Cases are named after the parties involved, with the name of the plaintiff or prosecutor preceding that of the defendant. Given the adversarial nature of proceedings, the convention is to place the initial 'v' (for 'versus') between the names of the litigants. In English criminal practice, where private prosecution is extremely rare, charges are brought and pursued on behalf of the state, or Crown, and this is indicated by use of the initial 'R' (for *Rex* or *Regina*, i.e. the reigning monarch, depending on whether a king or a queen is on the throne), e.g. 'R v Smith'.

---

[6] Davies, Rachel: 'Record Company cannot Apply Penalty Clause against Invoices'. *FT Law Reports. Financial Times* (March 21, 1990).

When spoken aloud, this is enunciated as 'the Crown against Smith', so that the written formula is more of an algebraic representation than an abbreviation as such. Similarly, in the title of a civil action, e.g. 'Lewis v Averay', the 'v' is enunciated as 'and'. In our example, the introduction reads:

> Ariston SRL *v* Charly Records Ltd. Court of Appeal. Lord Justice Mustill, Lord Justice Beldam and Lord Justice Leggatt.[7]

Reason for the decision setting the precedent (*ratio decidendi*)

Judicial decisions are based on closely, sometimes intricately argued interpretations of legal principle as they apply to the facts of the given case. It is therefore impossible for everything a judge says to be binding on future courts. The law reporter's task is to isolate the ultimate reason for the decision (called the *ratio decidendi, motif décisoire, Entscheidungsgrund*) from the rest of the argument (called *obiter dicta, opinions incidentes, gelbeiläufige Äußerungen,* i.e. remarks made by the way). The rule is that only the *ratio* is binding for the future; remarks made *obiter* are said to have 'persuasive force' but are not binding. In identifying the *ratio*, the reporter will strip it as far as possible of the circumstantial detail of the particular case and enunciate it in the form of a general principle or rule, almost as if it were a section or subsection of an Act. In our example, the *ratio* was defined thus:

> SUMS AGREED between parties to a contract, to be payable in the event of specified breaches, cannot be a genuine pre-estimate of damage if they are to apply equally to serious and minor breaches. They are therefore not liquidated damages but a penalty which is unenforceable for the purpose of the whole contract, including in respect of those breaches to which they are proportionate.

---

[7] In professional law reports and in written judgements, the convention is to abbreviate judges' titles. Crown Court, County Court and High Court judges are called Mr/Mrs Justice X; Appeal Court judges are called 'Lord Justice X'; and the 'Law Lords' sitting on the judicial committee of the House of Lords are known simply by their titles ('Lord X'). The latter is never abbreviated, but the first two are shortened respectively to 'J' and 'LJ' (plural 'LLJ'), with the abbreviation being placed after the name, e.g. 'Littledale J' or 'Middleton, Fletcher and Rowley LLJ'. The senior English civil law judge has the honorary title of 'Master of the Rolls', abbreviated 'MR', whilst the head of the British judiciary is styled 'Lord Chancellor', or 'LC'. Translators into languages in which these hierarchical distinctions are not usually marked might wish to use some courtesy formula in their place, e.g. 'Su Señoría, el juez Littledale', 'Su Señoría el juez Wilkinson, presidente del Tribunal Superior de Apelación /decano de la Sala de lo Civil del Tribunal Superior de Apelación', or 'Su Señoría el juez Loftus, presidente del Tribunal Supremo'. The title 'Lord' could, of course be retained untranslated, but in a sense it is misleading to do so, since judges are made 'lords' for purely professional reasons unconnected with hereditary rights or political expediency.

The decision of the court

The decision of a court as a matter of law on the facts of the case leads to an outcome, which can take only one of two forms: a finding in favour of the plaintiff or the Crown or judgement for the defendant – a verdict of not guilty in criminal cases. Courts are bound to come down on one side or the other, however narrow the margin, and to deliver a judgement; they cannot declare a draw. In law reports, this crucial decision is usually signalled by the term 'held' (*falló, resolvió, décidé, entschieden*), which is often printed in capitals in professional reports to make it easier to spot at a glance. The formula found in our example is the most common one ('The court... so held when dismissing an appeal...'), since it neatly brings together the principle of law upheld by the court and the consequence for the two parties concerned:

> The Court of Appeal so held when dismissing an appeal by the defendant, Charly Records Ltd, from a decision by Judge Hayman on a preliminary issue that a clause in a contract between Charly and the plaintiff, Ariston SRL, was a penalty clause and therefore unenforceable.

The recital

The recital consists of a summary of the major facts and the relevant law, including, in appeal cases, the judgement of the trial court or other lower court (*tribunal a quo*) from whose opinion appeal is brought. The facts, which are often very complex, are usually laid out first, as in our example:

> LORD JUSTICE BELDAM said that Charly specialised in producing and marketing re-issues of quality popular records of jazz, blues and rock music. It bought the rights of records released under other labels and re-issued them under its own. For that purpose it acquired master tapes of the performance and the metal parts and lacquers used for pressing out the records. It also obtained the negatives, films, artwork and labels necessary to produce record sleeves and protective inner envelopes. It did not have the facilities to manufacture the records but contracted with specialist record-making companies which did. Ariston was an Italian company in Milan which produced record pressings. On July 1 1982 Ariston and Charly entered into an agreement under which Ariston undertook to manufacture long playing records and to print colour sleeves and plastic coated and printed inlay bags. Charly was to entrust Ariston with the necessary metal parts, lacquers, negatives, artworks and label information. All those items were essential to the production of record pressings and of considerable value to Charly. Accordingly, by clause 7 of the agreement, Ariston undertook to return all the items within 10

working days of Charly's request. The clause provided that 'a penalty' of £600 per day would be paid by Ariston for late delivery. In 1985 Charly transferred its production order from Ariston to another company. Just under £14,000 was outstanding on invoices for records supplied by Ariston...

The summary of the facts is then followed by the court's view of how the facts relate to the decisions in similar cases relied on in argument by counsel. Once again, the emphasis falls on the reasons given by the earlier judges for adhering to or departing from specific principles of law, including both judgements and relevant legislation:

In *Clydebank Engineering [1905] AC 6* Lord Halsbury emphasised that the court must construe such a clause according to the real nature of the transaction and that the mere use of 'penalty' or 'damage' would not be conclusive as to the parties' rights....

In *Wallis v Smith (1882) 21 Ch D 243* the relevant clause provided that if the defendant were to commit a 'substantial breach' of the contract, he should pay £5,000. It was held that the inclusion of 'substantial breach' meant that trifling breaches were excluded and the clause could therefore be construed as providing for liquidated damages...

In *Dunlop/1915] AC 79,102* Lord Parmoor said that if the agreed sum applied equally to stipulations of varying importance and was a penalty in respect of any of them, it was a penalty for the purpose of the whole contract, 'since it could not in the same contract be construed both as a penalty and as liquidated damages'.

The finding

Finally, the court's decision is recorded concisely, and even tersely, in phrases such as 'The appeal was dismissed', 'Appeal allowed', 'Judgement for the defendant', 'The appeal was allowed and the convictions quashed', and so on.

6.   Judgements

Despite the fact that judgements constitute a separate genre, they underlie law reports and, though they are naturally much longer and the format is more open, the breakdown is very similar. They may be pronounced extempore (in an improvised way), but modern practice is for judges to write their opinions and read them out in open court. Copies, known as 'handed-down judgements', are usually distributed to the parties and later published by specialist firms (and increasingly on the Internet). Written judgements are commonly laid out in numbered paragraphs and may run from anything from 40 or 50 lines to 60 or 70 densely argued pages. When the judgement is not the work of a single judge but contains the opinions of a bench of three or five judges (or, in rare cases, more than five) the paragraphs are numbered consecutively in the order in which the opinions were delivered, forming a single coherently presented document. A good example of a contemporary judgement is that delivered by the High Court (Queen's Bench Division) on 15 February, 2000,[8] which effectively put an end to the 'Pinochet case' in Britain. Here, Lord Justice Brown's opinion runs from paragraph 1 to paragraph 57; this is followed (paragraphs 58-67) by the opinion of Mr Justice Latham; and finally comes the opinion of Mr Justice Dyson (paragraphs 68-88).

As for format, the judgement commonly begins with an Introduction, in which the nature of the issue is identified and the parties are introduced together with a brief explanation of their legal relationship. Where the official title of a party or body involved is inconveniently long, a shortened form of the name will be given in brackets following its first appearance, e.g. 'The Chief Constable of South Yorkshire (the Chief Constable)' or 'The South of Scotland Electricity Board (the Board)'. The use of 'hereinafter' to indicate that the given short form will be used throughout the remainder of the document is much more formal and is more likely to be encountered in the preamble to a contract or a warranty than in the text of a written judgement.

Next comes a section headed 'The Facts', in which the principal matters of fact assumed, admitted or proved are set out as coherently and succinctly as possible. Curiously enough, translators should be prepared for this to be the most difficult part of their job, since the case may well involve highly technical discussion of working parts, industrial processes, chemical reactions, complex financial operations or pathologists' reports analysed in minute detail. This is followed by separate sections devoted to description of and comment upon the parties' contentions based on these facts and on what they perceive to be the relevant law, i.e. a summary of pleadings. For example, Lord Justice Brown's judgement is subdivided for convenience into a number of separate sections, each with a descriptive heading: 'The Application Below' [paras. 21-23]; 'The Context of the Secretary of State's Decision' [paras. 24-28]; 'The Secretary of State's Argument' [29-36]; 'The Secretary of State's Assurance of Confidentiality' [paras. 37-40]; and 'The Applicants' Argument' [paras. 41-46]. Finally we have the court's conclusions, in this case simply headed as such [paras. 47-57].

---

[8] *R v Secretary of State for Home Department, ex parte the Kingdom of Belgium and R v Secretary of State for Home Department, ex parte Amnesty International Limited and five other applicants*, Case Nos. CO/236/2000 & CO/238/2000, Supreme Court of Judicature, Queen's Bench Division, Tuesday, 15 February, 2000.

The final decision is very simply expressed: 'For the reasons given earlier, this application succeeds'.

When a number of opinions are presented together, as happens with handed-down judgements in cases of judicial review or on appeal to the higher courts, it is customary for the summary of facts to be left to the judge providing the leading opinion; the others are usually content to acknowledge the accuracy of the summary by some such formula as 'The facts have been set out in the opinion read by my learned friend, Lord X'. For the same reason, the later judges may, if they wish, begin by stating the decision they have reached and work back from that to the reasons for their judgement. Finally, where one or more of the later judges entirely concur in the opinion of another, they may simply state this, e.g. 'For the reasons given by Lord X, I too think that this appeal should be dismissed'.

In keeping with the British tradition of strongly reasoned judicial opinion, judgements are often couched in a style that is flavoured with the personality of their maker. Flashes of verbal wit, veiled sarcasm and ironic or pointed comment on particular submissions are not unusual. There is some acerbity, dryness or latent sarcasm, for example, in the italicized portions of the following remarks from Lord Brown's speech:

> "*Shorn of the applicants' more exorbitant demands*...this is the essence of their complaint." [para. 2]

> "France and Switzerland, we are told, have made representations, *to what effect we know not*." [para. 20]

The irony is more barbed in the same judge's comment in paragraph 39:

> "...had the report not, *uniquely amongst such reports*, concluded that no significant improvement can be expected in Senator Pinochet's condition, it would in any event have been disclosed to the requesting states."

The final example taken from this text [para. 42] is in fact a quotation from a much earlier judgement by Megarry J (as he then was). It is an elegant combination of judicious colloquialism, irony, buried metaphor and sustained rhetorical use of paradox and antithesis which, if it does not exactly make for deathless literary prose, is a far cry from the aridity of legal jargon and pomposity which are thought to be the hallmarks of judicial style by those who have, perhaps, not taken the trouble to read all that many judgements:

> "The path of the law is strewn with examples of open-and-shut cases which, somehow, were not; of unanswerable charges which, in the event,

were completely answered; of inexplicable conduct which was fully explained; of fixed and unalterable determinations that, by discussion, suffered a change."

In translating this passage, the style and tone would have to be preserved, along with the rhetorical flourishes we have indicated. For reasons of clarity, the translator might feel the need to explicate the first instance of paradox by reviving the suppressed term 'apparently' or 'seemingly' ('[seemingly] open-and-shut cases'). This is the kind of decision the literary translator is constantly being forced to make, a fact which stresses how close the non-technical side of legal translation is to its literary counterpart. We suggest the following Spanish version:

El camino del Derecho está sembrado de ejemplos de casos [aparentemente] clarísimos que, por una razón u otra, después no lo fueron tanto; de acusaciones irrefutables que, a la hora de la verdad, quedaron refutadas hasta el último detalle; de comportamientos inexplicables que encontraron perfecta explicación; y de resoluciones fijas e inmutables que, tras la oportuna deliberación, sufrieron mudanza.

Incidentally, on the subject of buried metaphor, the legal translator will not infrequently come across a courtroom vocabulary whose figurative origins are recognizably martial, though habitual usage has dulled their impact to the point where the reader or listener has probably ceased to be aware of their metaphorical associations. In the Pinochet judgement, for example, Mr Justice Latham, comments [para. 50] with some vividness: "Those are *the battle lines drawn up* by *the protagonists*...". Among a very long list of martial terms commonly used in the language of the courts we might mention obvious instances such as 'defence', 'attack', 'marshal [arguments]', 'resist', 'contend/contention', 'victor', 'vanquish', 'sword', 'shield' (the doctrine of equitable estoppel, which is only available to the defendant and never to the plaintiff, has been called 'a shield and not a sword') and, of course, the newspaper favourite 'courtroom battle'.

Another feature of English judicial style that the translator should notice is that, as in report- and essay-writing, the first person singular is the norm for the expression of opinion. The use of the first person plural is confined to objective references to the activity or thinking of the judges as a body or group, or else it is to be understood as expressing not the judge's personal view but the collective awareness of the whole court and of any members of the public who have followed the case. A single judge sitting alone will never say 'we' when 'I' is meant. Examples from Lord Brown's speech, selected almost at random, include "*I have not found* this an easy case" [para. 47]; "*I readily see* the force of much of Mr Sumption's argument... *I recognise*..." [para. 48]; "*I find myself driven to conclude...*"[para. 50].

Finally, in contemporary judgements we not infrequently encounter slight departures from the formal register that is the rule. This occasional admixture of more colloquial utterance is presumably designed to temper the severity of the law, to make the opinion sound more humane and to create an impression of reader-friendliness suited to the democratic tone of our times. Lord Brown, in the judgement we have quoted from, remarks at the start of his speech that "*it is high time* the decision was taken" [para. 1]; in his summary of the facts he settles into a relaxed narrative tone that includes the phrase "I can *pick up the story* with the final House of Lords decision" [para. 5]; he keeps up the person-next-door tone with his comment at para. 57 that "Comity, like fairness, is *a two-way-street*"; and he indulges in a somewhat outmoded colloquialism in his thirty-seventh paragraph, where we read "Although *at first blush* that express assurance might be thought of some importance...". Since these features affect only the tone and style of the judgement and are in no way concerned with matters of law, it would clearly be the translator's duty to reproduce them as faithfully as possible in the target language, even though the linguistic habits of the local judiciary tend toward greater restraint or formality than is exhibited by their English counterparts.

7.   Oral genres (I). The examination of witnesses at the public hearing

We mentioned earlier that the term 'genre' can apply to both written and oral text types. In the case of the oral genres, it will be obvious that the spoken medium favours variety and spontaneity, and the speech of judges and lawyers is just as much subject to this element of unpredictability as anyone else's. Secondly, the content of courtroom speeches depends very much on the particular facts of the case, so that by far the greater percentage of the actual utterance is free, unpredictable or indeterminable in advance. But once again, the linguistic reality is quite different. As a matter of fact the vast majority of addresses of the kinds we have mentioned conform to predictable and very specific patterns that we shall examine in their place. The reason, plainly, is that both the purpose of these speeches – to elicit information from witnesses and to persuade the jury in the case of the lawyers, and to enlighten the jury as to its duty in the case of the judge – and the existence of very strict rules of procedure determining what may and what may not be said in court act to restrict the theoretical freedom of form. The result is that, though they are delivered orally, these addresses are just as much genres as their written counterparts, and can be formally described with a reasonable degree of accuracy. Naturally, translators will come up against the occasional unfamiliar term of art, as they do in working on any text form.

But they will rarely be surprised by the format once they have mastered the key issues that determine the models: the function of the speeches and the procedural rules governing them.

In the Examination of Witnesses at the public hearing the basic rule is that leading questions are not allowed, i.e. counsel is not permitted to suggest the expected or desired answer to any question put to a witness, or in any way to seek to trap witnesses into making statements or admissions that do not flow naturally from the testimony they wish to give. Witnesses, after all, take an oath when they take the stand in the classic form:

> I swear by Almighty God that the evidence I shall give shall be the truth,
> the whole truth and nothing but the truth.

(Witnesses who prefer not to 'swear by Almighty God' can instead take the oath in the form 'I affirm'). There is therefore a presumption that the witness will tell the truth, as well as the threat of legal sanctions for perjury if they tell lies or suppress the truth or deliberately mislead the court, so it would seem unfair to allow counsel to browbeat (intimidate) witnesses or attempt to twist their words or otherwise restrict their voluntarily offered versions of events.

Examination of witnesses is further patterned by the conventions controlling the order in which they are called and the party calling them. The basic rule is that the prosecution, in criminal trials, or counsel for the plaintiff in civil proceedings, state their case first, followed by the defence. Each side has the privilege of being first to examine the witnesses it calls. However, each side is entitled to cross-examine (*repreguntar, mener un contre-interrogatoire, ins Kreuzverhör nehmen*) the other side's witnesses when counsel calling them has finished conducting the examination-in-chief or 'direct examination', as American lawyers prefer to say. Finally, witnesses may be re-examined by the side calling them with a view to rebutting evidence given by them that appears to favour the other side, or to removing or diminishing the effect of damaging admissions made during cross-examination. Let us now consider each of these stages in turn. We shall take our examples from criminal trials, since a majority of readers will be more familiar with the conduct of these than with that of civil trials:

(a) Direct examination or examination-in-chief

Although it is true that counsel for the side calling a witness frames their questions selectively and seeks to elicit answers favouring their side's case, the questions must be put as neutrally as possible. It is absolutely against the rules for counsel to ask a question like "When the accused attacked you from behind in that dark alley, how did you defend yourself?" unless the witness has already made these accusations without undue prompting. Instead the lawyer must elicit the answers by carefully framed open questions, e.g. "Where were you at 10 p.m. on the night in question? – Did you see anybody else there? – Is that person present here in court? – Can you please tell the court what happened next?", and so on. This is laborious, but it is scrupulously in accordance with the principles of fairness, objectivity and the accused's right to a fair trial. The most counsel can get away with is the making of an indirect, open-ended accusation, which traditionally takes the form 'I put it to you that...' (*Diga ser cierto que..., N'est-il pas vrai que...?, Ist es nicht wahr, dass...?*).

It is assumed that a witness called by one party will generally provide a version of events in keeping with the case that side wishes to present. Indeed, that is the reason why the witness is selected by the side in question. But it sometimes happens that when the moment arrives for that person to take the stand, they change their story and give evidence favourable to the other side. If this happens, the side calling the witness is allowed to ask the judge to direct the jury that the testimony is that of a hostile witness. The side affected may also be allowed to cross-examine the witness, which means that they will be able to ask leading questions that in normal circumstances they could not have asked.

An accused person is not, of course, obliged to answer incriminating questions or even to enter the witness-box. Moreover, in the US a person who feels compromised by a question is entitled to refuse to answer it by 'taking the fifth [amendment]' (to the Constitution of the United States). However, the judge or the jury are likewise entitled, in such a case, to draw a negative inference from the witness's behaviour. In any event, the main point is that counsel must not lead the witness in examination-in-chief or re-examination.

(b) Cross-examination (examen contradictorio de la prueba, contrainterrogatorio, contre-interrogatoire, Kreuzverhör)
Obviously the purpose of this examination by the opposite side is to cast doubt on the accuracy of the testimony of the other side's witnesses, to exploit any inconsistencies in it or to destroy or undermine the witness's credibility. In the latter case, the examination is sometimes called 'cross-examination to credit'. In cross-examination leading questions are allowed, and it is legitimate for counsel to draw attention to any discrepancy between witnesses' answers and any other statements previously made by them and which stand on the court record, e.g. depositions (declarations) taken during the committal stage (*fase de instrucción, pendant l'instruction,* perhaps *Ermittlungsverfahren*) or in answering questions asked by the police. If the witness's evidence is crucial to the prosecution case and the inconsistencies are so marked that the entire case collapses, counsel for the defence may make a formal submission of 'no case to answer'. If counsel for the prosecution agrees and the judge takes the same view, the case is withdrawn from the jury, the judge directs (orders) them to return (give)

a formal verdict of not guilty and the accused is acquitted and discharged.

(c) Re-examination *(segundo interrogatorio, nouvelle interrogation,* perhaps *erneute Prüfung)*

As we have said, the essential point of this second chance for the side calling the witness is to dispel doubts raised in cross-examination and to restore lost credibility or reinforce points that have been weakened or questioned. Since the degree of doubt in the jury's mind is crucial in criminal trials, given that the standard of proof required for a verdict of guilty is 'proof beyond reasonable doubt'[9], it is very important for the prosecution in particular to ensure there are no loose ends. After all, an accused person does not have to prove their innocence; it is up to the prosecution, who normally bear the burden of proof, to establish guilt. Doubt therefore almost always favours the defence on the old principle *in dubio pro reo* (in cases of doubt, the law finds for the prisoner.) Finally, there is a rule that in re-examination only matters arising out of the cross-examination are normally allowed. Leave of the judge (permission) is required to raise new issues and the other side is given the opportunity to oppose any such request.

8.   Oral genres (II). Counsels' closing speeches to the jury (jury summation). Judge's summing-up and charge to the jury

Criminal trials in the English-speaking countries traditionally end with counsel's final speeches to the jury and the judge's summing-up before the jury retire to consider their verdict. These speeches are also called 'closing statements', 'closing arguments' or 'final arguments' (cf. Walter 1988). In Britain and in some American states, the order is the same as in the examination of witnesses,

---

[9] This is the classic formula. However, juries down the years have often found it difficult to understand the technical distinction between 'doubt' and 'reasonable doubt', as is obvious from the many anomalous verdicts that have been returned. In recent times, judges have often preferred to use simpler or clearer expressions of the standard of proof to help juries. Thus, judges may tell a jury that the phrase means "so that you are really sure" or they may mix the two and tell them that to convict they must be "satisfied beyond doubt so that you feel sure of the defendant's guilt" (cf. Osborne 1993/1999:237-8). If judges feel justified in explaining or slightly altering the venerable formula, there seems to be no good reason why translators of it into another language should be constrained to literal versions which may actually be unclear in the TL. For example, our classroom experience has shown us that Spanish translators are often unsure of what exactly is meant by the standard translation *más allá de la duda razonable*, which is syntactically dubious (what does '*más allá de*' [beyond] actually mean?) and conceptually complex. It is a relief to translators to know that all that is really implied by the phrase is that the jury has no major doubts about the guilt of the accused.

i.e. counsel for the prosecution speaks first followed by counsel for the defence, but in some US jurisdictions the defence counsel speaks first and the prosecution has the final word. (This latter practice is frowned on by many British lawyers, who regard it as contrary to the presumption of innocence, i.e. the idea that accused persons have a right to a fair trial and are assumed to be innocent unless they are proved guilty.)

Whatever the order, the format of the speeches is highly conventional and standardized, though the content, of course, varies enormously depending on the facts of the case. However, the style tends to be relaxed, and counsel may even permit themselves a certain amount of colloquialism of expression. As we have seen in our analysis of the examination of witnesses, the lawyers are at all times on the lookout for tactical advantage, and so they tailor their remarks to suit their audience. Psychology and manner are just as important as content. Barristers can easily 'lose' a jury if they do not pitch their speeches properly. Thus, the normal approach is to stress repeatedly that all that is required is that the jury should not worry about legal subtleties, but should consider all the evidence, apply common sense to the matters of fact which they are asked to decide, and generally come to the conclusions that any sensible and responsible group of ordinary people would reach in their position. Naturally enough, counsel for each party will select the evidence which best suits their own case and try to persuade the jury that this evidence points to the right and commonsense verdict. However, in Britain, though usually not in the US, counsel for the prosecution is supposed not to press for a conviction at all costs but to act as a 'minister of justice' and so stress the jury's duty to act fairly and reasonably and come to a just decision based exclusively on the evidence.

In their speeches, counsel will choose the plainest and most everyday words in their attempts to convince the jury, and will avoid complex legal terminology as much as possible. They will remind the members of the jury that they are in a very special position and that they alone, and not the judge, are responsible for deciding the facts of the case by bringing in (giving) a verdict of guilty or not guilty, while it is for the judge to acquit or convict the accused and to pass sentence if the verdict is one of guilty.

The judge's summing-up is usually somewhat more formal and certainly less rhetorical, since it is not the judge's business to persuade the jury but simply to ensure that they have understood their duty. Stylistically, then, and even in part of the content, there is some similarity between counsels' representations and the judge's remarks to the jury, though there are some legal requirements of content in the judge's address that we shall comment on in their place. To sum up, the normal order of the three speeches is as follows: (a) closing address to the jury by the prosecuting counsel; (b) closing address to the jury by counsel for the defence; (c) judge's summing-up and charge to the jury. This concludes the trial proper and the jury then retires to consider its verdict, so the effect of these speeches is critically important to both litigants. The judge's comments are equally important, since the summing-up is their last chance to explain the jury's role to them as a group and, as we shall see, a misdirection by the judge will lead inevitably to an appeal and to the quashing of the verdict. Let us now look at some examples of the actual content and possible wording of these oral genres.

Address by counsel for the prosecution

As we have said, the prosecution normally bears the burden of proof. Technically, to establish guilt, two things must be proved: first, that the prisoner committed the unlawful act of which they stand accused; and secondly, that the act was accompanied by the criminal frame of mind appropriate to the particular offence. These two elements of the crime are respectively known as *actus reus* (unlawful act, i.e. *hecho punible, comportement délictueux, strafbare Handlung*) and *mens rea* (unlawful frame of mind, i.e. *dolo, intention delictueuse, verbrecherische Absicht*). The test for the first is objective: if an act or failure to act is deemed criminal in a statute, then it is an offence whether the accused knew it or not. This is the meaning of the well-known phrase that 'ignorance of the law is no excuse'. But the second issue, concerning the accused's frame of mind, is more complex. *Mens rea* is sometimes translated as 'criminal intention', but this is an oversimplification, since people do not always intend every single consequence of their acts in the literal sense of desiring the outcome. However, it would clearly be wrong in some cases for accused persons to get off with the crime simply by saying 'Yes, I did it, but I didn't mean it'. The law sometimes imposes criminal liability for unreasonable behaviour, the use of excessive force, negligence, indifference or a failure to foresee the likely or probable consequences of certain acts. The concept of 'constructive malice' can be used by the prosecutor who wants to convince the jury that the accused *should have been aware* of the criminal nature of a given act, even if criminal intention as such is denied or is difficult to establish.

All of these points have to be proved on the evidence led by each side. Counsel for the prosecution will therefore make a speech appealing to the jury's sense of justice and ability to read the evidence sensibly. If the crime charged is theft, or dangerous driving, or causing someone personal injury or bodily harm, the prosecutor will stress the victim's suffering and society's need to find means of protecting itself against such behaviour, and of teaching criminals that 'crime doesn't pay' and that they cannot go unpunished.

The prosecution may also use the speech to attack the defence's case. The accused may have lodged one of the 'general defences' available in law, such as insanity (*enajenación mental, aliénation mentale, Geisteskrankheit*), automatism (*conducta involuntaria, réflexe automatique, Reflexhandlung*), necessity (*estado de necesidad o miedo insuperable, besoin, Notstand*), mistaken identity (*identificación errónea, identification erronée, Irrtum über die Person*), alibi (*cortada, alibi, Alibi*), duress (*coacción, contrainte, Zwang*), self-defence (*legítima defensa, légitime défense, Notwehr*) or intoxication (*estado de embriaguez, ébriété, Betrunkenheit*). Some of these defences, especially those involving insanity or mental derangement, have the effect of reversing the burden of proof (*la carga de la prueba, la charge de la preuve, Beweislast*), which then falls on the defendant. But in any case, they may all give the prosecution the chance to attack the credibility of the accused or the defence witnesses.

We shall conclude this section with a brief list of the type of remarks commonly used by counsel for the prosecution in the closing address to the jury. They are intended merely as illustrations of the content and tone of a speech that will generally follow the outline we have just provided:

> How, ladies and gentlemen, does the defendant's explanation appeal to your reason or common sense?
> I think you will agree that this witness looked very uncomfortable giving testimony.
> I have no doubt you will bring back the true and correct verdict in this case.
> You have a chance now to see to it that justice is done.
> The name of that, ladies and gentlemen, is first degree murder.
> I ask you to find D. guilty of causing the victim grievous bodily harm.

Address by counsel for the defence

In the light of what we have said, defence counsel will commonly use the final speech to plant the seeds of doubt in the minds of the jury. Obvious tactics include reminding them that it is for the prosecution to prove the guilt of the accused and that if they are in doubt they must acquit; stressing contradictions and inconsistencies in the prosecution's case in contrast to the solid evidence led by the defence; drawing attention to the defendant's previous good character; or, when the charge is one of wounding, pointing to evidence of provocation.

There follows a list of comments typically made by defence lawyers in their final speeches:

> We have no burden at all. It is the prosecution who has a burden of proving to you...
> Is there any reasonable doubt in your mind?
> I would ask you to go carefully through each piece of evidence and use your common sense.
> You become a part of the jury institution, an institution that has a history

of eight hundred years.
I submit to you that a proper verdict in this case is 'not guilty'.
We submit that the case has not been proved to the high level required.
Everyone has a right to defend themselves and their family.
It could be you or me standing in the dock there.
If you believe that, then your verdict must be not guilty.
I ask you to acquit my client in this case.

Judge's summing up and charge to the jury

In US courts, the judge's final speech to the jury is usually brief and concentrates on the second point of the two indicated in the above heading, summary of the evidence and the parties' positions being left to counsel. In Britain, however, the judge has an absolute duty to summarize the evidence and direct (give instructions to) the jury concerning the value they should attach to it. As we have seen, in criminal trials in which a judge sits (presides) with a jury, the jury is the 'trier' or judge of fact, and the judge's role is to ensure the law is correctly applied. Since the law of evidence is very complex, the judge often has to spend quite a long time explaining in ordinary language what the jury is or is not entitled to do in the particular case. The judge must avoid leading the jury but it may be necessary to remind them that certain inconsistencies in testimony mean that a particular witness's evidence is unreliable or that certain parts of the evidence the jury has heard improperly have been ruled inadmissible or have been withdrawn by the party who tried to lead them, and so must be disregarded.

Clearly the judge has to remain impartial at this and every other stage of the trial, but impartial does not mean inactive. In fact English judges have always played a very active role in the conduct of criminal trials, intervening to clarify matters of law that arise during argument, or to restrain unruly witnesses or bullying barristers. In recent times, new rules of practice, some of them promoted by a professional body known as the Judicial Studies Board, allow judges to request the active assistance of counsel involved in a trial in preparing the directions to be given to the jury in the summing-up. The idea is to ensure as far as possible that the judge does not make any fatal error of fact or law that would constitute a misdirection and thus lead to a quashing (*revocación, révocation, Aufhebung*) of the verdict on appeal. (One effect of this, of course, is that the defence must cooperate within reason; counsel for the defence can no longer 'sit tight' and hope that the judge will make a false step in the summing-up.)

Within this general framework of the summing-up, judges are likely to make comments like the following to the members of the jury:

You are the only triers of the facts in this case.
You must disregard the testimony of X, which has proved to be unreliable.

It is your duty to consider all the evidence and to reach your verdict, without fear or favour, on that basis alone.

You have over two hours to reach your decision, but if you need more time, within reason, there will be no difficulty about arranging it.

If at all possible, your verdict should be unanimous, but if you cannot all agree, a majority verdict will be acceptable, provided at least ten of you agree.[10]

Should you require further guidance from me, or wish further clarification of any matter relating to the evidence you have heard here, you must all return together and ask your questions in open court

If you are satisfied beyond doubt so that you are really sure of the defendant's guilt, you must bring in (give) a verdict of guilty. Otherwise, you must find the accused not guilty.

---

[10] If for any reason (usually illness or family problems) one member of the jury is excused after the trial has begun, a majority verdict returned by ten of the eleven remaining jurors is acceptable; if two are excused, at least nine of the remaining ten must agree. After time extensions have been granted, if the jury is still unable to agree on a unanimous or a majority verdict within these limits, the jury will be discharged. In that case, either a new trial will be ordered, with a different jury, or (more probably) the prosecution will withdraw its case. In the US, failure by the jury to reach a verdict is called a 'mistrial' (*juicio frustrado, procès ne pouvant aboutir, ergebnislose Prozess*). In both Britain and the US, the term 'mistrial' also means a trial that is vitiated by some major procedural defect (*juicio nulo, procès entâché d'un vice de procédure, wegen Verfahrensfehlern in der Prozessführung*).

6.   Genres in the Translation of Legal English (II)

In the previous chapter we examined some of the major legal genres found in the domains of statute law, public law and judicial decisions. In these text types, and especially in statutes, the macrostructure is extremely predictable and the technical content is at its densest, just as one would have expected. Texts of these types thus place very considerable constraints on translators. The translator is generally forced to work within the narrow confines of legislative and quasi-legislative tradition, drawing the appropriate vocabulary and sentence structure from target-language texts displaying equivalent conventions (codified statutes, judgements, densely worded pleadings, and so forth).

However, there are two further classes of genres found in legal text typology which, by comparison, are more flexible and more open in their subject-matter, though they still possess distinctive macrostructural features that make them instantly identifiable as legal genres. These are, respectively, texts setting out legal arrangements made by private individuals in their voluntary dealings with one another, and academic writings on the law (textbooks, studies of particular fields of law, professional articles, and suchlike).

The leading type within private law genres is the contract, but the category includes other major types such as wills and deeds. Here flexibility is seen in content rather than in form. In modern democratic societies, people are free to make any kind of arrangement, agreement or bargain they like and to dispose of their property as they see fit, so long as they remain broadly within the law. The subject-matter of a contract may therefore be virtually any object or service that exists at present or is conceivable, makeable, doable or performable in the future. This, in its turn, means that variation in the language in which the contract can be expressed is potentially almost infinite. Moreover, the principle of freedom of contract (*la libertad contractual, la liberté contractuelle, Vertragsfreiheit*) means that the parties are not confined to any particular form of words. Indeed, in the event of dispute between the parties as to the meaning to be attached to particular terms, the usual principles of construction apply (see chapter 2 above). The courts will interpret all the words used in the contract, however technical they may appear, in their ordinary or habitual sense, in the sense they are commonly deemed to have in the place where the contract was made, or in traditional commercial practice.

However, for convenience, contracts do in fact tend to conform to standard formats, or even to be written on standard forms. By far the majority of commercial agreements the translator is likely to have to deal with will fall into these conventional categories. It is thus possible to establish a working macrostructure that covers most cases, as we shall shortly see.

By contrast, academic work on the law belongs to one of the classic written genres. It is wide-ranging in subject-matter though relatively constrained in form, and is likely to be densely technical in its references to the entire gamut of public and private law subgenres we have already noticed and described. Obviously the macrostructure in this case is determined not so much by legal constraints and traditions as by the conventions of the genre to which such texts truly belong, which is the essay in one or other of its forms. A specimen arrangement of the material as found in this genre is provided below.

Finally, for the sake of completeness, we have provided a brief overview of some fictional representations of the oral legal genres studied in this chapter. Our purpose in doing so is simply to stress that the translation of legal texts is conditioned by contextual as well as by textual factors and that translations will therefore vary in accordance with the requirements of the particular target audience.

1.   Contracts

In today's world contracts are the legal documents ordinary people are likely to be most familiar with. When we buy a car or a video player, take a lease on a property, arrange for a bank loan or a mortgage, change jobs, pay for meal at a restaurant, arrange for delivery of groceries from the supermarket and, in general, enter into any of hundreds of everyday agreements for the sale or purchase of goods or the exchange of services, we are making contracts. It is important to remember that a contract does not have to be formally written down and signed by the parties to it (*partes contratantes, les parties contractantes, Vertragsparteien*) in order to be valid and binding (*vinculante, bindend*). Oral contracts are good in law (*legalmente válidos, légalement valides, qui engage, qui lie, rechtlich begründet*), though there may be difficulty in proving them if there are no witnesses.

Given this freedom of form, it is as well to be clear on the basic elements that distinguish contracts from other forms of agreement and which must be present for a contract to be recognized as such and therefore enforceable. In the first place, there must be an **agreement** (*acuerdo, accord, Parteivereinbarung*) between the two parties, who may be individuals or groups, a natural or juristic person (*persona física o jurídica, personne physique ou juridique, natürliche oder juristische Person*). This agreement is often described as a 'meeting of minds' or *consensus ad idem*. Second, there must be **valuable consideration** (*prestación, contraprestación, contrepartie à titre onéreux, entgeltliche Gegenleistung*) given and received by each party. In other words, each party promises to give something in exchange for the other party's promise to give something else in return. Habitually this consideration takes the form of money, goods or services, but it may be practically anything so long as it has some identifiable value. Thus, in this mutual arrangement of offer and acceptance, each of the two parties may be viewed, vis-à-vis the other party, as both 'offeror' or 'promisor' (*oferente, prometiente, offrant, promettant, Anbietender oder Versprechens-geber*) and 'promisee' (*compromisario, receptor de una oferta o promesa, récipiendaire d'une promesse, Versprechensempfänger*). Third, the parties must intend their promises to be acted on and to be legally binding. Trivial or vague undertakings are not construable as contracts, nor are 'promises' to undertake the impossible. Fourth, the subject-matter of the contract must not be illegal or 'tainted with illegality'; so-called 'contract killings' are not contracts in law. Fifth, the contract must be freely entered into by both parties and both should be of equal bargaining power (*igualdad de capacidad negociadora, equalité de pouvoir de négociations, gleiche Verhandlungsstärke*). Any agreement induced by fraud, undue influence or oppressive means may be set aside, as may a 'catching [or unconscionable] bargain' (an agreement that is clearly unfair or one-sided).

In view of what we have said about the freedom of the parties and the diversity of possible contracts, it should be clear that the macrostructure described here is only one among many of the formats in which such agreements can be drawn up. Readers are encouraged to compare the structure presented here (based on Borja 1998:402-49) with that of any of the 'standard-form' contracts that are now in daily use, e.g. hire-purchase contracts.

(a) Commencement or premises

In the prefatory section there is commonly some descriptive phrase identifying the type of undertaking. Thus a contract of sale (*de compraventa, contrat de vente, Kaufvertrag*) will begin 'This Sale and Purchase agreement'; a licensing agreement or assignment (*cesión de propiedad, accord de licence, Lizenzverein-barung*) will begin 'This Assignment'; a securities contract (*contrato para la emisión de valores, contrat de valeurs, Sicherungsvereinbarung*) will start with the words 'This Underwriting', etc. It is customary to identify the parties to the contract in this section, using a formula like 'by and between X and Y', together with the date in full legal style, thus:

> This SALE AND PURCHASE AGREEMENT is made this fourteenth day of March 2000, by and between X and Y...'

(b) Recitals or preamble

In very formal contracts, such as those binding the Member States of the European Union to one another, the High Contracting Parties normally wish to set out the historical, social or economic reasons that have led them to take this step. In English, these factual matters are traditionally introduced by a set of clauses beginning 'Whereas' (*considerando, considérant, in Anbetracht*), which gives them something of the air of statute law. Commercial contracts sometimes follow this tradition in supplying details of the parties' identities, interests and relations to one another, and the overall object of the contract, as in this example:

> Whereas (One) Lotsastock Inc. (hereinafter referred to as 'the Company'), domiciled in Canada, is a commercial stock corporation of mixed economy organised and existing under the laws of Canada and having its registered office at 12, Easy Street, Vancouver, British Colombia, Canada.
>
> (Two) Seller is the beneficial owner of 3,786,583 series B shares each of a nominal value of 1.5 Canadian dollars, representing forty-six and seven hundred and seventy-five thousandths percent (46.775 %) of the issued and outstanding share capital of the Company (hereinafter called 'the Shareholding').
>
> (Three) Seller desires to sell and Purchaser desires to purchase the Shareholding and those shares to which Seller would otherwise become entitled on and subject to the terms and conditions contained in this Agreement...

(c) The operative provisions

This section begins with a clause declaring the existence of an agreement between the parties and giving force to it by the use of a performative verb (e.g. 'agree', 'promise', 'undertake', 'commit oneself to') governing the following clauses:

> NOW IT IS HEREBY AGREED by and between the parties as follows....

The remainder of the section is devoted to a detailed specification of the overall bargain and the parties' commitments (*compromisos, obligations, Verpflichtungen*), divided for convenience into clauses (*cláusulas, dispositions, Klauseln*), covenants (*pactos, convenios, clauses, Vereinbarungen*) or articles (*estipulaciones, articles,* perhaps *Vertragsbestimmungen*). Collectively these specific clauses are known as 'terms and conditions'. However, translators should be careful not to assume that the two words are synonymous. In technical use, a 'term' is any provision of the contract, so that the really important distinction is not between 'term' and 'condition', but between a fundamental or essential provision ('condition') and a more secondary provision ('warranty').

In this strict sense, a distinction may be made between an 'express term' and an 'implied term'. The primary distinction is a matter of the importance accorded to the individual terms of the contract, i.e. it is a question of content, whereas the secondary distinction is a matter of form (the contract either expressly includes it or it does not, and any dispute concerning implied terms is resolved by judicial construction of the whole within the appropriate legal and commercial context). Translation of these terms will therefore depend on the overall context, and descriptive adjectives (equivalents of essential, fundamental, explicit, implicit, secondary, conventional, and so on) may well be required to ensure accuracy. An example of a warranty appears in section (f) below.

(d) Definitions

We have already seen that the macrostructure of statutes often includes sections providing definitions of key terms, and the same is true of contracts. If the parties decide that definitions are necessary in order to make their intentions absolutely clear, they are invariably contained in the operative provisions. Definition, as explained in chapter 1 above, may be provided in accordance with either of the logical categories of extension or intension. Thus, a definition by extension specifies the individual categories or subtypes comprehended in a generic term, as can be seen in the following explanation of 'expenses' and 'notice':

> 'expenses' include costs, charges and necessary outlays of every description;'notice' includes a demand, consent or waiver.

Definition by intension, on the other hand, limits the possible range of meanings or connotations in which the given term is to be understood in the context of the particular contract, as we see in this gloss on the word 'business day' (*día hábil, jour ouvrable, Werktag*):

> 'business day' means a day on which banks and foreign exchange markets are open for business in London and New York.

Sometimes the definition applies only to one particular clause or term of the contract. If this is the parties' agreement, it will be clearly stated in the defining formula, as in the following example involving careful restriction of the sense of the term '*force majeure*':

> For the purposes of this condition, 'force majeure' means fire, explosion, flood, lightning, act of God, act of terrorism, war, rebellion, riot, sabotage or official strike or similar official labour disputes, or events or circumstances outside the reasonable control of the party affected thereby.

(e) Consideration

> In consideration of Seller's undertaking to sell the shareholding, Pur-
> chaser shall pay Seller on the date hereof an amount equal to the sterling
> equivalent of twenty thousand US dollars ($20,000).

The legal rather than the everyday sense of 'consideration' is clarified here
by the use of the prepositional phrase 'in consideration of ', which implies the
mutual nature of the bargain. The sense is therefore 'in exchange for, in return
for' (*a cambio de, como contraprestación, en contrepartie de, im Tausch gegen*).

(f) Representation and Warranties

This clause (or set of clauses) sets out any matters of fact necessary to guarantee the good faith of each party, such as assurances as to the quality of the goods
sold or the services provided, the right of each party to act in the contract, and
the legal assumptions on which the contract is entered into. The term 'representation' is here to be understood in the sense of 'assurance, undertaking,
declaration, guarantee'. As we have mentioned already, the 'warranties' are regarded as secondary guarantees. This is not because they are not crucial to the
contract – a breach of warranty can have very serious consequences – but because they are not the basis of the agreement as such, which is to buy and sell
goods, to exchange services for payment, to provide transport at a stated price,
etc. Here is an example:

> Seller represents and warrants to Buyer that Seller is legally consti-
> tuted under the laws of England with adequate power to enter into this
> agreement....

(g) Applicable law

It is usual, especially in commercial contracts, for the parties to state which set
of laws (*ordenamiento jurídico, ensemble de lois, Gesetzessammlung*) is to gov-
ern the agreement. This provides greater security and certainty for both parties
as regards the meaning to be attached to the specific terms. It also clarifies
which courts are competent in the event of dispute. If it is not stated on the face
of the contract, it will be implied from the circumstances in which the agreement was made (place, language, participants, standard commercial practice,
etc). A simple example follows:

> This Agreement shall be governed by, and construed in accordance with,
> the law of England.

(h) **Severability** (*divisibilidad del contrato, divisibilité du contrat, Teilbarkeit des Vertrags*)

This is an optional section in which the parties may agree that if any part of the contract is deemed inoperative or unlawful, the rest of the agreement will remain valid and binding:

> Any term, condition or provision of this Agreement which is or shall be deemed or be void, prohibited or unenforceable in any jurisdiction shall be severable herefrom [...] without in any case invalidating the remaining terms or conditions hereof....

(i) **Testimonium [testing clause]**

This is similar to the testing clause of a will that we described earlier, except that the crucial signatures are those of the contracting parties. It is worth pointing out here that, under the doctrine of privity of contract (*exclusividad contractual, effet relatif du contrat, connexité contractuelle* in Canada), only the parties to it have any enforceable claim under it. This means that no 'stranger to the contract' (*tercero, un tiers au contrat, Dritter*) can sue under it, even if he or she was an intended beneficiary. Here are two examples:

> IN WITNESS WHEREOF the said parties have hereunto set their respective hands and seals the day and year first above written.

> IN WITNESS WHEREOF the parties hereto have duly executed this agreement this 22nd day of June nineteen hundred and ninety-nine.

(j) **Signatures**

The signatories' names are printed legibly above or below their signatures, and if any of the parties are juristic persons, the legal or professional capacity in which individual signatories are acting is also appended. If a contract is signed by proxy (*por apoderado, par procuration écrite, in Vertretung*) this is indicated as follows:

> SIGNED by
>
> John Smith
>
> for and behalf of
>
> Peter Stuart
>
> under a power of attorney dated 15 October, 1998.

(k) Schedules

These are also known as 'exhibits', 'appendices' or 'annexes'. As in the case of statutes, they contain miscellaneous information of interest to the parties (e.g. shipping documents, copies of deeds or certificates relating to the subject-matter of the contract, technical specifications, manufacturers' guarantees or warranties, bank statements, powers of attorney, and other such materials).

These, then, are the usual textual features of contracts, although, as we have said, there can be almost limitless variation. Many contracts, for instance, contain 'boilerplate clauses' (standard or template clauses), dealing with such matters as 'delivery', 'expenses', 'assignment' (*cesión de derechos, cession de droits, Zession von Rechten*), 'warranty of good title and quiet possession' (*garantías de titularidad, garantie de titre valide et possession paisible, Garantie für unbestreitbares Eigentum*), 'force majeure', etc.

Valid contracts are enforceable and are discharged in one of four ways: by **performance** (*por cumplimiento, par exécution, der Form halber*), i.e. when each party does what was agreed; by **agreement** (*por mutuo acuerdo de las partes, par un commun accord, nach Vereinbarung*), i.e. when each party releases (*exonera, exonère, entbinden*) the other from performance, or some specified event takes place, e.g. in a contract of employment the agreed period elapses and the contract is not renewed; c) by **frustration** (*por imposibilidad, par inexécutabilité, Unmöglichkeit*), i.e. when something unforeseen happens to prevent the contract being carried out; or by **breach** (*por incumplimiento, par rupture de contrat, Vertragsverletzung*), i.e. when one of the parties fails to perform their side of the bargain.

If the defaulting party fails to give the innocent party satisfaction, the usual remedy is an action for damages. However, there are also equitable remedies of rescission (*rescisión, resolución, resiliation, Anfechtung*) and specific or part performance. Since it is sometimes difficult to quantify damages after a breach has occurred, the parties may agree to include a clause in the contract specifying the amount of damages payable in the event of breach. This pre-estimate of damages is known as liquidated damages (*daños líquidos, indemnité forfaitaire, im voraus der Höhe nach bestimmter Schadensersatz*). Otherwise damages are unliquidated (*ilíquidos, a criterio del tribunal, dommages et intérêts non fixés au préalable, unbestimmter Schadensersatz*).

Finally, a distinction is made between a contract that is 'void' (*nulo, nul et non avenu, ungültig*) and one that is 'voidable' (*anulable, annulable, anfechtbar*) (see chapter 7 below). A void contract is a legal nullity (*viciado de nulidad, nulo con nulidad absoluta, une nullité juridique, rechtlich ungültig*); for the law it is as if the contract had never existed and no claim can be entertained under it. This happens, for example, if one or more of the basic elements described above is missing, or if the contract is unlawful, or where there has been an 'operative mistake' (a shared unrectifiable error concerning the subject-matter of the contract). On the other hand, a voidable contract is one that can be avoided (declared void) by only one of the parties, e.g. on the grounds of fraud, misrepresentation (*declaración falsa o errónea, déclaration erronnée, Vorspiegelung falscher Tatsachen*) or mistake by the other party. But if the innocent party does not avoid the contract within a reasonable time, or chooses to affirm it, then it remains good in law and is binding in the usual way.

2. Deeds and indentures

The terms 'deed' and 'indenture' are now synonymous (rendered as *escrituras, actes de propriété, Vertragsurkunde*). However 'deed' is far more common, while 'indenture' tends to be used, if at all, to refer to a deed creating or transferring an estate in land (*escritura de traslado de dominio, un titre créant ou trasférant une propriété en droit foncier, Grundstücksübertragungsvertrag*). In the latter sense the term 'deed of conveyance' ('convey' meaning to transfer property) is also used.

As documents, the 'deed poll' and the 'indenture' were formerly distinguished from one another by their physical appearance. The word 'poll' is an old adjective derived from a verb meaning 'cut short, shear, clip' and it described the smooth edge of the parchment, which was cut even . The name 'indenture', on the other hand, comes from the indented or serrated edge of the paper it was written on. There was originally a practical reason for this. Since the deed poll was in the form of a unilateral declaration, no copy was required and the original manuscript had the standard plain edge. However, the indenture was a bilateral deed in the nature of a formal contract, and so the text was copied twice on the same parchment, which was then cut in two, with each party being given a copy for safe keeping. To ensure that there could be no question about the genuineness of the deed if the two copies came to be collated, the original manuscript was not cut evenly but with an indented or wavy edge. Obviously only the two original halves would exactly match. The names then stuck for many centuries after the primitive checking system had been abandoned, and the unilateral deed poll and the bilateral indenture continued to be regarded as different types of documents. However, since the 1920s this rather artificial distinction has been dropped. All documents of this type are now usually known as 'deeds', even though in common speech the contract binding apprentices to their employer is still called an 'indenture' and both lawyers and non-lawyers speak of people legally 'changing their names by deed poll'.

In form and in function, deeds are very similar to contracts. Since we have already examined contracts in detail, we shall confine our remarks here to a few essentials. As regards the macrostructure, the main difference between the two genres is that deeds are not usually divided into clauses, but take the following shape:

(a)   Recitals (the preamble)
(b)   Operative part
(c)   Witnessing part (or 'testatum')
(d)   Premises (identification of the parties and declaration of the subject-matter of the deed)
(e)   Parcels (details of the property or good concerned)
(f)   Testimonium (or testing clause)
(g)   Locus sigilli (space for the seal).

The 'witnessing part' (point *c* above) should not be confused with the 'testimonium' (point *f* above). As in contracts, the latter is merely the concluding section in which signatories and witnesses swear to the truth and accuracy of the contents of the document, usually by means of a formula like 'in witness whereof' (*en fe de lo cual, en foi de quoi, zum Zeugnis dessen*) preceding the signatures. The witnessing part, on the other hand, is some solemn formula like 'Now this deed witnesseth as follows', which introduces the operative part of the deed and is performative in nature. In other words, it declares the maker's solemn promise to be bound by the deed. Appropriate translations would be along the lines of *Por esta escritura yo, el otorgante, declaro mi voluntad como sigue..., Cet acte témoigne comme suit..., Durch dieses Schriftstück erklärt der Aussteller seinen Willen, sich wie folgt zu binden... .*

Section (g), it will be noticed, specifically indicates that a seal is expected. The reason is that, unlike contracts, which are essentially agreements between two parties, deeds, as we have seen, may be the expression of the will of a single individual, and so the greatest solemnity and formality is required to ensure that there is no doubt as to the identity and the true wishes of their makers. This, in its turn, explains why deeds must necessarily be written documents and why there is a requirement in law that, once made, they must be signed, sealed, and delivered. The same applies when a deed is really a form of contract, e.g. for the sale of land or the conveyance of property, for both of which the law prescribes the formal or written contract known as a 'specialty contract' or 'contract under seal'.

Conceptually speaking, the major difference between deeds and contracts is that the latter, as we have seen, are worthless unless they involve a consensus, and non-existent unless each party gives and receives consideration, whereas deeds may be the formal, legal expression of unilateral undertakings, e.g. a deed of gift or a deed of conveyance on grounds of charity, esteem or natural affection. Secondly, a contract is a private agreement whereas the whole point of making a deed is to ensure public and universal recognition of the matters contained within it. A good example of this dual unilateral and public nature of some deeds is the 'deed poll' by which a person, for entirely private reasons, legally changes his or her name.

The public and universal effect given to a deed containing a unilateral declaration is emphasized by using the archaic opening formula 'Know all men by these presents...'. A neutral or natural translation of this would probably silently modernize (*Por la presente se hace saber que..., Qu'il soit certifié par les présents..., Hiermit wird Ihnen mitgeteilt...*), thus gliding over the old-fashioned jussive or subjunctive force of the verb (*que sepan todo..., que tous sachent...*) and eliminating the quaintness of the phrase 'these presents' (meaning the present document, the deed at hand). However, translators might bear in mind that the banns, edicts and proclamations of Spanish mayors traditionally end with the formula *Lo que se comunica para general conocimiento* ('Which is [hereby] announced that it may be generally known'). As we saw earlier in examining the macrostructure of certificates, the information content of a given genre tends to be very similar in different languages even though the distribution of the functional parts is different. In other words, a case might be made in certain circumstances for postponing this part of the deed until the end of the text.

It is in the 'recitals' and 'parcels' sections of deeds (headings 4 and 5 of our outline above) that the specific matters and personalities involved are described, and the particular function of the deed is clarified, e.g. property conveyancing (*traslado de dominio o de transmisión patrimonial, le transfert de propriété, Vermögensübertragung*) or bailment (*contrato de depósito, contrat de dépôt, Verwahurung, Aufbewahrung*). Bailment is the act by which the owner of goods, known as the 'bailor', places them temporarily at the disposal or in the care of the 'bailee', and it may be either gratuitous (*gratuito, desinteresado, gratuit, unentgeltlich*) or for reward (*por precio o remuneración, pour rémuneration, Vergütung*). The wording of the deed will clarify the precise purpose of the bailment of the goods (e.g. for storage, repair, alteration or carriage, on loan, as security for a debt owed by bailor to bailee, to be used by the bailee for hire, etc.) and also whether it is gratuitous or otherwise. It will also specify that during the time the goods are under the bailees' care and control (*custodia, contrôle, Gewahrsam*) they undertake to look after them as if they were their own and are liable for any loss or damage. Finally, the bailment entitles the bailees to act in all respects as the temporary owner sof the goods and, where necessary, to bring proceedings against any third party who unlawfully damages the goods while in their possession. The bailee is therefore in the position of a specially privileged agent of the bailor.

Finally, translators should be aware that, despite the similarity of the wording found in deeds and contracts, the legal implications are often very different. A case in point are the agreements contained in deeds which, though similar to the promises made in contracts, are given the special name of 'covenants' (*pactos promisorios, cargas, clauses,*perhaps *Vertragsabreden*). Unlike contractual undertakings, they are sometimes binding on third parties. For example, a covenant in a sale or lease of land specifying that the land is never to be used for industrial purposes may be registered as a land charge (*gravamen, servidumbre,* perhaps *servitude foncière, Grundschuld*). If so, it is binding on any later assignees to whom the leasehold is transferred. A few examples of covenants follow. We have deliberately chosen an old-style indenture to give the reader the full flavour of a solemn deed (here a contract under seal), but translators will readily appreciate that it is the format of the document and not the particular form of words that really distinguishes this genre from others:

> X DOTH HEREBY ASSIGN onto Y, his executors, administrators and assigns ALL AND SINGULAR the several chattels and things specifically described in the schedule hereto annexed by way of Security for the payment of the sum of £10,000 and interest thereon...

> And the said X doth further agree with the said Y that during the continuance of this security:

> 1. He will at all times pay the rent, rates and taxes of the property or premises wherein the said chattels and things shall be...
> 2. He will at all times keep the said chattels and things insured against loss or damage by fire...
> 3. He will not at any time remove the said chattels and things or any of them from the premises where they now are or to which (with the consent of the said Y) they may hereafter be removed without consent in writing of the said Y....

3.   Insurance policies

Like the deed or indenture, the insurance policy may be regarded as a special form of contract. There are two parties to it, the insurer (*asegurador, assureur, Versicherungsgeber*) and the insured (*asegurado, l'assuré, Versicherungsnehmer*). The agreement involves the giving and receiving of consideration by each party, viz. a premium (*prima, prime, Prämie*) paid by the insured and the insurer's guarantee to cover the insured property against certain risks.

The risks normally covered are death, personal injury, loss or damage to property caused by illness, accident, equipment malfunction or natural disasters. But it is also possible to insure against the loss of legal rights and against legal liability (*responsabilidad civil, responsabilité civile, gesetzliche Haftpflicht*). The descriptive name of the policy generally makes the type of risk clear, as when we talk about 'accident insurance' (*seguro contra accidentes, assurance accident, Unfallversicherung*), a 'fire policy' (*póliza de seguros contra incendios, police type incendie, Feuerversicherungspolice*)', a 'life assurance[1] policy' (*póliza de seguro de vida, police d'assurance sur la vie, Lebensversicherungspolice*) or a 'liability policy' (*póliza de seguros de responsabilidad civil, police d'assurance de responsabilité civile, Haftpflichtpolice*). However, a policy can be mixed and so include a number of different risks, connected or otherwise. For example, in marine insurance it is standard practice to take out a policy covering the ship itself, the cargo and the shipowners' legal liability to third parties for injury or damage. Insurers also provide different types of policy for protection against the same kind of risk, e.g. motor vehicle insurance may be fully comprehensive (*a todo riesgo, tous risques, Vollkaskoversicherung*) or may cover only the legal minimum (*seguro obligatorio, minimum juridique, Haftpflichtversicherung*) of third party, fire and theft (*contra terceros, assurance au tiers, Teilkaskoversicherung*). Moreover, with fully comprehensive insurance the insured has the choice of paying the full premium in return for cover against any type of damage, or of taking out a slightly cheaper policy which entails an excess (*franquicia, excès,* perhaps *Selbstbeteiligung*). In the latter case, in the event of an accident the insured pays up to an agreed amount out of his own pocket and the company pays any amount in excess of that sum. Finally, companies usually run a bonus system under which the insured is entitled to a 'no-claims bonus' (a bonus or reduced premium if they have not presented any claims).

Insurance policies belong to the group of contracts described in law as being *uberrimae fidei*, i.e. based on the utmost good faith. This means that both parties undertake to be scrupulously frank and honest in disclosing any facts that are, or may become, relevant to the agreement. If, for instance, an insured who has taken out a health insurance or life assurance policy conceals or misrepresents information about their medical history, the policy is voidable.

The macrostructure of insurance policies is, once again, essentially the same as that of any other type of contract, and readers are referred to section 7 above for the main outline. Here, we shall be examining the linguistic features of two risks traditionally covered in marine insurance policies: damage to the hull and to the cargo. As a result of the long-established hegemony of Lloyd's of London in the marine insurance and underwriting market, it is sometimes thought that the rules adopted internationally for this type of policy are basically the English or British ones. In fact the laws governing marine transport are not the domestic laws of any one nation. They are a nineteenth-century compromise, reached after negotiation at York and Antwerp. These York-Antwerp rules have

---

[1] Though the word 'insurance' is usual in common speech, there is a technical distinction between it and 'assurance'. Where the event insured against may never happen, the proper term is 'insurance'; but where payment is guaranteed under the policy either after a fixed period or because the event is inevitable (e.g. death), the term 'assurance' is preferred.

since enjoyed wide international currency and have long been the standard in international trade. Translation therefore tends to conform to the model described below under the heads 'risks covered' and 'exclusions':

(a) Risks covered

Under this head the translator can expect to find three main clauses: the 'General Average Clause' (*cláusula de avería general, clause d'avarie commune, Havarie-grosse Klausel*), the 'Risks Clause' (*cláusula de riesgos, clause de risque, Risikoklausel*) and the 'Both-to-Blame Collision Clause' (*cláusula de abordaje culpable bilateral, clause de responsabilité partagée en cas d'abordage, Klausel über Schiffskollisionen bei beiderseitigem Verschulden*). The first point to be made here is that the word 'average' does not have its usual sense of 'arithmetical mean', but rather means damage or loss to ship or cargo due to an accident or event at sea. Hence the proportional contribution made by each of the owners to cover the loss. (As it turns out, the everyday meaning of 'average' derives from this secondary sense of 'proportional contribution', and not the other way round as might have been thought.)

The General Average Clause includes all losses and expenses reasonably incurred by the master and crew of the ship in trying to avoid the loss of the ship itself, such as cargo jettisoned in dangerous weather conditions or after the ship has suffered damage. These charges are determined and adjusted in accordance with the contract of affreightment (*fletamento, contrat d'affrètement, Befrachtung*) and/or the governing law and practice, i.e. usually the York-Antwerp rules, as the following example illustrates:

> General average to be settled [paid] according to York-Antwerp Rules, 1974. Proprietors of cargo to pay the cargo's share in the general expenses even if same have been necessitated through neglect or default [failure to perform a duty] of the Owner's servants [employees].

Among the contingencies covered in the risks clause it is usual to include losses reasonably attributable to fire or explosion, but also to such characteristic marine mishaps as the vessel being stranded, grounded, sunk or capsized and the enforced discharge of cargo at a port of refuge/distress. If the clause refers to loss of or damage to the subject-matter insured caused by general average sacrifice (*sacrificio por avería general, sacrifice d'avarie commune, Aufopferung der grossen Havarie*), this should be taken as referring to jettison (*echazón, jet à la mer, Überbordwerfen von Gütern*), as we said earlier. This must be one of the few situations in which the law regards deliberate destruction of the subject-matter of the contract as a rational and legitimate act, upheld and even dignified by the use of the word 'sacrifice'.

(b) Exclusions

The purpose of these clauses, also known as 'exemption clauses' (*cláusulas de excepción, clauses exonératoires, Freizeichnungsklauseln*), is to restrict or limit the liability of the insured in specified circumstances, an intention most often signalled by the use of the phrase 'free from' (*exento de, exempt de, befreit von...*) the responsibilities not covered. An example is 'free from capture and seizure', often abbreviated to 'FCS' (*exento de la responsabilidad que surja por actos de piratería, exempt de capture et saisie, Frei von Aufbringung und Beschlagnahme*). A somewhat fuller version of this same exemption is 'Free of capture and seizure, strikes, riots and civil commotions', sometimes known as a 'strikes, riots and civil commotions clause'.

Among the various exemption clauses used in marine insurance that more directly affect risks arising from the condition of the ship and its cargo or from the conduct of the insured or their agent, the captain, some of the most common are the 'general exclusion clause' (*cláusula de exclusiones generales, clause d'éxclusion générale, Generalausschlußklausel*), the 'unseaworthiness and un-fitness clause' (*cláusula de exclusión por innavegabilidad o inaptitud del buque para los fines propuestos, clause relative à la non-conformité aux normes de navigabilité, Seeuntüchtigkeits und Untauglichkeitsklausel*) and clauses excluding loss, damage or expense 'attributable to wilful misconduct of the insured' (*imputables al quebrantamiento intencionado de los reglamentos por parte del asegurado, attribuable à la mauvaise conduite de l'assuré, zurechenbar vorsätzliche Pflichtverletzung des Versicherungsnehmers*).

4. Last will and testament

A will is an instrument (or document) by which a person makes a disposition of their real and personal property, to take effect after their death, and appoints executors (*albaceas testamentarios, exécuteurs testamentaires, berufener Testamentsvollstrecker*) to administer their estate (*patrimonio, caudal hereditario, patrimoine, Nachlaß*) in their name. The testator (*testador, testateur, Erblasser*) may alter the will during their lifetime by amending or destroying it or by adding codicils (*nuevas disposiciones, avenant, Testamentsnachtrag*). In theory, the term 'testament' refers only to personal property and not to land, but in contemporary usage the two words 'will' and 'testament' are regarded as synonyms. In any case, the latter is now never used alone and it is common practice for lawyers and non-lawyers alike to speak simply of a 'will'. Those who inherit the property of the deceased are termed 'beneficiaries' (*beneficiarios, herederos, les bénéficiaires, Begünstigte*), though in common speech the word 'heirs' is still often used. Minor beneficiaries who receive legacies (*legados, mandas, legs, Vermächtnisse*), or gifts of personal property under a will, are known as 'legatees' (*legatarios, légateurs, Vermächtnisnehmer*). A person who dies without having made a will is said to have died 'intestate' (*intestado, sans testament, ohne Testament*) and there are separate legal rules for dealing with intestacy.

Probate (*derecho testamentario, validation de testaments, formelle Testamentsbestätigung durch das Gericht*) is the branch of law that deals with matters relating to wills, such as succession (*sucesión, succession, Erbfolge*), inheritance (*las herencias, héritage, Erbschaft*) and administration (*ejecución, administración, administration, Verwaltung*) of the deceased's estate, or, where a will is disputed, any probate action brought by interested parties. The aim of probate is twofold: (a) to ensure compliance with the testator's wishes for the distribution of his estate; and (b) to secure (guarantee) the rights of the beneficiaries and successors of the deceased.

In order to give effect to the testator's wishes, the executors (*albaceas, exécuteurs testamentaires, Testamentsvollstrecker*) must apply to the Family Division of the High Court for a grant of probate (*certificado de autenticidad del testamento, concession de validation de testament, Testamentsvollstreckerzeugnis*). Along with the application they should enclose a number of documents, including a copy of the will, an affidavit (*declaración jurada, déclaration écrite sous serment, eidesstattliche Versicherung*) in which they undertake to administer the estate in accordance with the deceased's wishes and an Inland Revenue account. Where the will is undisputed, probate is granted in 'common form' (*certificado ordinario, suivant un modèle-type, allgemeine Form*), but in contentious probate cases the resulting certificate is issued in what is called 'solemn form'. In both cases, the certificate declares the validity of the will that has been proved and authorizes the executors to proceed with the administration of the estate.

Contentious probate proceedings (*los juicios de testamentaría, les procédures de succession litigieuse, Gerichtsverfahren*) are heard in the County Court or in the Chancery Division of the High Court, depending on the value of the estate, though such cases are the exception rather than the rule, since most wills are undisputed and grants of probate are usually a mere formality. In cases of intestacy, an administrator (*ejecutor, albacea judicial, administrateur, Verwalter*) is appointed by the court at the request of an interested party. This is done by granting a 'letter of administration' authorizing the person named to oversee the distribution of the estate.

There is no prescribed form for wills, which may take any form compatible with common sense, clarity and the unambiguous expression of the testator's wishes. However, for convenience most people have their wills drawn up by a solicitor, who may very well include some of the traditional clauses outlined below. The highly formal and somewhat archaic language used in some of the following examples can, of course, be avoided without loss of legal force, but the translator should be prepared to meet it, especially in wills drafted by fussy or old-fashioned family solicitors:

(a) Debt clause

FIRST: I direct that the Executor (Executrix) hereinafter named pursuant to this Last Will and Testament, pay (as soon after my death as practical) all of my just debts and obligations, including funeral expenses and the expenses incident to my last illness, but excepting those long-term debts secured by real or personal property which may be assumed by the receipt heir(s).

(b) Distribution clause

SECOND: All of the rest, residue and remainder of my Estate, both real and personal, of whatsoever kind or character, and wherever situated, I give, devise and bequeath unto...

Here the stylistic device of accumulation of synonyms or near synonyms ('rest, residue and remainder', 'kind or character', 'give, devise or bequeath') illustrates the fussiness we referred to earlier. The translator may decide to omit some of the repetition in the TL version as being unnecessary and imprecise, or simply unnatural. However, it is worth stressing that 'residue' and 'remainder' can, on strict construction, be regarded as distinct concepts: the former can mean the part of an estate left over once debts, death duties, specific legacies and sundry charges have been subtracted; and the latter in old-fashioned contexts may be taken to mean the interest (*titularidad, titularité, Anrecht*) in real property on the death of the holder of a life interest (*dominio vitalicio o usufructuario, propriété viagère et usufruit, lebenslänglicher Nießbrauch*). On the other hand the complete phrase may be an imprecise formula, i.e. a longwinded way of saying 'everything else'.

As usual, the golden rule for translating is to proceed with caution and never to lose sight of the context. Similarly, the terms 'devise' (*dejar en herencia, legar, léguer, vermachen*) and 'bequeath' (*legar, mandar, léguer, vermachen*) refer to different things, respectively real and personal property. Since it may be difficult to find equivalent terms in other languages, translators should consider the possibility of transferring the distinction from the verbs to the nouns that are their objects. After all, a list of distinct objects belonging to different categories is less likely to cause awkwardness or an impression of semantic clutter than a redundant series of practically interchangeable verbs. In our example, the distinction is already clear enough from the use of the phrase 'all my property, both *real* and *personal*', but it can do little harm to the sense, and may help convey the tone and register of the original, if the translation reads something like this:

> *Instituyo como heredero y legatario de todos mis demás bienes y pose-*
> *siones, tanto muebles como inmuebles, de cualquier naturaleza, clase o*
> *condición, y dondequiera que se encuentren situados, a...*
> [I name as heir and legatee of all my further goods and possessions, both
> movable and immovable, of whatever kind, class or condition, and
> wheresoever they may be, ...]

This rather heavy-handed version is further justified by the distinctly old-fashioned flavour of the original, with its pedantic redundancies and its insistence on pompous and archaic phrasing ('whatsoever', 'wherever situated', 'unto' and so on).

(c) Common disaster clause

Properly drafted wills made by married couples always make arrangements for every possible contingency, including the possibility that both could die simultaneously, e.g. as the result of an accident. Such provisions are contained in the 'common disaster clause', the purpose of which is to indicate the testator's wishes in the event that he or she is not survived by the named beneficiary. This is done by creating a legal fiction whereby the beneficiary is deemed (*se presume a efectos legales, est supposé être, angenommen, daß*) to have predeceased or survived the testator, as in the following example:

> THIRD: If my spouse, or any other person named in this Last Will and
> Testament, shall die as a result of a common disaster with me, then my
> spouse or such other person(s) shall be deemed to have survived me [**or**
> predeceased me].

It will be noticed in this and other similar clauses that for the main verbs the 'shall' form is used, much as in the text of a statute, to convey a forceful idea of finality and command. However, in the example quoted, the 'shall' form is also used in the conditional clause ('if my spouse....*shall die*') to somewhat different effect, viz. to stress the remoteness or contingency of the possibility described. In a Spanish translation, an equivalent effect would be achieved by use of the future subjunctive, now largely confined to legal hypothesis (*si conmuriere*) and therefore eminently suitable here.

(d) Survivorship clause

The aim of this clause is to arrange for distribution of the estate, or a share in it, in the event that a beneficiary named in a will has predeceased the testator. However the clause is phrased, the term 'survivors' is taken to mean the heirs of the beneficiary who were still alive at the time of distribution. This can be somewhat complicated, as we see in the following example:

> FOURTH. If any heir named in this Last Will and Testament (other than my spouse) shall not survive me, then that share of my estate which would be distributed to such heir(s) had he (she) (they) survived me, shall be distributed *per stirpes* [**or** to the survivors of them].

Translators are not, of course, concerned with the legal difficulties such disposal may give rise to in particular circumstances, but they do need to be aware of the linguistic implications of the clause. The *per stirpes* (by lineage) arrangement in our example involves distribution of that part of the estate equally among surviving representatives of each 'branch' or 'stock' of the family; the alternative is distribution among the deceased beneficiary's own 'survivors' in any appropriate sense.

(e) Executor appointment clause

The title of this clause is self-explanatory. Optionally, the testator may make alternative arrangements, as in this example:

> FIFTH: I hereby nominate, constitute and appoint...as the Executor (Executrix) of my Estate; provided, however, that in the event she (he) is unable or unwilling to so serve in such capacity, then I nominate, constitute and appoint....

(f) Guardians appointment clause

Where used, this clause is similar to the previous one in both purpose and wording, as can be seen in the following example:

> SIXTH: I hereby nominate, constitute and appoint...as the guardian of any minor children of mine: provided, however, that in the event she (he) is unable or unwilling to so serve in that capacity, then I nominate, constitute and appoint....

(g) Saving clause

This is an attempt by the testator to guard against the possibility of the whole will's being declared invalid in a probate action because of some technical illegality in one of its parts. The court could, of course, reach this decision of its own motion (*motu proprio*) but is more likely to do so if the clause is included, since the presumption is that the testator's clearly expressed intentions are to be respected so far as they are not incompatible with law. Here is an example of a saving clause:

> SEVENTH: In the event any separate provision of this Last Will and
> Testament is held to be invalid by a Court of competent jurisdiction,
> then such finding shall not invalidate this entire Last Will and Testament
> but only the subject provision.

(h) Signature

(i) Attestation clause, or testing clause or testimonium

This type of clause is not found only in wills, but is regularly used in certificates, affidavits, deeds, notarized statements and other documents whose
probative value depends on their being read and signed by witnesses. A very
common formula is 'In witness whereof...' (*en fe de lo cual... en foi de quoi,
zum Zeugnis dessen*). However, the function of the clause is fulfilled by any
form of words conveying the idea that the will has been duly executed in the
presence of witnesses who, in the presence of the testator and of one another,
saw, heard and understood the making of the will and can swear to the accuracy
of its contents:

> The foregoing instrument consisting of two pages was signed and de-
> clared by the testator to be his last will in the presence of us, who, at his
> request, and in his presence and the presence of one another, have sub-
> scribed our names as witnesses.

5. The power of attorney

The document known as a 'power of attorney' entitles the holder or attorney (*el
apoderado, mandataire, Bevollmächtigte*) to act on behalf of (*en nombre de,
pour la compte de, im Namen von*) the donor (*poderdante, mandate, mandant,
Schenkungsgeber*), defend the principal's legal rights and interests and represent them in court where necessary. It is therefore a particular type of contractual
agreement by which a principal empowers an agent to act for them. Just as there
are contracts that are required by law to be drafted in the form of deeds, a power
to execute a deed must be given by a deed. To ensure that the attorney[2] does not
cheat the donor or go beyond their wishes, the power specifies the acts, or kind
of acts, the attorney may perform. It is normally itself a document under seal
(*documento protocolizado, document formel, unter Siegel*) acknowledged

---

[2] Especially in the US the 'attorney-in-fact' is usually distinguished from the 'attorney-in-
law' or 'attorney-of-record'. The former may be any trusted representative, but the latter has
to be a lawyer.

(*otorgado, constaté devant, förmlich anerkennt*) in the presence of a solicitor or notary public. It can be revoked at any time and is revoked automatically on the death of the donor. The macrostructure, which is very simple, is as follows:

(a) Commencement and performative act

In the pragmatic way common to most legal documents, the power habitually refers to itself as such in the opening phrase ('By this power of attorney...') and goes on to identify the donor and the attorney, yoked together by the performative verb ('appoint'), which both describes and activates the legal relationship:

> BY THIS POWER OF ATTORNEY, John Smith, hereinafter called the Donor, does appoint James Wright as his general attorney, to whom he gives all the necessary powers and more particularly...

The use of 'does' in the example here should not necessarily be taken as an emphatic. Old-style legal texts often use the archaic form 'doth' in declarative sentences, a fossilized form without emphatic intent but with a stylistic impressiveness that our example perhaps rather lamely attempts to ape with its half-way-house approach. Translators in such cases are well advised to modernize silently (*nombra, nomme, benennt*), since it could make no conceivable difference to the meaning if the text read 'appoints' or 'has appointed'.

(b) The operative part

In this section the attorney's rights and duties are explicitly laid out, often under a series of heads. It is very important for this part of the document to be carefully worded and for the powers conferred on the agent to be sufficient for the purposes for which it is issued. This is always thoroughly checked when attorneys display their accreditation, so translators too must ensure that they provide a scrupulously accurate version of the original. Here are a few examples of a power of attorney granted to an administrator:

(a) To manage and administer
1. To receive any monies, whether of the nature of income or capital, give receipt therefor and release (*cancelar, céder, auflösen*) against payment (*mediante el pago correspondiente, contre paiement, gegen Zahlung*) any sureties (*garantías, cautions, Wertpapiere*) whatsoever.
2. To acquire, subscribe for and sell any shares, debentures and any securities (*títulos, valeurs, Sicherheiten*) quoted on a stock exchange.
3. To attend any meetings of companies, associations or organizations, carry out any duties thereat, vote and sign any minutes.

(b) Investment and disposition
1. To acquire, sell and exchange any immovable property subject to

such terms and conditions as the Attorney shall deem fit.
2. To grant and modify any easements (*servidumbres, servitudes, Grunddienstbarkeiten*) and abandon the same.

(c) To lend and to borrow
1. To borrow any monies on such terms and conditions as the Attorney shall deem fit and as security for such loans to grant any mortgages (*constituir hipotecas, hypothèques, Hypotheken bestellen*) and generally any securities whatsoever.
2. To lend up to the principal sum of $100,000, subject to such conditions as the Attorney shall deem fit.

(d) Acting in legal proceedings
1. To represent the Donor in legal proceedings both as plaintiff and defendant, appoint any counsel and other legal representatives, take or require any legal proceedings or any interlocutory measures or measures for execution.
2. To compromise and compound. To appoint any arbitrator.

(e) Substitution. Sundry powers
1. For the above purpose, execute and sign any deeds and minutes, give an address for service substitute (*sustitutoria, suppléant service, Ersatzzustellung*), waive (*renunciar a, renoncer à, verzichten auf*) any registrations including those arising by operation of law, to make all declarations of civil status and generally do whatever may be necessary.
2. On the terms that no defect or inaccuracy in the powers above set out (which are set out by way of example and not by way of limitation) shall invalidate the acts of the attorney and that he shall have the power to appoint a substitute.

(f) Testimonium clause
This takes the usual form and is as in contracts, wills and deeds:

IN WITNESS whereof (*en testimonio de lo cual, en foi de quoi, zum Zeugnis dessen*) I have hereunto set my hand this 14th day of May nineteen hundred and ninety-nine.

6. The professional article

So far, all the legal genres we have examined in this and the previous chapter have been formal and technical documents or texts intended to stand on the record or to create, promote, consolidate or cancel legal relations and consequences. But there is another written genre which, though it has no status as a legal document, is extremely influential in legal circles and is a kind of text that translators are frequently asked to deal with. This is the professional article on some specialist area of law, written by a jurist, an academic or a practising lawyer and published in one of the many learned journals brought out by universities or legal bodies and associations.

Compared to the highly technical texts we have been examining, it is a mixed genre in that it is written in a style that mingles the formulaic language of the law with the more personal, though still formal, discourse of argument, analysis and illustration and the rhetoric of persuasion. The purpose of an article, however scientifically and cogently written, is not to lay down the law but to comment on it or to deliver a scholarly opinion on some aspect of it. Clearly, therefore, the translator is called upon to combine the skills required by the essay with the accuracy demanded by the technical text. This is work that requires translators to read very carefully before putting pen to paper, or finger to key, since they need to be alert to nuances and niceties of tone as well as to matters of precise legal diction and vocabulary.

Before we describe the macrostructure of scholarly articles on legal topics, we should say a few words about the different types, or subtypes, commonly found. The following may be distinguished:

(a)   Articles that discuss the historical origins, scope, implications or limitations of specific statutes or judgements;
(b)   Articles on comparative jurisprudence, suggesting improvements or innovations in legal method;
(c)   Articles on the social benefits or otherwise of particular laws or decisions.

It seems obvious, for conceptual reasons, that types (a) and (b) will involve more constant and exhaustive analysis of both substantive and adjective law than type (c), which is likely to be more discursive in approach. Since the whole purpose of this section of our analysis of legal genres is to stress contrasts, we shall base our discussion on an article of type (c) entitled 'The Evolving Controversy over Insider Trading' (Bagby 1986), which is typical of texts of its kind in displaying the following overall structure:

(a)   Brief introductory remarks;
(b)   A statement of the topic dealt with and/or the writer's aims and a brief synopsis of the problem examined;
(d)   The body of the article, i.e. an extensive discussion and analysis of the ways in which legislators and judges have approached the problem;
(e)   Conclusions and Suggestions for improvement.

(a) Brief introductory remarks

The first paragraph immediately addresses the dilemma faced, under the rules restricting insider trading (trading in the stock market by someone who has privileged information), by the directors of a company with access to confidential information, and identifies the relevant rule ('disclose or abstain') that forces them either to make the information public or to stay out of the market. The paragraph also provides a definition of, or gloss on, the underlying concept of 'insider trading' itself:

> The restriction of insider trading is widely accepted as a principal enforcement goal under various provisions of the federal securities laws. These provisions deny certain trading opportunities to persons with knowledge of material, non-public, confidential information about an issuer, its business prospects, or external events that may affect the market for the issuer's securities. This trading restriction is often termed the 'disclose or abstain' rule, since the 'insider' usually has a choice either to trade after disclosing the confidential information or to refrain from trading altogether until the information becomes public.

The main purpose of the second paragraph is to provide a historical context in which recent legal approaches to the problem by professional bodies, parliament and the courts can be understood and assessed. Reference is thus made to the market watchdog (*organismo supervisor, organe de surveillance du marché, Marktwächter*) and its role in providing safeguards (*salvaguardias, normas de vigilancia y control, protections, Sicherungsmaßnahmen*):

> The insider trading restriction originated in state common law. The first congressional restriction of insider trading was imposed by section 16(b) of the Securities Exchange Act of 1934 (1934 Act) [...]. However, a considerable insider trading jurisprudence has also developed around the separate anti-fraud provisions in section 10(b) of the 1934 Act and Rule 10b-5 of the Securities and Exchange Commission (SEC) [...]. The SEC has reinforced the insider trading restrictions with promulgation of Rule 14e-3 of the SEC, an independent provision prohibiting insider trading in connection with tender offers. Congress has further reinforced these trading restrictions by providing the SEC with the power to seek a treble penalty under the Insider Trading Sanctions Act of 1984 (ITSA), etc.

(b) Statement of aims and synopsis of problem discussed

In our example, the third paragraph very efficiently sets out the writer's aims in the article and indicates the structure of the piece, the issues dealt with and the order in which the elements are presented:

> This article <u>traces</u> the development of the public policy debate surrounding these insider trading provisions. <u>To facilitate an evaluation</u> of the restriction, <u>it relates</u> this philosophical evolution to prevailing economic

theory. <u>After</u> a brief introduction summarizing the case law history of Rule 10b-5 and insider trading, <u>the theoretical and economic arguments are explored</u>. <u>Next</u> the article <u>analyzes</u> recent legislation and the emergence of the expansive misappropriation theory, and <u>makes some observations about </u>the ironies recreated by the disjunction between the theory and the practice of the trading provisions. <u>Finally</u>, the article <u>offers some new perspectives on insider trading analysis</u> that avoid the pitfalls of past analysis and of the contemporary approach, and <u>provides insight</u> into the costs and benefits of the trading restrictions.

(c) The body of the article (discussion of the issues)

Thereafter, the matters highlighted in the introductory framework are dealt with systematically and with a wealth of illustration in the way customary in academic writing. For obvious reasons of space we shall not reproduce the article here.

(d) Conclusions and suggestions for further discussion

The last part of the article summarizes the major points dealt with and often closes with an invitation, or an indirect challenge, to interested colleagues and fellow researchers to contribute to the debate along specific lines indicated, as we see in the following examples:

> The issues raised here will, it is hoped, contribute to a better understanding of the international dimension of modern property law, but we are a long way short of a full understanding of all the matters discussed. There is still much work to be done, as I feel sure my colleagues in the field of Private International Law will acknowledge.

> To enable us to address the problem more effectively what we really need, of course, are reliable and continuously updated statistics on the crime rate in the Member States. Unfortunately, this is a matter beyond my expertise and beyond the modest scope of this article.

7. Legal English in popular fiction

The last legal genre we shall deal with is the fictional representation of the law commonly found in popular novels of the detective story or thriller type. Though they are intended for mass consumption and usually have no pretensions beyond providing entertainment, these texts and the film scripts which are often made out of them are sometimes written by authors who either have some legal training or have researched the legal material quite carefully. As a result, translators of this kind of fiction have to strike the same delicate balance in their versions as the original author. In both the source and target languages, this may involve 'educating the audience' in the meaning or implications of certain legal technicalities, hitting the right note in dialogues between lawyers using the slang of their profession, or accommodating the formal idiom of the law to the everyday, colloquial or familiar register that usually predominates. It is therefore an exercise in linguistic tact as well as a test of the translator's overall accuracy, and these are the features, we suggest, that give this text type its status as a genre in its own right. Here are a few brief passages from recent legal thrillers:

(a) On 'probable cause'

In this passage, a firm under investigation is suspected of being a cover (*tapadera, couverture, Tarnung*) for illegal activities. The FBI agents are discussing the next move: should they apply for search warrants (*órdenes de registro, les mandats, Durchsuchungsbefehle*) or should they wait until there is more evidence?

> 'Once there is probable cause, we can go in [...] We gotta have a very tight and solid case before we go crashing in with search warrants' (Grisham 1991:236).

Clearly the hard-bitten tone of the second sentence ('gotta have', 'tight and solid case', 'go crashing in') gives the translator the clue as to the register that is required. The phrase 'search warrants' is too obvious to need glossing or explanation, but the remark about having 'a tight and solid case before crashing in' (*una justificación legal a prueba de bomba antes de entrar por las bravas, un dossier solide avant de se lancer,* perhaps *...eine vollständige, solide Ermittlungsakte, bevor wir richtig losgehen*) not only keeps the dialogue plausibly colloquial; it also explains the formal legal term 'probable cause' (*razones fundadas, motifs raisonnables et suffisants,*perhaps *handfester Grund*) to any reader who did not know it or recognize it.

(b) On objections raised by counsel

During the examination and cross-examination of witnesses, as we have seen, there are rules about what counsel may and may not do or say. If counsel for one side oversteps the mark, counsel for the other side is entitled to object (*protestar, objecter, einwenden*), briefly stating the grounds. The judge then either sustains (*acepta, admet, anerkennt*) or overrules (*deniega, passe outre, weist ab*) the objection. Our next two passages economically handle this typical courtroom situation:

1. 'Is it true that your son was convicted of selling marijuana?'
   'Objection! [...] The criminal record of the victim is inadmissible!'
   'Sustained!' (Grisham 1989:404).

2. 'And did you hear who started this alleged argument...?'
   'No.'

'So for all you know, [...] may have provoked the argument?'
'Objection. Calls for speculation.'
'Withdrawn.' (Hoag 1999:208)

Once again, the onus is on the translator to use the target-language style and
register appropriate to the situation and the expectations of the readership but
without sacrificing the accuracy of legal terminology. In passage (1), it will be
noticed that the ground of the objection is stated elliptically: what counsel means,
of course, is that the victim's criminal record is inadmissible *as evidence*, not
that it is morally deplorable. In some languages the translator may have to convey this without ellipsis to avoid confusion (e.g. '...is inadmissible as evidence').
Similarly, 'sustained', like 'withdrawn' in passage (2), will probably have to be
expanded in translation. The reason is not only to ensure naturalness of style
but also to make allowances for the pragmatics of dialogue in different languages. In the English texts, the responses respectively of the judge and counsel
for the other side are understood to apply to the *whole* of the previous message,
i.e. the objection and the reason given for raising it. However, in a language
like Spanish, utterances such as *se acepta* ('it is accepted') or *se retira* ('it is
withdrawn') would probably sound gnomic or unclear in this context. (Can the
judge be saying that it is acceptable to refer to the victim's criminal record? Is
counsel telling the court that someone is leaving the room?) Fortunately it is a
simple enough matter to clarify this (*se acepta la protesta* ['the objection is
accepted'], *Se retira la pregunta* ['the question is withdrawn']) without seriously compromising the terseness of the exchanges.

In passage (2), for similar reasons, the translator should probably restore
the deleted subject of 'calls for speculation'. The source-text lawyer's verbal
economy here is born of long practice: he is reciting from memory one of the
grounds of objection he was taught at law school. The equivalent effect in
Spanish is achieved by the opposite means: a textbook-quoting expansion such
as *la pregunta invita al testigo a especular* ('the question invites the witness to
speculate').

(c) On plea bargaining

Our last fictional snippet involves an instance of plea bargaining (negotiation
between the parties and the judge with respect to possible charges, testimonies
and sentences):

'I'll walk into a courtroom, face the Judge...and I'll plead guilty to the
felony charge of mutilating the corpse. But I get no jail time.' (Grisham
1997:380).

Here the essential point for the translator is to reproduce the cynicism and bravado of the defendant's tone. His very familiarity with the language of the law ('the felony charge of mutilating the corpse') is part of this; but so is the crucial switch from future to present tense in the last phrase. He is no longer imagining the figure he will cut; he is driving a hard bargain, which must come across as an ultimatum in the target language. In Spanish this use of tenses could simply be reversed: the vivid present for the imagined scene in court and the categorical future for the refusal to go to prison (*'Pero no iré a la cárcel'*). The alternative is to end on a swagger with a verbless sentence like *'Pero nada de ir a la cárcel'* (literally, 'nothing about going to prison') or *'nada de chirona'* (perhaps 'no time in the nick', or '...in the can' for Americans). The whole passage might run something like this:

> *'Entro en la Sala, me encaro con el Juez...y me declaro culpable de mutilar el cadáver, que es un delito grave. Pero nada de ir a la cárcel.'*

> [I enter the courtroom, I face the judge... and I declare myself guilty of mutilating the body, which is a felony. But no way will I get prison.]

7.   Practical Problems in Translation Explained (I)

1.   Translation as problem-solving

Like the researcher, the translator must relish the challenge posed by the fresh problems that continually arise in the course of providing a reliable version in one language of texts produced in another. In any type of translation the problems that crop up are likely to be not merely linguistic but sociocultural too. In a specialist field like legal translation, where the asymmetry of the two systems of law is at least as important an issue as the asymmetry of the languages involved, the translator must expect to have to cope with alien modes of thought and unfamiliar conceptualizations of the underlying subject-matter, as well as performing the more obvious task of wresting the original terms and syntax into a shape acceptable to users of the target language. In doing so, the translator, as cultural mediator, will often have to rely on the unsatisfactory counsel of hunch and intuition, much as the researcher has to learn to live with doubt and even to build a system of enquiry on this uncertain basis. The method of proceeding from doubt to something approaching certainty, or of conceiving of the work on hand as a continuous process of problem-solving, is at least as old as Descartes, but in the field with which we are concerned here there is nothing abstract about the procedure. Like the researcher, the translator of legal texts moves forward by constantly referring back to what is known to work, both in the tapping of available linguistic resources and in the handling and adjustment of legal concepts.

All of this means that translators of this particular type of text must add continuously to their stock of knowledge of legal terminology and procedure in both systems as well as replenishing their linguistic repertoire. Since lawsuits can turn on literally any area of human experience, the resources of the language of the law are coextensive with those of the common tongue. It is a mistake to think that 'legal language' comes down to a few hundred fossilized or semi-fossilized terms, as anyone who has read a dozen law reports or studied a textbook of cases and materials can testify. Conceptual adaptation and stylistic adjustment are, then, required skills in this field just as much, though perhaps not so obviously, as they are in the field of literary translation. That is why chapters 1 and 2 were devoted to some of the characteristic features and problems of legal English as a linguistic system, while chapters 3 and 4 have explored different features of the legal system and its linguistic consequences for the translator. The aim of chapters 7 and 8 is to complete this information, starting from the assumption that translation is neither a completely erratic nor an absolutely systematic task (Toury 1995:67). The aim here will be to identify certain patterns of regularity, understood as the most frequent and uniform ways of dealing with specific problems found in the versions of legal texts provided by a plurality of translators. In other words, chapters 7 and 8 will attempt to identify certain regularly recurring features of legal language which, because of their predictability and frequency of use, appear to provide reliable pointers and guidelines for the translator of texts of this kind. The following are the chief points dealt with:

(a)   Methodological problems in the translation of specialist vocabulary.
(b)   Common collocations in legal English.
(c)   Frequent semantic fields in legal English.
(d)   The temptations of paronymy: false cognates and unconscious calques.
(e)   Translation techniques: transposition, expansion and modulation.
(f)   Problems with the translation of syntagms.
(g)   Simple and complex syntax and the use of double conjunctions.
(h)   Thematization.
(i)   Textual coherence and lexical repetition in the language of legal English.

2.   Legal vocabulary (I)
The translation of purely technical vocabulary

For obvious reasons, one of the primary aims of the legal translator must be to achieve a contrastive awareness of legal vocabulary, i.e. a comparative mastery of the appropriate vocabulary in the source and target languages. It will be remembered that in Chapter 1, Section 5, legal vocabulary was divided into the symbolic (*court, judge, adjudge, contract, misrepresentation, convict*, etc.) and the functional (*subject to, whereas, under, hereinafter*, etc.). It was also suggested that the symbolic type could be further subdivided into three groups or subtypes, but that this subdivision was merely operative and therefore tentative. Given the haziness of the borderlines between one group and the others, some of the terms included in the second subtype could drift into the first, while some of the words assigned to the third group could equally well belong to the second.

2.1. Problems in the translation of one-word purely technical terms

The terms assigned to this group, whatever their origins may have been, now belong almost exclusively to the vocabulary of the law, or are firmly attached to this sphere in their everyday usage. Some are archaic terms, often Anglo-Norman in origin, such as 'seisin' (feudal property rights), 'escheat' (the reversion of property to the state in cases where a decedent dies intestate or when the property is abandoned) or 'estovers' (among several variants, the right to take wood from a property to supply basic needs). However, many of the commonest terms of modern law belong in this group, as witness such obvious examples as 'legal', 'illegal', 'lawful', 'unlawful', 'manslaughter', 'theft', 'judge', 'barrister', 'solicitor', 'bailiff', 'bail', 'tort', 'contract' and hundreds more which the reader will readily be able to think of. Some of them may occasionally stray into common speech when they are used in a figurative sense. For instance, someone may be said to be 'a good judge of a horse' (or of a painting, or of practically anything requiring skill, experience, discernment or shrewdness for its appraisal). Similarly a verb like 'mortgage' (*hipotecar, hypothéquer, hypothekarisch belasten*), though it appears most often in legal contexts, may be used metaphorically, as in a sentence like 'Senator McDonald mortgaged his political career by taking an unpopular stand on abortion'.

English expressions of this type seldom present serious problems to the European translator, since, if we discount the figurative usage mentioned above, they tend to be monosemic and often overlap with legal concepts which are well established in neighbouring cultures sharing a similar history. Indeed, the only problem in certain cases is to decide whether to translate the terms or to leave them in the original English, thus marking them as technical peculiarities, the product of specific local conditions with no exact parallel elsewhere. Taste enters such decisions, as well as the desire for terminological accuracy and respect for cultural uniqueness. It is unfortunately rather difficult to determine at what point a translator's alleged respect for linguistic peculiarity becomes mere laziness or cowardice. Nor is it easy to distinguish the supposed desire for technical accuracy from the cultural snobbery implicit in the use of needless Anglicisms so prevalent at the moment, especially in the field of technical translation (IT and the Internet in particular). However, legal translators, especially those not trained to the law, as is most often the case, must heed the advice of legal practitioners, who are not infrequently reluctant to accept adaptations of terms they regard as alien technicisms to be held at arm's-length by means of textual reproduction, i.e. non-translation. This is particularly so with words and phrases deriving from Latin or Norman French[1]. Some lexical units belonging to the group we are dealing with, such as *common law* or *estoppel*, may appear untranslated in the target language, either because they are distinctive and very well known even to moderately cultivated jurists, or because they are extremely complex technically, so that it is easier to understand them conceptually than to translate them. Sometimes both reasons may be adduced in support of non-translation, e.g. the English terms 'estop' and 'estoppel' regularly appear

---

[1] However, the mere fact that a legal expression is taken over directly from Latin does not by itself justify non-translation. Frequently-used terms of English law such as *actus reus, mens rea, non compos mentis* or *ex parte* will in all likelihood be translated into some appropriate target-language equivalent, even though it could be argued that many target-language lawyers will be either fully conversant with their technical meanings or in a position to make an intelligent guess at them.

untranslated in non-English texts within the field of Private International Law, and attempts to translate them are often frowned upon by European lawyers concerned with strict terminological accuracy. Similarly, though there would seem at first sight to be no insuperable difficulty in rendering 'common law' by *derecho consuetudinario, derecho común or droit coutumier*, many writers in European languages prefer to leave the original English term untouched in their versions.

Among many other terms that could be cited in this first group, the following may serve as examples:

lien (*derecho prendario, droit de rétention, Retentionsrecht, Pfandrecht*): e.g. The repairer of a car often has a lien over the vehicle until the cost of labour and materials has been satisfied.

magistrate (*juez de primera instancia, juez lego, juez de paz, juge de paix, Friedensrichter*): e.g. A warrant for the arrest of a suspect must be signed by a magistrate.

abscond (*fugarse, s'esquiver, se soustraire à la justice, Friedensrichter*): e.g. The prisoner was released on bail and later absconded before he could be brought to trial.

easement (*servidumbre, derecho en predio ajeno, droit de passage, Grunddientsbarkeit*): e.g. The owner of the house was prevented from raising the height of the garden wall by his neighbour's enjoyment of an easement of light.

charter (*fuero, privilegio, charte, Privileg*): e.g. The Town Council's original rights over the land were created by a royal charter.

The terms illustrated in the above examples all have single meanings. Other words in the group are more complex in that their precise senses may vary with context, though the overall field of reference remains the legal one. An example is the term 'jurisdiction', which has three distinct senses. In the first place, it may mean the power of the courts to take cognizance of matters referred to them; in this sense it is equivalent to 'competence' or 'authority'. A second meaning of the word is the particular area or class of law in which this power is exercised, as when we talk of civil jurisdiction or criminal jurisdiction. Finally it is applied to the region, district or geographical area over which a given court has authority; a case will normally be heard or brought in the nearest court of the appropriate rank to the place where the crime was committed or reported, or to the address for service provided by the plaintiff, and in this sense the term is synonymous with 'venue'.

A more complicated instance is the term 'remand', which may be translated in a variety of ways depending on the particular grammatical or semantic context of use. Etymologically the word means 'to send back', an obsolete sense still listed in dictionaries compiled on historical principles, though it is related to the usual modern meaning of the verb, which is to make an order disposing judicially of the person of a prisoner when proceedings are adjourned. This usually occurs after the preliminary hearing at the magistrates' court and the effect of it is that the prisoner is delivered back to the keeping of the appropriate authority, which generally means the police or the officers of a prison. Depending on the nature and gravity of the charge, the accused may be 'remanded in custody' or 'remanded on bail'.

We have already remarked that there is no real equivalent in the English judicial system to the concept of *instrucción* (Spanish) or *instruction* (French), which is such a characteristic feature of criminal procedure in many European countries. However, perhaps the preliminary enquiry by a magistrates' court is as close as one gets in English criminal law to the process of preliminary examination by a judge which is what these terms designate. At any rate, putting together all the semantic and contextual features of the term 'remand' – the making of a court order, the decision to put the accused on trial at a later date and the judicial determination of their situation in the interim – our suggested translation of the phrase 'remand on bail' is *dictar auto de procesamiento en libertad provisional bajo fianza (libérer sous caution, Freilassung gegen Kaution bis zur neuen Verhandlung)*. It then follows that 'remand in custody' would be *dictar auto de procesamiento con ingreso inmediato en prisión (mettre en détention préventive, in Untersuchungshaft behalten)*. Naturally the translator will have to make the relevant adjustments when 'remand' occurs as a noun or when it is used attributively in phrases like 'remand prisoner' or 'remand home'. (Incidentally, the expansion required in translating the word 'remand' is a technique the legal translator must develop, since it is one common way of overcoming the asymmetry of the legal systems to which we have referred again and again. Many further examples of the technique will be seen later in the chapter.)

2.2. Problems in the translation of multiple-word technical terms

So far, all the examples given of technical vocabulary belonging to this first type have been single-word terms. The translator who sets out to systematize the vocabulary of the law will nevertheless quickly discover the prevalence of phrases that are meaningful only in a legal context, even though the individual words of which they are composed may belong to the general vocabulary of everyday speech. Here are some examples:

burden of proof (*onus probandi*): "One consequence of the principle of the presumption of innocence is that the burden of proof (*la carga de la prueba, charge de la preuve, Beweislast*) in criminal cases is borne by the prosecution."

accessory after the fact: "Anyone who knowingly harbours a criminal is liable to be prosecuted as an accessory after the fact (*encubridor, complice par assistance, nach Begehung der Tat Beteiligter*)."

accessory before the fact: "The three accomplices who helped the prisoner plan the robbery were convicted as accessories before the fact (*colaboradores necesarios, instigateurs, vor Begehung der Tat Beteiligter*)."

duty of care: "In accordance with the principle of the duty of care (*diligencia debida,* perhaps *précautions nécessaires, l'obligation de soins, Sorgfaltspflicht*), manufacturers of goods are bound to ensure that ultimate consumers of their products do not suffer personal injury as a result of using them as directed."

interlocutory issue: "An interlocutory issue (*un incidente procesal, incident de procédure, question interlocutoire* in Canada, perhaps *Verfahrensfrage*) arose concerning the validity of the plaintiff's passport."

power of attorney: "Mr Smith granted his agent a power of attorney (*poder notarial, procuration, Vollmacht*) to enable her to negotiate the contract."

In all the foregoing examples, it will be seen that although the paramount decisions for the translator concern the specialist items of vocabulary highlighted, any target-language versions also involve complex issues of word order, syntactic arrangement, thematization, modulation, anaphora and stylistic choices. Some of these points will be dealt with later in the chapter, but we take this opportunity to stress that specific problems of translation, legal or otherwise, can never be addressed in isolation. Translators of legal texts who take the trouble to systematize their approach to the selection of technical vocabulary will, we believe, produce versions possessing the advantages of clarity, regularity and predictability. But their task will be far from done until they have taken on and solved the accompanying problems of stylistic adaptation and adjustment.

3.   Legal vocabulary (II)
The translation of semi-technical vocabulary

For the translator, semi-technical vocabulary is a more complex group, since it contains terms that have one meaning (or more than one) in the everyday world and another in the field of law. It is here that the translator must be particularly careful to take nothing for granted and to exercise extreme caution in selecting from among the various options apparently available. Some of the potential pitfalls are, of course, more obvious than others. On the other hand, it is an unfortunate fact of contemporary life that certain seemingly standard translations of law terms popularized by journalists and by films and TV series of the 'courtroom drama' type are inaccurate, inappropriate, highly dubious, misguided or simply wrong. The only model for the legal translator is the language actually used by target-language legal practitioners when they are going about their professional business; anything else is suspect, including the evidence of the translator's own eyes and ears, especially when the latter are particularly attuned to habitual (i.e. non-technical) usage. The following examples should clarify the nature of the problem:

(a) Defence:
General meaning: the contrary of 'attack', e.g. 'Italian football puts the emphasis on defence' (*defensa, défense, Verteidigung*).

Legal meaning[1]: synonymous with 'reply' or 'answer', e.g. 'If no defence is filed within 15 days, the plaintiff may apply for judgement in default' (*contestación a la demanda, resistencia, oposición, excepción, défense, Klagebeantwortung*).

Legal meaning[2]: referring to the defendant and their counsel, e.g. 'The defence based its case on the testimony of two key witnesses' (*la defensa, avocat de la défense, défenseur, Verteidigung*).

Legal meaning[3]: special ground of defence or plea alleging mitigating circumstances, e.g. 'The accused set up a defence of temporary insanity' (*eximente, causa de inimputabilidad, défense, Verteidigung, Rechtfertigunggrund*).

(b) Discharge:
general meaning: synonymous with 'unload, disencumber, free', e.g. 'The ship was discharged of its cargo' (*descargar, descarga, décharger, entladen, löschen*).

legal meaning[1]: synonymous with 'annul, avoid', e.g. 'The contract will be deemed to be discharged if any of these conditions are not satisfied' (*extinguir, extinción, décharger, décharge, aufheben*).

legal meaning[2]: synonymous with 'perform/performance', e.g. 'The manager was dismissed for serious misconduct in the discharge of his functions' (*ejercicio, desempeño, exécution, exercice, Erfüllung*).

legal meaning[3]: synonymous with 'acquit, free, acquittal', e.g. 'In view of the accused's age and previous behaviour, the magistrate who had found him guilty granted him an absolute discharge' (*lo puso en libertad sin imponerle pena alguna, libération, acquittement, relaxe, Freispruch*).

legal meaning[4]: a special case of point 3 above, e.g. 'The bankrupt's liability is terminated when the court makes an order of discharge' (*auto de rehabilitación en su favor,* perhaps *ordonnance de libération,* perhaps *Restschuldbefreiung*).

(c) **Case**:
general meaning: a specific set of circumstances; a particular instance or representative sample, e.g. 'You must do what is best in each case' (*caso, situación, cas, situation, je nach Lage der Sache*).

legal meaning[1]: litigation, action, suit, prosecution, e.g. 'The case was heard by the High Court' (*proceso, causa, pleito, juicio, asunto, querella, affaire, procès, litige, Rechtsstreit*).

legal meaning[2]: legal grounds for proceeding, e.g. 'There is no case to answer', 'You have no case' (*fundamento jurídico de la demanda o la acusación, legitimación, cause, Gründe, Argumente*).

legal meaning[3]: arguments put forward by counsel, technical side of pleadings sustained by either side, e.g. 'The entire defence case depended on the construction of one clause in the contract'(*tesis, argumentación, argumentos jurídicos, arguments, affaire, Plädoyer*). [2]

(d) **Consideration**:
general meaning: attention, thought, deliberation, e.g. 'The arguments were given careful consideration' (*consideración, reflexión, considération, Überlegung*).

legal meaning: whatever is given or accepted by each party in return for the other party's reciprocal promise, e.g. 'If A promises to pay B a sum of money for the purchase of some goods, A's consideration is the payment of the amount agreed and B's is the handing over or delivery to B of the goods themselves' (*prestación o contraprestación, causa contractual, contrepartie, cause, Leistung, Gegenleistung*).

(e) **Find:**
general meaning: 'Police have found a gun at the scene of the crime' (*encontrar, trouver, finden*).

---

[2] 'Case' is often a much more difficult word than translators seem to realize. It might be tentatively suggested that the legal sense is closest to the general meaning when reference is to the particular *facts at issue*, and furthest from it when the context indicates some *technical or procedural matter* (venue, type and stage of proceedings, justification of the steps taken or proposed by either side, etc.).

legal meaning: deliver a formal judgement or judicial decision on the facts held proved and the applicable rules of law, e.g. 'The court found for the plaintiff' (*fallar, declarar, déclarer, fallen, entscheiden, fällen*).[3]

(f) Information:

general meaning: 'For further information please contact our head office'.

legal meaning: 'Criminal prosecution often begins when the police lay an information before the magistrates' (*denuncia de un delito ante un juzgado o tribunal, dénonciation,* perhaps *eine Anzeige erstatten*).[4]

It would be pointless to attempt to provide an exhaustive list of terms of this type, or even to try to classify the semantic fields such words might belong to. All that can be usefully said is that translators should get into the habit of consulting specialist dictionaries whenever something in the context alerts them to a usage distinct from the standard or everyday one. Sometimes this will be obvious enough, as when the verb 'entertain' is followed, in a legal text, by a word like 'claim' (and thus means 'to admit that a claim has grounds') or 'doubt' (thus meaning 'to harbour a doubt'). In other cases the blanket nature of the term will trigger the appropriate response from the experienced translator. Faced for instance with the verb 'bring', the translator will discard the literal sense in expressions like 'bring proceedings/a case/an appeal' in favour of formally more acceptable versions that take account of the synonymy with terms such as 'commence' or 'institute'. Finally, the translator is bound to come up against wholly unfamiliar collocations of common words, explicable only as survivals in the formal context of legal English of connotations remote from the everyday sense. For example, we find 'prefer a charge / an indictment', where the meaning (to present or formulate the charges or indictment) is unrelated to the usual one and can only be reconciled with it by etymological analysis of the components (Latin *prae + ferre*).

---

[3] This elliptical usage is very common in legal texts and means, of course, that the court gave judgement in favour of the party named. A frequent alternative is the verb 'hold', the past participle of which ('held') is often used at the end of law reports to indicate the final decision. An equally concise and elliptical formula is 'Judgement for the plaintiff/defendant'. Both the verb 'find' and the noun 'finding[s]' imply a decision on facts as well as law; where a court's decision exclusively involves questions of law, as is often the case on appeal, the preferred term is 'ruling'. Finally, in criminal cases the judge or jury 'finds the accused guilty/not guilty'; despite a recent tendency to translate the English phrase literally (e.g. *encontrar culpable*), in Spanish it is more naturally rendered *declarar culpable/inocente*.

[4] This expression is highly formal, and is used exclusively to refer to the mechanism by which prosecution is instituted. The ordinary citizen is normally said to 'make a complaint' to the police, or to 'report' a matter to them. It is then up to the police to decide whether to proceed and how to do so. The tone and context will be the safest guide for the translator in choosing between a more formal version or a more everyday expression.

Given the polysemy of these terms, and the stylistic fact that English, unlike a language like Spanish, is relatively tolerant of repetition when a given term is customary and expected in a particular context, the translator should be prepared to find a word of this class occurring more than once in the same sentence or paragraph in two or more different senses (or even in the same sense if no acceptable synonym is available). Thus, in a legal dispute involving a singer's contract, it is perfectly possible that terms like 'perform' and 'performance' will occur in two distinct senses (referring to entertainment on the one hand, and to legal processes on the other). Here is a real example of repetition of the word 'provide' in two distinct senses ('to give' and 'to allow' or 'to stipulate'):

> Congress was aware of the problems of consumer reluctance in the absence of EFT regulations, yet at the same time Congress believed that the array of financial services that were *provided* under EFT systems had the potential to be of great benefit to consumers [...]. EFTA section 910, entitled 'Liability of Financial Institutions', *provides*, in part: '(a) Subject to subsections (b) and (c) of this section, a financial institution shall be liable...'.

4.   Legal vocabulary (III). Problems in the translation of everyday vocabulary in legal English

Following our discussion of exclusively legal vocabulary (class 1) and mixed general and legal terms (class 2), it seems logical to consider a third class of words which, without losing their everyday sense, occur frequently in the formal contexts we are analyzing. As a general rule, it may be said that the terms included in this group are more commonly found in one area of the law, or one legal genre, than in others (e.g. usually in judgements, or more commonly in the criminal law, or most frequently in contracts, etc.). Translators are advised to get into the habit of making their own lists of words or expressions of this type. They will probably find that the terms are easier to understand than to translate, precisely because they tend to be contextually bound. For this reason we suggest that students should bear in mind the macrostructural hints contained in the previous chapter on genres.

For present purposes, we shall take two particularly rich terms, 'develop' and 'qualify', as examples, but as ever the list is potentially a long one, and would take in such words as 'argument', 'report', 'issue', 'create', 'application', 'succeed', 'fail', 'challenge', 'disclosure' and literally hundreds of others. For the translator, the point here is not so much to be aware of the potential meaning of the original, which in these cases is never far from the ordinary sense of the terms, as to be alive to stylistic and contextual constraints. In other words, the best choice is a matter of literary accuracy (in the broad sense) rather than of technical precision:

(a) Develop

This verb and the noun derived from it ('development') are widely overused, as are their literal equivalents in other languages, as Torrents dels Prats (1977:145-57) has argued. However, we shall confine our illustrations to the purely legal, or quasi-legal, sphere. In each case our aim is to show that the apparently obvious versions (*desarrollar, développer, entwickeln*) are not always the best, though no doubt some pragmatists will take a different view:

'the developed law' (*el Derecho sustantivo tal como se ha evolucionado,* le *droit tel qu'il a évolué, hergeleitetes Recht*)
'the arguments developed by Counsel for the defence' (*las tesis expuestas por el abogado defensor, les arguments élaborés par la défense, die Argumente, die vom Verteidiger vorgebracht wurden*)
'a new development in the case' (*novedades en el asunto/caso, nouveauté dans l'affaire, das Verfahren nahm einen neuen Verlauf*)
'development project' (*plan de urbanización, projet d'urbanisation, Bebauungsplan*)
'develop a theory' (*trabajar sobre una hipótesis, travailler sur une théorie,* perhaps *eine Theorie ausbauen*)
'develop a point raised earlier' (*profundizar en/ampliar una cuestión mencionada con anterioridad, expliquer un point déjà soulevé, einen zuvor aufgetauchten Punkt ausführen*)

(b) Qualify

This is a notoriously difficult word to translate, along with its derivatives 'qualification', 'qualifying' and 'qualified'. Possibly some of the confusion surrounding translation of the terms is owing to the hasty literalism and mistranslation frequently found in recent sports journalism, a field in which the pressure of satisfying large audiences and being first with the news leads daily to slack usage and instant coinages that translators with time on their side are advised to place on their suspect list. In the sentence 'Scotland failed to qualify for the finals', the sense of 'qualify' (*clasificarse* and not *calificarse*) is 'meet the required standard, fulfil the required conditions' and hence 'prove one's worth or competence' or 'gain entitlement to inclusion in a privileged category'. In other words, the term is being used in the formal or administrative sense it often has in legal contexts. Here are some more obviously legal or quasi-legal examples:

'to qualify as a barrister' (*sacar/obtener el nombramiento/la habilitación para ejercer de abogado/actuar ante los tribunales,* something like

être reçu avocat, als Rechtsanwalt zugelassen werden). [In this example
the asymmetry of the two systems may force the translator to modify as
well as adapt the term. Clearly we must find a version which would not
merely mean 'take a law degree', while at the same time indicating that
the specific function or privilege of a barrister is to represent clients before the courts.]

'highly qualified lawyers' (*juristas de toda solvencia/de entre los más
destacados de su profesión, avocats renommés, très expérimentés,* perhaps *angesehene Rechtsanwälte*). [Here again, modulation may be
necessary. Since 'qualifications' in English include both relevant diplo-
mas and professional accreditation and experience, the translator has to
come up with a phrase that implies prestige and proven ability as well as
basic entitlement. It does not seem a good idea to resort to forced
equivalences like *altamente cualificados*, however popular they may have
become in adverts.]

'a qualified opinion' (*una opinión matizada, una opinión favorable pero
con matices,* perhaps *avis atténué, sous condition, avec réserves, nicht
uneingeschränkte Auffassung*)

'qualified privilege' (*inmunidad limitada, privilège conditionnel,
immunité relative,* perhaps *bedingte Immunität*). [As in the previous example, the sense of 'qualified' is close to 'limited' or 'in specified
circumstances'. Etymologically this is not far from the French or Spanish sense of the equivalent term when it is used to mean 'describe' or
'specify', but neither language seems to have developed the absolute usage of the participle found in the English instances.]

'qualifying date' (*fecha límite, plazo, date limite, délai, Stichtag*). [De-
spite appearances to the contrary, we are back here to the sense mentioned
in the first example. This is an interesting case of a translation in which
semantic equivalence is achieved through logical rather than grammatical analysis. The sense is that one will 'qualify' for the right or privilege
in question provided one has applied by the date in question, which therefore becomes a time limit or deadline. Both these terms would be
acceptable English equivalents in most cases.]

'qualifying period' (*período de carencia [de un seguro, etc.], délai
d'attente, période de carence, Karenzfrist*). [Yet another instance of the
sense in which 'qualify' means 'have or obtain the right'. Here again, the
explanation of the translation is to be found in logic, this time because
the condition specified in the insurance policy is a negative one. Implicit
in the English phrase is a term such as 'Cover will not begin until...' or
'Claims will only be entertained after...'. In other words, there will be a
period during which no cover can be guaranteed, a logical condition,
since insurance companies will clearly not want to provide cover against
the risk that the new client may break a leg if his or her leg is already
broken at the date when the policy is signed!]

We have suggested above that in legal translation similar problems constantly arise with a host of other terms, including 'argument', 'report', 'issue', 'create', 'application', 'succeed', 'fail', 'challenge' and 'disclosure'. None of these words belongs to our first group and, at first sight, none of them appears to present major problems to the translator. However, the difficulties we have illustrated in the cases of 'develop' and 'qualify' ought to be sufficient to alert the reader to the potential traps of legal texts in which terms of this type lie in wait for the incautious user of standard dictionaries. To end this section, without going into specific detail, translators might wish to reflect on how they would go about dealing with phrases like 'the *issue* between the parties', '*challenge* a decision', 'listen to *argument*' or 'the appeal *fails*'. In each case, we suggest, the high-lighted word will prove to be crucial, and the resulting choice will necessarily colour the entire version of the phrase, most probably involving the translator in some kind of syntactic and stylistic rearrangement.

5. The translation of functional vocabulary in legal English

By functional vocabulary we mean the terms used to interrelate the major linguistic elements, or blocks of meaningful words, in a text. Every specialist field has its own functional vocabulary. For instance, phrases like 'evolve into', 'branch into', develop from' or 'be in good agreement with' belong mainly to scientific discourse, while logical connectors of a formal kind, such as 'hence', 'thus' or 'whence' are found in philosophical, discursive or scientific language generally. In formal legal parlance, two phrasal groups stand out: adjectives/adverbs, or adjectival/adverbial groups, on the one hand, and conjunctions or prepositional phrases on the other. In many cases, the expressions, in keeping with the highly conservative nature of legal language, are otherwise antiquated or fossilized. Examples include the following:

(a) Adverbs
'hereineafter' (*en adelante, en lo sucesivo, más abajo, ci-après, nachstehend, im nachstehend, im folgenden*), e.g. 'The Richman Air Travel Company, hereinafter 'The Company'.'

'forthwith' (*de forma inmediata, con efecto inmediato, prendre effet immédiatement, sofort, unverzüglich*), e.g. 'In this event the contract shall be terminated forthwith'

'aforesaid/aforementioned' (*dicho, susodicho, mencionado, aludido, susdit, susmentionné, précité, vorher erwähnt, vorgenannt*), e.g. 'In our dealings with the aforesaid company...'. [Translators should note that these forms are perceived to be archaic even by practising lawyers and may be avoided in modern-style contracts by means of the simple deictics ('this,

that', etc.), more formal deictics ('the former, the latter') or supposedly
less archaic formulations such as 'said' with ellipsis of the article, e.g.
'our dealings with said company'. On the other hand, their archaic nature
may be stressed by deliberate placement after the noun, e.g. 'the condition aforesaid'.]

(b) Conjunctions and prepositions

'under' (*según, de acuerdo con, a tenor de, en vertu de, conformément
à, gemäß*), e.g. 'under section 33 above'. [In translating phrases of this
type into Spanish, there is little to be said for literal versions involving
bajo, which seem to lack historical warrant.]

'subject to' (*sin perjuicio de, con la salvedad de, salvo, a tenor de,
siempre de acuerdo con lo dispuesto en, sous réserve de, abhängig von*),
e.g. 'Subject to section 4(1), witnesses may be sworn...'. [An entire chapter
could be devoted to this phrase! The essential point to bear in mind is
that unlike 'under', it imposes a condition, so that it always introduces an
exception to some other term, clause, rule or section contained in the
same text. Take the example 'Subject to s 25(1), the seller may...'. Whatever subsection 1 of section 25 may say, it will not be saying the same as
the present subsection, which only makes sense as a partial exception to
it. Thus, any translation that states or implies 'in accordance with, as set
out in, pursuant to' will be contradicting the true sense of the text.]

'concerning' (*en relación con, relacionado con, en lo tocante a, au sujet
de, à propos de, über hinsichtlich*), e.g. 'I have nothing further to say concerning my relations with the plaintiff.' [Often in English this is a
somewhat formal way of saying 'about', but translators should bear in
mind that, fussy though it may be, it is by no means unusual in everyday
speech. Spanish *concerniente a* does not, therefore, seem the most appropriate translation, recent newspaper and political usage notwithstanding.]

'pursuant to' (*según, a tenor de [lo dispuesto en], en aplicación de,
suivant, zufolge*), e.g. 'Pursuant to section 13 of the Act, it is my duty
to...'. [Contrast with 'subject to'; here the sense is clearly 'as stated in, in
accordance with, as a consequence of', and so on. Very formal but
unproblematic.]

'without prejudice [to]' (*sin perjuicio de, salvando, con la salvedad de,
sans préjudice de, ohne Schaden für*), e.g. 'This letter is to be read without prejudice to the rights of X...'. [The phrase is unusual in legal English
outside of the communications between parties, since the 'without
prejudice' clause acts as a safeguard when potentially damaging or incriminating statements or admissions are being made privately. It is
therefore unlikely to occur in the texts of laws or judgements. However,

the fact that in English it is not at all the same as 'subject to' does not prevent the appropriate translations of that phrase from being considered as possibilities here.]

6.   Lexical resources in translation (l)
The collocations of legal English

In building up two-way repertoires of lexical equivalents in the field of law, the translator might usefully consider two further principles of textual arrangement, namely frequently recurring collocations and semantic fields. We shall deal with them in that order in this and the following section. By 'legal collocations' we simply mean particular lexical combinations found with some regularity in legal texts. In the examples that follow we have selected the five major terms 'contract', 'act', 'appeal', 'judgement' and 'witness', but translators could easily assemble further lists of collocations based on such items as 'proceedings', 'motion', 'application', 'charge' and many others.

(a)   Contract[5]

Verbs:
enter into a contract (*formalizar/celebrar un contrato, passer un contrat avec, einen Vertrag abschließen*)

sign a contract (*firmar/suscribir un contrato, passer un contrat, einen Vertrag unterschrieben*)

perform a contract (*cumplir un contrato, exécuter un contrat, einen Vertrag erfüllen*)

honour a contract (*cumplir un contrato, honorer un contrat, einen Vertrag einhalten*)

breach/break a contract (*incumplir un contrato, rompre/ casser un contrat, einen Vertrag brechen*)

set aside a contract (*resolver/denunciar/rescindir un contrato, rejeter/annuler un contrat, einen Vertrag aufheben*)

avoid a contract (*anular un contrato, éviter un contrat, se soustraire d'un contrat, einen Vertrag annullieren*)

draw up a contract (*redactar un contrato, dresser/rediger un contrat, einen Vertrag aufsetzen*)

negotiate a contract (*negociar un contrato, négocier un contrat, einen Vertrag aushandeln*)

renew a contract (*renovar un contrato, renouveler un contrat, einen Vertrag erneuern*)

---

[5] See section 2 in chapter five.

Nouns:

void contract (*contrato nulo, contrat nul, nichtiger Vertrag*)

voidable contract (*contrato anulable, contrat annulable/résiliable, anfechtbarer Vertrag*)

binding contract (*contrato vinculante o de obligado cumplimiento, contrat de force obligatoire*, perhaps *verbindliche Vertrag*)

exclusive contract (*contrato exclusivo, contrat à exclusivité, Alleinbezugsvertrag*)

breach of contract (*incumplimiento de contrato, rupture/violation de contrat, Vertragsbruch*)

terms of a contract (*condiciones de un contrato, termes / stipulations d'un contrat, Vertragsbestimmungen*)

the law of contract (*el derecho contractual, droit contractuel, Vertragsrecht*)

rules of contract (*normas que regulan el derecho contractual, règles contractuelles, Vertragsregeln*)

Adverbial phrases:

in contract (*según las normas del derecho contractual, conformément au droit des obligations, en matière contractuelle,* ADD perhaps *vertraglich*)

under contract (*contratado, obligado por las condiciones de un contrato, sous contrat, vertraglich verpflichtet*)

under this contract (*según lo estipulado/pactado en el presente contrato, conformément au présent contrat, nach den Bestimmungen des Vertrags*)

(b) Act

As object of verbs:

introduce an Act (*promulgar una ley, promulguer une loi,* perhaps *ein Gesetz verkünden*)[6]

repeal an Act (*derogar una ley, révoquer une loi, ein Gesetz aufheben*)

enforce an Act (*hacer cumplir una ley, velar por su cumplimiento, appliquer une loi, dem Gestez Geltung verschaffen*)

As subject of verbs:

an Act provides (*una ley dispone, une loi stipule,* perhaps *ein Gesetz sieht vor, dass...*)

an Act establishes (*una ley determina, une loi établit,* perhaps *ein Gestez stellt fest, dass...*)

---

[6] The formal term 'enact' is found in the same sense (e.g. 'The government intends to enact new legislation to deal with the drug problem') but for obvious reasons of euphony and logic, the tautology 'enact an Act' is avoided. In the less formal context of newspaper reporting, the word 'enact' is likely to be replaced with more reader-friendly terms like 'pass', 'introduce' or 'bring in', but in the preamble to the Act itself, the classic formula ('the enacting words' by which a bill becomes law) is still the old jussive form 'Be it enacted that...'.

an Act abolishes (*una ley deroga, une loi abroge / abolit*, perhaps *ein Gesetz hebt auf*)

an Act consolidates (*una ley consolida o refunde, une loi consolide*, perhaps *verfestigt*)

(c) Appeal

As noun
bring an appeal (*interponer un recurso, lancer un appel, Rechtsmittel / Einspruch /Berufung einlegen, in die Berufung gehen*)

lodge an appeal (*interponer un recurso, loger un appel, se pourvoir, Rechtsmittel / Einspruch /Berufung einlegen*)

allow an appeal (*estimar un recurso, accueillir un pourvoi*, perhaps *Rechtsmittel zulassen, dem Einspruch / der Berufung stattgeben*)

dismiss an appeal (*desestimar un recurso, rejeter un appel*, perhaps *Rechtsmittel abweisen*)

As verb
appeal against a decision/judgement/sentence, etc. (*recurrir una resolución/un fallo/una sentencia/una condena*, etc., *réclamer contre une décision*, perhaps *gegen ein Urteil Berufung einlegen*)[7]

grant leave to appeal (*admitir a trámite un recurso, concéder l'autorisation d'appel*, perhaps *Rechtsmittel zulassen*)

refuse leave to appeal (*inadmitir un recurso, no admitirlo a trámite, réfuser la permission de faire appel*, perhaps *Rechtsmittel nicht zulassen*)

Prepositional phrase
on appeal (*en la instancia de apelación, a raíz del [oportuno] recurso, tras la interposición de un recurso, en instance d'appel*, perhaps *in Revision*)

(d) Judgement

give judgement (*fallar, resolver, dictar sentencia, pronunciar el fallo, accorder un jugement, ein Urteil fällen*)

judgement for the plaintiff (*fallo condenatorio, jugement en faveur du demandeur*, perhaps *Urteil im Sinne des Klägers*)

judgement for the defendant (*fallo absolutorio, jugement en faveur du défendeur*, perhaps *Urteil im Sinne des Beklagter / Anbeklagter*)

default judgement (*fallo condenatorio por incomparecencia del demandado, jugement par défaut, Versäumnisurteil*)

---

[7] In standard American English the verb 'appeal' is normally transitive, e.g. 'appeal a decision, appeal a sentence'.

deferred judgement (*sentencia dictada tras un intervalo discrecional para deliberación*, perhaps *jugement déféré*, perhaps *aufgeschobene Beurteilung*)[8]

(e) Witness

Adjectival phrases:

casual witness (*testigo fortuito, témoin fortuit*, perhaps *zufällig Zeuge*)

character witness (*testigo convocado para aportar testimonio sobre la solvencia moral del acusado, témoin de moralité, Leumundszeuge*)

chief witness (*testigo principal, témoin principal/en chef, Hauptzeuge*)

compellable witness (*persona que puede ser obligada a testificar, témoin contraignable, zur Aussage gezwungener Zeuge*)

Crown witness/witness for the prosecution (*testigo de cargo, témoin à charge, Kronzeuge*)

defence witness/witness for the defence (*testigo de descargo, témoin à décharge, Zeuge der Verteidigung*)

eyewitness (*testigo ocular/presencial, témoin oculaire, Augenzeuge*)

witness statement (*testimonio, declaración, déposition, Zeugenaussage*)

As verb:

witness a will (*firmar un testamento como testigo, attester/certifier l'authenticité de, contresigner [witness with signature]*, perhaps *bestätigen*).

7.   Lexical resources in translation (ll)
The semantic fields of legal English

A further technique that may prove helpful to legal translators in the task of systematizing lexical items and developing the available contrastive vocabulary is the division of the subject-matter into semantic fields. Whereas in the previous section we dealt with habitual combinations of terms involving specific lexical items, in this section we will look at a variety of words or terms linked by their shared semantic relation to given concepts or central sense units. For the sake of illustration, let us take some introductory lists based on the common semantic fields of civil proceedings, criminal proceedings, employment contracts, company law and admiralty law:

(a) Civil proceedings

civil action (*demanda, action civile, Zivilprozeß*)

---

[8] In straightforward cases, English judgements are extempore and are delivered orally in open court. Where the matter is more complex, or requires a closely argued written analysis, or where judges decide to take more time for deliberation or consultation, the judgement is said to be 'deferred'. Since this seems to be the norm in many European systems, and is increasingly frequent in English cases, the translation may sound rather strained as well as somewhat pointless.

tort (*agravio extracontractual, ilícito civil, derecho de daños, derecho extra-contractual, délit civil, zivilrechtliches Delikt*)

breach of contract (*incumplimiento de contrato, violation / rupture de contrat, Vertragsbruch*)

claim form ([*escrito que contiene la*] *demanda, escrito de pretensiones, formulaire de demande, Antragsformular*)

claim (*pretensión, prétention, Anspruch*)

judgement (*sentencia, fallo, resolución, jugement, arrêt [judgement of an appeal court], Urteil*)

decree (*sentencia, fallo, décret, Urteil*)[9]

claimant/plaintiff (*demandante, demandeur, Kläger*)

defendant (*demandado, défendeur, Beklagte*)

service (*notificación, notification, Zustellung*)

acknowledgment of service (*acuse de recibo de la demanda, accusé de notification, Bestätigung der Zustellung*)

defence (*contestación a la demanda, oposición, excepción, défense, Klagebe-antwortung*)

counterclaim (*reconvención, demande reconventionnelle, reconvention, Gegen-anspruch*)

case management (*gestión procesal, dirección judicial de las actuaciones*, perhaps *gestion de la cause*, perhaps *Behandlung des Falles*)

procedural judge (*juez de procedimiento, juez encargado de la fase inicial de una acción judicial, juge de procédure, juge d'instruction, Verfahrens-rechtrichter*)

particulars of claim (*cuerpo de la demanda, détails de la demande, Klagebe-gründung*)

statement of case (*alegaciones, exposé des allégations, Darlegung des Stand-punktes*)

track (*vía procesal, voie, Spur*)

public hearing (*vista oral, audience publique, öffentliche Verhandlung*)

(b) Criminal proceedings

offence, crime (*delito, infraction, délit, Straftat*)

offender (*delincuente, reo, condenado, contrevenant, délinquant, Straftäter*)

arrest (*detención, arrestation, Festnahme*)

---

[9] Semantically, 'judgement' and 'decree' are synonymous, but, except in Scots law, where the latter term is dominant in judicial usage, 'judgement' is overwhelmingly preferred. However, judgements in divorce cases are known as 'decrees'; the initial dissolution of the marriage bond is the 'decree *nisi*' and the final judgement is the 'decree absolute' . Note the position of the adjectival element, which follows the noun in both cases. This is an occasional feature of highly stylized or formal registers in English, such as legal and administrative language (e.g. 'court martial', 'director general', etc.).

information (*denuncia, inculpation, accusation, Anzeige, Anklage*)
arrest warrant (*orden de detención o de busca y captura, mandat, Haftbefehl*)
in due process of law (*con las debidas garantías judiciales, dans les processus de la justice, ordnungsgemäßes Verfahren*)
caution (*leer los derechos al detenido, informer de ses droits, über seine Rechte belehren*)
trial (*juicio, vista oral, audiencia, procès criminel, [Gerichts-]Verhandlung*)
sentence (*pena, sentencia, peine, Strafurteil*)
acquittal (*absolución, acquittement, décision absolutoire, Freispruch*)
conviction (*condena, condamnation, Verurteilung*)
probation (*libertad condicional o vigilada, liberté surveillée, denuncia, inculpation, accusation, Anzeige, Anklage*)
on parole (*en libertad condicional, en liberté conditionnelle, bedingte Entlassung*)
parole board (*junta de tratamiento, conseil chargé d'étudier les dossiers de mise en liberté conditionnelle, Ausschuß für Gewährung der bedingten Entlassung*).

(c) Employment contracts

employer (*empleador, patrono, employeur, Arbeitgeber*)
employee (*empleado, employé, Arbeitnehmer*)
full-time job (*empleo a tiempo completo, travail à plein temps, Vollzeitbeschäftigung*)
part-time job (*empleo a tiempo parcial, travail à temps partiel, Teilzeitsbeschäftigung*)
retirement age (*edad de jubilación, âge de la retraite, Pensionsalter*)
early retirement (*jubilación anticipada, retraite anticipée, vorzeitige Pensionierung*)
unfair dismissal (*despido improcedente, licenciement abusif, ungerechtfertigte Kündigung, perhaps unfaire Entlassung*)
constructive dismissal (*despido indirecto o analógico, congédiement déguisé, Verhalten des Arbeitgebers, das als Kündigung auszulegen ist*)
health and safety at work (*seguridad e higiene en el trabajo, sécurité et hygiène au travail, Gesundheit und Sicherheit am Arbeitsplatz*)
paid holidays (*vacaciones retribuidas, congés payés, bezahlter Urlaub*)
right to strike (*derecho a la huelga, droit de grève, Streikrecht*)
picket (*piquete, montar un piquete, formar parte de un piquete, organiser un piquet de grève, Streikposten*)
exclusive clause (*cláusula de exclusividad, clause exclusive, Ausschlußklausel*)

(d) Company law

partnership (*sociedad limitada, société en commandite, Personengesellschaft*)
company/firm (*empresa, firma, sociedad, mercantil, société, compagnie, Gesellschaft*)
sole trader (*empresario autónomo, empresa unipersonal, commerçant indépendant, Alleinhändler*)

firm name (*razón social, nom commercial, Firmenname*)

equity (*capital social en acciones, fondos propios, capitaux propres, fonds propres, Eigenkapital*)

passing off (*usurpación comercial, imitación fraudulenta, contrefaçon, fraude, Unterschieben eigener Ware[n] als fremde*)

board of directors (*consejo de administración, conseil d'administration, Vorstand*)

board member (*vocal, membre du conseil d'administration, Vorstandsmitglied*)

managing director (*consejero delegado, administrateur délégué, General-direktor*)

Chief Executive Officer, CEO (*presidente ejecutivo, directeur général, Unter-nehmensleiter*)

bankruptcy (*quiebra, faillite, Bankrott*)

winding-up (*liquidación, disolución, liquidation, Liquidation*).

(d) Admiralty law

wrecked vessel (*buque naufragado, vaisseau naufragé, schiffbrüchiges Schiff*)

salvage (*salvamento, premio de salvamento, prime / indemnité de sauvetage, Bergung, Bergelohn*)

towage (*servicio de remolque, remorquage, Schleppen*)

rescue (*rescatar, sauver, récupérer, retten*)

cargo (*cargamento, cargaison, faculté, fret, Ladung*)

collision (*abordaje, abordage, Kollision*)

prize (*presa, prise, Prise*).

8. Lexical traps for the translator: false cognates and unconscious calques

Any systematic approach to lexical equivalence in the field of translation will have to deal with the problems posed by various kinds of literalism, of which the false cognate, or 'false friend', is a leading example. Legal translation is no exception and it might even be argued that, given the predominance of formal register and the abundance of Latinisms in the core vocabulary of this field, the problem is especially acute in texts of this type. Take an apparently straightforward term like 'case': how often will the obvious cognates *caso* or *cas* be appropriate and when and why will they prove unsuitable? Clearly there is no simple statistical answer to this question; as usual, the translator will be forced to consider both semantics and contextual issues. By and large, all that can be safely said is that the closer the sense of the word 'case' approximates to 'the particular facts, this specific instance', the more likely the selection of the cognate will be, and conversely, the further it is from that sense, the greater the probability that some alternative will have to be sought.

In the following examples, 'case' is used in a variety of common legal acceptations, for each of which an equivalent is suggested that takes account of source-language semantics, target-language usage and, most importantly, context. The reader will observe that the mere cognates (*caso* or *cas*) can be avoided in the first example and must be resisted in the other eight:

(a) 'The <u>case</u> was a particularly complex one' (*caso, asunto, affaire, Fall*)

(b) '<u>There is no case to answer</u>' (*la acusación carece de fundamento, l'accusation manque d'argument convaincant, der Anklage fehlt die Beweisgrundlage*)

(c) 'the <u>case</u> for the defence' (*versión de los hechos, tesis, les arguments en faveur de l'accusé, zusammenfassende Klagebeantwortung*)

(d) 'The <u>case</u> was heard in the High Court' (*causa, asunto, affaire, Fall*)

(e) 'present <u>a strong case</u>' (*argumentos sólidos o poderosos, présenter de bons arguments, überzeugende Argumentation*)

(f) 'win/lose one's <u>case</u>' (*juicio, pleito, affaire, Prozeß*)

(g) 'The <u>case</u> dragged on for months' (*proceso, affaire, Prozeß*)

(h) '<u>case</u> law' (*[repertorio de] jurisprudencia, droit de jurisprudence, Fallrecht*)

(i) 'appeal by way of <u>case stated</u>' (*argumentos jurídicamente motivados, argument juridiquement motivé*).

Similar care should be taken in translating the terms 'process', 'proceeding[s]' and 'procedure'. Even native speakers of English unfamiliar with the niceties of legal usage occasionally experience difficulty in distinguishing between the two latter terms, and for the translator there is the added problem that the target language may very well not possess a matching set of etymologically interrelated words. As a result, makers of versions will have to pay scrupulous attention to context, where necessary sacrificing symmetry for the sake of accuracy and ignoring inappropriate cognates, as in the following examples:

(a) 'an abuse of the *process* of the court' (*las normas del enjuiciamiento [criminal o civil], las actuaciones judiciales, el procedimeinto establecido en derecho, la procédure, Verfahren*)

(b) 'in *due process* of law' (*las debidas garantías judiciales, clauses de sauvegarde des libertés individuelles, ordnungssgemäßes Verfahren*)

(c) 'serve *process*' (*auto, notificación, cédula de citación, notification de procédure, gerichtliche Verfügung*)

(d) 'bring *proceedings* against a party' (*demanda, querella, acciones judiciales, entamer une procédure contre, Klage*)

(e) '*stage of proceedings*' (*fase procesal, stade de la procédure, Stand des Verfahrens*)

(f) '*stay proceedings*' (*archivar las actuaciones, sobreseer la causa, arrêter les procédures, das Verfahren einstellen*)

(g) 'a *record of proceedings*' (*acta de las sesiones, memoria de lo actuado, sumario, autos,* perhaps *compte-rendu du procès, procès-verbal, Verhandlungsprotokoll*)

(h) 'rules of *procedure*' (*normas procesales, règles de procédure, Verfahrensregeln*)

(i) 'correct *procedure*' (*trámite, procedimiento, procédure [normale], Verfahren*).

Perhaps unexpectedly, the translation of the word 'legal' itself by the Spanish cognate *legal* or the French *légal* is not unproblematic. In a very general sense, of course, the terms are semantic equivalents, but it seems to be the case that the English word is wider-ranging than some at least of its Continental counterparts. When the predominant sense is 'allowed by law, lawful' or 'concerning the law', the literal translation is generally unexceptionable, e.g. 'the contract is legal', 'a legal wrangle', 'legal matters', and so on. But the following examples are instructive illustrations of the imperfect equivalence of the cognates in certain collocations, in which alternative adjectives (*legítimo, reglamentario, jurídico, légitime, judiciaire, juridique, rechtmäßig, rechtsgültig, juristisch*) are usually available and sometimes unavoidable, to say nothing of adverbial usage, where 'legally' could, and often should, be translated by phrases such as *en derecho/conforme a derecho, según la ley, en droit, juridiquement, conformément à la loi, auf dem Rechtswege*:

'legal English' (*el inglés jurídico, l'anglais juridique, juristisches Englisch*)

'the legal profession' (*la profesión de abogado, la abogacía, los letrados, la profession juridique, la robe, Anwaltschaft*)

'[take] legal action' (*demanda, querella, [proceder] judicialmente, intenter une action en justice, rechtliche Schritte einlegen*)

'legal advice' (*asesoramiento jurídico, conseil juridique, juristische Beratung*)

'the legal department' (*el departamento jurídico, la consultoría jurídica, service juridique, service du contentieux, Rechtsabteilung*)

'the legal owner' (*el legítimo propietario, propriétaire en droit, formeller Eigentümer*) 'a legal nullity' (*nulo de pleno derecho, nullité/invalidité légale, rechtlich ungültig*).

The terms we have examined provide particularly rich illustration of the dangers lurking in apparently innocent and straightforward correlations of cognates which prove to be false or inaccurate, but it is relatively easy to supply a miscellaneous set of words that legal translators should earmark for special treatment. Once again, the following list is very far from being exhaustive and our aim in presenting it is simply to underline the need to exercise the greatest caution in dealing with specious equivalents which, on closer inspection, turn out to be traps opening beneath the feet of the unwary translator:

'accessory before the fact' (*inductor, instigateur, vor Begehung der Tat Beteiligter,* not *accesorio antes del hecho*)

'accessory after the fact' (*encubridor, complice par assistance, nach Begehung der Tat Beteiligter*; not *accesorio después del hecho*)

'legal aid' (*asistencia letrada al detenido, assistance judiciaire,* Prozesskostenhilfe; not *ayuda legal*)

'magistrate' (*juez de primera instancia de lo penal, juge de paix,* perhaps *Friedensrichter*; not *magistrado* in Spanish, given the junior ranking of English magistrates in the judicial hierarchy and their narrowly defined function at first instance in criminal matters)

'court' (*tribunal, tribunal, Gericht*; not *corte*, which is rarely used in this sense in peninsular Spanish)

'sentence' (*condena, pena impuesta, castigo, peine, Strafe*; usually not *sentencia* in Spanish, which is a much wider term, embracing both civil and criminal judgements and including the decision itself as well as its legal consequences. In English, of course, 'sentence' refers exclusively to the punishment imposed on an offender following a guilty verdict in a criminal case, and must be carefully distinguished from 'decision', 'verdict', 'judgement', 'finding' and 'ruling'.)

'verdict' (*fallo, verdict, Urteilsspruch,* but not usually *veredicto* in Spanish; strictly speaking, only a jury or a judge in a criminal or defamation case records a verdict; there may well be a need to avoid *veredicto* and choose the more general word for 'decision' or 'judgement', depending on target-language usage.)

'prorogue' (*aplazar, suspender, interrumpir, ajourner la chambre, vertagen,* but not *prorrogar* in Spanish, since the sense is to postpone, suspend or end rather than extend, e.g. a session of Parliament. Readers alert to the cunning byways of semantics will note here a surprising instance of the unpredictable logic of etymology: the divergent paths of the languages have here ended in cognates so false that their meanings are almost completely opposite. However, the term 'prorogate' in Scots law is closer to the Spanish cognate; it is applied to the broadening or extending of a court's jurisdiction or of a time limit. This is just one instance of a linguistic phenomenon which legal translators should be aware of: for historical and cultural reasons, Scots law is often considerably closer than English to its Continental counterparts, both in concept and in terminology.)

'continuance' (*aplazamiento, suspensión, suspension des délais, ajournement, Vertagung,* but not usually *continuación* in Spanish: though the English word often does mean 'the act or fact of continuing', so that *continuación* is not necessarily wrong, the suggested translations will frequently be appropriate in legal usage, especially in American English).

Before leaving this brief discussion of spurious synonymity, we should perhaps stress that cognates are not the only traps leading the incautious translator into unwarranted imitation of the source text. The lure of non-lexical parallelisms involving prepositions or prepositional phrases, for example, can be equally beguiling and must be equally strongly resisted. We have already noticed the case of 'subject to'. In the context of false imitation we might add a warning about the misuse of literal equivalents of 'under' in such phrases as 'under the present agreement' or 'under section 16'. Here, the sense is 'in accordance with' or 'according to the terms of', and this indicates how the phrases should be translated: *según el presente pacto* or *de acuerdo con el artículo 16; selon/ suivant, conformément à l'article 16; in Übereinstimmung mit, gemäß Abschnitt 16*), and not *bajo, sous, unter* [under] in either case.

8.   Practical Problems in Translation Explained (II)

1.   The translator at the crossroads: techniques of legal translation

So far we have dealt with problems of translation concerning the selection of vocabulary, with the focus on specific issues relating to lexical units and technical terminology. However, anyone who has ever translated legal texts knows that such complex choices are not amenable to pure laws of predictability. The selection of the best, or the most appropriate, or the most natural or effective term will always depend also on other factors, such as context, traditional usage, genre and even subgenre, as we have suggested in the previous chapter.

In other words, in choosing the most appropriate terms, it is not enough for the translator to know that the text for translation belongs to a given genre. It is equally essential to bear in mind the particular subgenre of the text type concerned. If it is a contract, the next question is what sort of contract (an employment contract? a contract of sale?). And the same goes for any other kind of subgenre: this is a judgement, the translator might think, but is it a debt judgement or a divorce decree? The answer to such questions will clearly entail a limitation of the lexical range of any acceptable translation of its specific terms, as well as determining the organizational macrostructure of the ensuing translation. Pressing the point a little, what this means is that lexical decisions will, to some extent, depend on requirements of syntax. To take a simple example, the 'facts as found' section of a judgement is likely to be arranged paratactically, whereas the syntactic layout of the clauses of a contract, or, more spectacularly, the provisions of an Act, will almost certainly be much more complex. In the latter case, it is crucial for the translator to realize that the resulting hypotactic structure of both source and target clauses is not, or is not primarily, an effect of mere inflation or rhetorical grandeur; it is intended to contribute to the clarity and unambiguousness of the fact, agreement, rule or norm described. Consequently, any translation should attempt to be as accurate as possible and should never take refuge in sheer literalism, approximate legalese or mere gobbledegook. However arid or pedantic they may appear, all the 'subject to', 'whereas', 'except as otherwise indicated' or 'any person who either...or...' clauses require extremely careful perusal and make exceptional demands on the translator's lexical skills as well as on their syntactic imagination.

What this suggests, then, is that the translator should be seeking dynamic rather than literal equivalence. By this we mean target versions that provide connotative as well as denotative parity with the original by dint of selecting the natural equivalent of source-language expressions, jettisoning where necessary inappropriate cognates, dubious paronyms and other spurious counterparts, such as homographic, homophonic and isomorphic terms. After all, the aim, in legal as in other forms of translation, is to provide target versions that are at least as readable and natural as their source predecessors.

The issue of syntactic equivalence is dealt with more fully later, in sections 5 and 6. For the moment, let us concentrate on the matter of literalism in the translation of legal texts and, more precisely, the question of what the term 'literal' is supposed to mean in this context. An extreme position, admittedly more commonly defended by legal practitioners with no knowledge of the linguistic niceties involved than by translators or linguists themselves, is that the target version should reproduce exactly and exclusively the words of the source text. To this, the short answer is that the requirement cannot possibly be satisfied. Anyone with even a rudimentary awareness of the various types of asymmetry that distinguish one language from another – syntactic organization, morphological features, verb tense and mood, deictic representation, markers of emphasis, register and style, and word order, to mention only a handful of the most obvious – knows that the notion of identity in translation is illusory. To take a simple instance, where an English law report concludes with the statement 'judgement for the defendant', a Spanish version like *juicio para el demandado* would be entirely unacceptable syntax. It would, in fact, be meaningless nonsense, since no combination of these target terms would convey anything to Spanish-speaking lawyers, far less to ordinary speakers of the language with no legal training, unless they happened to know a fair amount of English and had a reasonable grasp of English legal idiom.

We could take our example further by extending the idea of asymmetry, as we must, to embrace the notions of asymmetries of linguistic concept, of the underlying legal systems and of the accepted formulae in which the peculiar doctrines and discourse of those systems are expressed and enshrined. Moreover, an acceptable translation would have to take account of local cultural factors, e.g. the expectations of readers of reports in general and law reports in particular. Our English example is couched in the habitual syntactic shorthand of texts of this class, but there is no reason whatsoever to assume that any given target language could achieve succinctness by the same syntactic means: what in English is concision and clarity would be abruptness and obscurity in Spanish. Not to labour the point, one acceptable Spanish equivalent would be *se dictó sentencia absolutoria* or, more succinctly, *sentencia absolutoria*. These, we could say, are *natural* equivalents, in accordance with cultural and linguistic tradition, immediately familiar to practising lawyers and readily comprehensible to the average cultivated reader.

Besides these considerations, it is obvious that major international organizations such as the EU or the UNO depend for their very existence on the ability of translators to adapt texts in this way and to provide versions that are accurate, natural and acceptable. There is simply no point in demanding what cannot be produced. Let us not forget that the very word 'literal' is a metaphor, albeit a buried one: the *literal* meaning of 'literal' is 'letter-by-letter' or 'word for word', so that *literally* speaking there can be no *literal translation* of any word or phrase from one language into another. What is conveyed or 'carried over' (*trans-lated*) is the sense, the tone, the register, the expected and natural equivalent in the *other language*, since strictly to reproduce a foreign word or expression is to repeat it *as it is*, e.g. *cogito ergo sum* for *cogito ergo sum*.

This is not, of course, what most of us mean by 'literal translation'. By and large, the expression refers to an attempt to carry over the primary sense of the source text in target-language words that remain as close as possible, in both form and meaning, to the original. But should this be our ideal? In the light of what we have been saying about false cognates and related problems of paronymity, the answer would seem to be not necessarily. Take a straightforward sentence like 'The court rose at 5 p.m.'. A headlong, mulishly unreconstructed Spanish version might read *La corte se levantó a las 5 de la tarde*. Applying the criterion of naturalness and acceptability, or dynamic equivalence, however, a more appropriate response to the original would be *Se levantó la sesión a las 17 horas*. It is this kind of necessary adaptation that we shall recommend and illustrate in the remaining sections of this chapter.

However, before we move on to describe and exemplify some of the main techniques of adaptation, we should clarify that we are not here advocating what is sometimes called 'free translation'. Whatever else this term may mean in particular cases, it appears to involve taking stylistic and cultural liberties with originals, and there is simply no place for such free-ranging adaptation in the translation of legal texts. No doubt there is a place for this approach in preparing versions of literary texts that are culturally, linguistically or historically remote from the intended audience of the target text, or in adapting the lyrics of a musical where the producer has decided, for whatever reason, that the words have to be sung in the target language though the original music is to be retained. The law may be an ass, as Dickens once suggested, but it must be allowed by the translator to bray in the appropriate tone.

If we must have a name for the type of legal translation we are proposing, we could do worse than call it 'indirect' translation. The essence of the method is to produce on the target reader an equivalent effect to that produced by the source text. Both terms suggest avoidance of calques and cognates and other forms of automatic reproduction of source syntax and terminology, while at the same time (we hope) implying that, by operating certain linguistic transformations, the translator should, as Hamlet puts it, "by indirections find directions out". Furthermore, the term 'indirect' is in common use in Applied Linguistics, to one branch of which translation partly belongs. That field has thrown up terms such as 'indirect communicative techniques' (e.g. understatement or indirect speech acts), 'indirect courtesy', and others, which make good sense and address issues not dissimilar to those which concern us here. For the terminology relating to the main techniques of indirect (or what is also called 'oblique' translation), we are indebted to Vázquez Ayora (1977: 251-313), whose useful book on the topic analyzes and illustrates some of the ways in which the translator may shake off the shackles of source-language syntax and vocabulary with the aim of producing natural, idiomatic and yet still accurate versions of the originals. The main techniques discussed here are transposition, expansion and modulation.

2. Transposition

By transposition is meant the substitution of one grammatical category for another, on the basis that both may be fairly said to possess the same semantic weight or equivalent semic density. For example, if the original reads 'The defendant *said...*' (a construction with a verbal nucleus) and the translation proposed is '*Según* el demandado...' ('according to the defendant', a prepositional phrase with a noun nucleus), we are looking at a transposition from the verb to the noun category. Likewise, a translation of 'for *late* delivery' by 'por *demora* en la entrega' ('due to delay in the delivery') shows a transposition from adjective to noun.

From these examples it will readily be seen that transposition can be of many kinds. What follows is a short list of some of the most common:

(a) Verb for noun

Whereas English tends naturally towards the noun phrase, other languages like French, Spanish and German, probably in that order, are often more inclined to expressions constructed around verbs and verb phrases:

> without the slightest <u>hesitation</u> (*sin <u>vacilar</u> lo más mínimo*, back-translation: 'without <u>hesitating</u> in the slightest')
> during the <u>remainder</u> of the term (*hasta que <u>expire</u> el mandato*, back-translation: 'until the term <u>expires</u>').

(b) Pronoun for noun

This kind of transposition, and its counterpart (noun for pronoun), are very common in every sort of translation, since they allow of greater clarity and variety, especially in languages like Spanish and Italian which systematically avoid repetition even of relatively simple elements. In legal texts the use of indefinite pronouns for common nouns is particularly useful:

> any <u>person</u> who (*todo <u>aquél</u> que*, back-translation: 'all <u>those</u> who')
> to <u>persons</u> with (*a <u>quienes</u> posean*, back-translation: 'to <u>those</u> who have')

(It will be noticed, incidentally, that in the latter example we have in fact a double transposition: pronoun for noun and verb for prepositional phrase.)

(c) Noun for adjective:

> when the invoice is <u>overdue</u> (*al <u>vencimiento</u> de la factura*, back-translation: 'on <u>expiry</u> of the invoice')
> <u>indecent</u> assault (*atentado al <u>pudor</u>, attentat à <u>la pudeur</u>* back-translation: 'assault on <u>decency</u>')
> He was set <u>free</u> (*fue puesto en <u>libertad</u>, il a été mis en <u>liberté</u>*, back-translation: 'he was granted <u>freedom</u>')

(d) Noun for verb:

The corollary of (a) above, which often provides a neat way round awkward use of the passive voice. However, nominalization and avoidance of the passive should not be undertaken lightly; the transposition may not always be innocent or neutral, since important information may be lost, e.g. modality may be unwittingly suppressed or the identity of the subject or agent of the verb deleted. This does not occur in the following examples:

> The claimant asked for the deposit <u>to be returned</u> (*El demandante solicitó <u>la devolución</u> de la fianza, le requérant a demandé la <u>restitution</u>, der Anspruchsberechtigte fragte nach der <u>Rückzahlung</u> der Sicherheitsleistung*)
> It was <u>argued</u> by the defence that... (*El <u>argumento</u> utilizado por la defensa fue que...* , *l'<u>argument</u> utilisé par la défense était que..., Der Verteidiger trug die <u>Begründung</u> vor, daß...*)

(e) Active or impersonal form for passive

It is a well established fact that English is much more given to use of the passive voice than many other European languages like French, Spanish or Portuguese. So long as the translator does not overlook the problem mentioned in (d) above, greater naturalism can often be achieved by transposition from one mode to the other. However, a slightly more subtle case occurs in the third example below, in which the unstated agent of the original passive is 'restored' as active subject in translation:

No country <u>should be prevented</u> from taking measures... (*No se debe impedir a ningún Estado tomar medidas..., il ne doit être interdit à aucun pays de prendre des mesures...*)
The plaintiff realized the case <u>had been lost</u> (*El demandante se dio cuenta de que <u>había perdido el pleito</u>, back-translation:* 'The plaintiff realized <u>he had lost the case</u>')
Claims <u>must be filed</u> within 72 hours (*<u>Los interesados deberán presentar las reclamaciones</u> en un plazo no superior a 72 horas, les intéressés <u>doivent présenter</u> leurs réclamations dans un délai de 72 heures*)

(f) Relative or noun phrase for gerund or prepositional phrase with 'with'

An entire chapter could be written on the asymmetry between the use of the gerund (or the gerundive or the present participle) in English and in other European languages. For present purposes, we shall confine ourselves to frequently occurring phrase types in legal and administrative language in which the transposition from gerund to relative clause is motivated by syntactic as well as stylistic considerations. The similarity of the relative for preposition transposition to the case of verb for prepositional phrase seen in (b) above is striking, hence the third example:

'policy-holders <u>wishing</u> to withdraw from the agreement' (*aquellos asegurados <u>que deseen</u> poner término a la póliza*, back-translation: 'policy-holders <u>who wish</u>...')
'anyone <u>witnessing</u> such a transaction' (*todo aquel <u>que actúe de testigo</u> en un negocio de estas características, quiconque <u>témoigne</u> d'une telle transaction*)
'people <u>with</u> these disabilities' (*<u>los afectados por</u> dichas discapacidades, les personnes <u>affectées par</u> ces handicaps*)

(g) Noun phrase for adverbial phrase

'<u>how best to deal with</u> the matter judicially' (*<u>el mejor enfoque</u> judicial del asunto, <u>la meilleure façon</u> juridique de traiter le sujet*)
'determine <u>when exactly death occurred</u>' (*determinar <u>el momento preciso de la muerte</u>, déterminer <u>le moment précis de la mort</u>, bestimme den <u>exakten Zeitpunkt des Todeseintritts</u>*).

3. Expansion

In comparison with the Latin languages, English syntax is often described as synthetic, and the contrast holds good in the way each tongue deals with noun phrases. Generally speaking, English synthesis is matched by Latin periphrasis, e.g. 'immigration law' has been officially translated into Spanish as *leyes reguladoras de la inmigración, relativas a la inmigración* and *en materia de inmigración*. This apparent circumlocution arises from the need to avoid the ambiguity implicit in adjectival equivalents or use of the 'pure' genitive. For example, a putative form like *leyes inmigatorias* (immigratory laws) might be understood in a sociological sense to mean 'laws accounting for [the prevalence or patterns of] immigration', whilst *ley de [la] inmigración* (law of immigration) could easily be taken to mean an obligation to immigrate. For the same reason, the 'Theft Act' should probably not be translated as *Ley del robo* (law of theft), as this could suggest that there are rules that somehow make theft legal. A clear, and certainly less alarming, alternative is *Leyes relativas al robo* (laws concerning theft), and adapting this to the linguistic habits of the Spanish legislator leads us to propose *leyes relativas a los delitos contra la propiedad* (laws concerning offences against property) as a full-blown and natural instance of expansion. (It is worth pointing out, incidentally, that any such translation will always sound artificial to those acquainted with the codified structure of Continental law, under which the laws concerning immigration or theft would be laid down in the relevant book, part, section or article of the civil or criminal code.)

Periphrasis or expansion is one of the techniques that may be called for in translating virtually any part of speech, often in conjunction with transposition, since the reason why it is technically necessary in the first place is the constraint of syntactic structure that requires the drawing out of the target-language equivalent. Thus, in translating a phrase like 'valuable consideration', we may both transform the adjective 'valuable' into an adverbial or prepositional equivalent and, in consequence, expand the original, to produce *prestación a título oneroso*. Similarly, the tricky term 'under' may call for expansion. For instance, 'any of his obligations under the contract' would require some such explicitation as *cualquiera de las obligaciones que le incumben conforme al contrato* (any of the considerations to which he is subject in terms of the contract). However, in an impersonal case (without the 'his'), it might be preferable to avoid the expansion and choose instead a transposition like *cualquiera de las obligaciones derivadas del contrato* (...the obligations ensuing from the contract). Since this leaves the choice theoretically very open, all we can safely say is that the translator must be alert to norms of collocation, semantic range and prepositional régime, e.g. that duties 'fall or devolve *on or upon* someone', or that he or she is 'obliged or forced *to* perform an act', or that an obligation 'concerns or affects them' or 'is incumbent *on or upon* them', or that they 'must do or should do or ought *to* do something' or that 'it is *up or down to* them to do it', etc.

No discussion of periphrastic translation from English would be complete if it did not deal with adverbials. Like all the Germanic languages, English uses the '-ly' (or equivalent) forms unabashedly, so that there is nothing unusual in a testator granting a right to his heirs 'absolute_ly, final_ly and irrevocab_ly'. In many of the Latin languages, on the contrary, literal reproduction of the adverbs would be stylistically inappropriate, and it is likely that a prepositional equivalent involving periphrasis would almost always be preferred. This might lead to something like *con carácter absoluto, definitivo e irrevocable* ('in an absolute, final and irrevocable way').

4. Modulation

Of all the techniques of indirect translation, modulation is usually the most thoroughgoing. Whereas transposition affects grammatical function, modulation involves changes to semantic categories or even alteration of the processes by which thoughts are expressed. If we translate the English sentence 'The new law has prompted thousand of citizens to *demonstrate*' into Spanish as *La nueva ley ha volcado a la calle a miles de ciudadanos* ('has brought them to the street'), we have introduced a modulation of the part (*la calle*) for the whole ('demonstrate'). The translation also involves the introduction of several figures of speech: synecdoche, or part for whole substitution, as the vehicle of articulation; metonymy in the selection of *calle* ('street') through its close association with the idea of public protest; and the semantic transference of the idea of incitement or instigation suggested by 'prompt' to that of spilling or pouring out, tipping or emptying contained in the term *volcar*. Similarly, if 'white collar offences' is translated as *delitos de guante blanco* ('white-glove offences'), though synecdoche is retained in that neither 'collar' nor 'glove' directly state the idea of superior social or professional rank, the Spanish version selects a different item of clothing to convey the same idea.

However, modulation need not involve figures of speech or thought. To take a simple example, the English sentence 'Under £14,000 pounds was outstanding on invoices' may conveniently be translated by *Quedaban pendientes de pago facturas por un importe no superior a 14.000 libras esterlinas* ('Awaiting payment were invoices to a value of no more than £14,000'). In this case the modulation is purely functional, 'under' appearing as 'not greater than' in a ploy aimed at greater naturalness of expression. (Even so, it could be argued that the Spanish version entails the introduction of the rhetorical device known as litotes, by which the positive is stated by denying the negative.)

Modulation, though extremely frequent in literary and general translation, is much less so in specialist and technical contexts. In the case of legal texts, it is unlikely to figure much in dealing with very formal documents such as laws, contracts or wills. However, it will often prove extremely useful to the translator of judgements and rulings, given the linguistic habits of the judiciary in the English-speaking countries, who often draw on everyday experience in formulating their opinions. Because they are trained in oral delivery and therefore tend to favour a certain colloqialism of utterance, they are more inclined than their Continental counterparts to express themselves vigorously and personally and to deck out their speeches with rhetorical flourishes. These factors may well lead the translator to consider the possibility of using modulation, as in the following examples:

> 'It is high time a decision was taken' (*Va siendo hora de que se adopte una determinación, l'heure est arrivée de prendre une décision,* but *Es ist höchste Zeit, daß*)
> 'I can pick up the story with the final House of Lords decision' (*Vuelvo a retomar el hilo narrativo a partir de la resolución final de la Cámara de los Lores*; literal back-translation: 'Again I take the narrative thread from the final decision of...')
> 'The point was made with great cogency by Counsel for the defence that...' (*Tiene mucha fuerza de convicción el argumento presentado por el abogado defensor al sostener que*...; back-translation: 'There is great force of conviction in the argument presented by the Counsel for the defence when maintaining that...').
> 'Those are the battle lines drawn by the protagonists on the central issue' (*Tales son las líneas de combate defendidas por cada uno de los protagonistas respecto de la cuestión principal en litigio*; back-translation: 'Such are the lines of combat defended by each of the protagonists with respect to the main question in dispute').

5. Modifiers

So far in this chapter we have been examining some of the problems involved in translating lexical units from English into other languages. It is time now to turn our attention to matters of syntax.

The complex noun phrase

The long noun phrase that is a feature of English and other Germanic languages presents problems to the translator of technical texts in particular. Some phrases of this type, especially in scientific texts, are obscure enough to deserve to be called 'incomprehensible monsters' as one commentator has put it (Norman 1999:57). Norman is referring to complex modifiers of the following type:

> Gonadotropin-releasing hormone-secreting neuron activity.
> Calcium-modulated membrane transport protein reactivation rate
> The vitamin D receptor protein DNA binding region.

Although legal English is unlikely to throw up modifiers of quite this complexity, the translator must expect to encounter problems of a similar nature. In fact, two types of noun phrase should be distinguished: those containing a single premodifier as well as an indeterminate number of postmodifiers, and those containing more than one premodifier. The following sentence illustrates the first type, with complex postmodification:

> <u>A defective affidavit sworn in support of an application for leave to serve proceedings out of the jurisdiction</u> does not necessarily invalidate leave.

Here the translation is relatively straightforward, since the nucleus, 'affidavit', is preceded by a solitary modifier, 'defective', and followed by several postmodifiers arranged in an order that coincides with that of many of the most widely known European languages.

However, matters are made more complicated for the translator who has to deal with noun phrases of the second type, i.e. with several premodifiers, since word order and overall structure will often need altering. When, for example, the premodifier is a noun used adjectivally, the strategies of transposition, expansion and modulation discussed in section 6 above will come into play. For instance, if we translate the phrase 'progress payments' as *pagos escalonados* ('staggered payments'), we are using an adjective for noun transposition, whereas the alternative translation *entregas periódicas de cantidades escalonadas* ('periodical payment of gradually differing amounts') is an example of modulation. In other cases expansion will be the preferred technique, e.g. in translating 'for the protection of its essential <u>security interests</u>' by *para la protección de sus intereses esenciales <u>en materia de</u> seguridad* ('...essential interests with respect to security'). Whenever several premodifiers are encountered, it is likely that the translation will require a combination of the strategies described. For example, one official Spanish translation of 'the highly technical extradition law' reads *la complejidad técnica de las leyes reguladoras de la extradición* ('the technical complexity of the laws governing extradition'). This version demonstrates a dual transposition (part of speech in *la complejidad técnica* and switch from singular to plural in *leyes*, since 'law' in the original implies <u>all</u> the rules rather than a single law) together with an instance of expansion (*leyes <u>reguladoras</u>*, clarifying that these are the laws governing extradition rather than enforcing it).

Verb phrase modifiers. Adverbs

There is seldom much difficulty with the translation of verb phrases except in certain cases in which the adverb is qualified. A particularly tricky instance is the translation of the adverbs 'wilfully' and 'knowingly' as used in section 1001 of the United States Criminal Code, which reads in part as follows (Solan 1993):

> Whoever, in any matter within the jurisdiction of any department or agency

of the United States <u>knowingly and wilfully</u> falsifies, conceals or covers up by trick, scheme or device a material fact [...] shall be fined not more than $10,000 or imprisoned not more than five years, or both. [*Emphasis added.*]

Judicial construction of the two terms has led to controversy as to their scope and meaning in the federal courts themselves, so that the translator must tread especially warily in dealing with them. The issue, as might be expected, is whether the two adverbs qualify only the phrase 'falsifies, conceals or covers up', etc. or if they should also be taken as applying to the restrictive clause 'in any matter within the jurisdiction of any department or agency of the United States'. The Supreme Court was called upon to give a ruling and decided that the two adverbs modified the whole sentence. In cases of this kind, when the translator may know or suspect that there is a legal issue involved, but may be unsure what the current judicial wisdom is, it is best to provide a version that sticks as closely as possible to the word order of the original. Any resulting awkwardness of style or phrasing will send out a signal to the target reader that there is more going on here than meets the eye and that the translator, if he or she has erred at all, has erred on the side of safety.

6.   The syntax of legal English. Double conjunctions

In the previous sections we were concerned with vocabulary problems as they affect individual phrases, but it is time now to look at the lexical choices faced by the translator of legal English in considering whole clauses and sentences. In this as in other text types, there are two main forms of syntactic construction: simple, or paratactic, clauses and their complex, or hypotactic, counterparts. As a starting point, each of these corresponds to a different legal English genre or subgenre. In the 'facts as found' section of a judgement, on the one hand, judges naturally aim to make their language as factual and objective as possible. The resulting grammar tends to be paratactic, with facts and events being presented as a series of 'stills' through juxtaposition and coordinate clauses, as in the following example:

> *The Evening Star* was a steel-hulled motor yacht built in 1962 according to Lloyd's Rules. *She* was regularly surveyed and was classed 100A1. *The Rules* required biennial surveys with a special survey every four years. On October 1984 *the owners' agents* instructed Lloyd's to carry out a special survey before sale of the vessel. *The survey* was conducted in November. *An interim certificate* was issued recommending that she remained as classed and be credited with passing special survey when certain repairs were carried out.

In reading a paragraph of this kind, the non-native speaker may silently supply 'missing' temporal, causal, conditional or consecutive links ('following', 'after', 'since', 'as', because', 'if', 'although', 'hence', etc.).

On the contrary, the style found in statute law, legal text-books, regulations and judicial rulings tends to be much more complex or hypotactic, with pride of place going to subordination and restrictive clauses of many different kinds, e.g.:

> *Subject to* subsection (6) below, *if an award* is made and, *on an application* made by any of the parties to the reference, (a) *with the consent* of all the other parties to the reference, or (b) *subject to* section 3 below, *with the leave* of the court, it *appears* to the High Court that...

The brakes put on swift comprehension of the meaning of this should, of course, be matched in translation of the phrases in italics, and it is worth pointing out that the complexity of the sentence is increased by the fact that the conditional clause, itself dependent on the 'subject to' insertion, is articulated as a dual condition ('if...and...'). In our view, it is neither the duty nor the right of the translator to minimize such complexity whenever it is clear, as in this case, that the writer of the original has deliberately opted for complex wording. Moreover there are strong grounds for arguing that even apparently avoidable complexity should be retained in translation when, for instance, it is a consequence of a particular judge's view of matters, or the means deliberately chosen by some arbiter or committee to communicate official findings. Hypotaxis would, in such a case, be the most reasonable approach to any translation of complex sentences.

However, the most elegantly planned sentences, like the best-laid schemes of mice and men, 'gang aft aglay'. When this happens, and the translator spots it, good manners as much as good grammar require silent emendation of obvious errors, as in the following instance:

> He said if the plaintiff 'by reason of the way in which he orders his affairs, including where he chooses to live and where he chooses to keep his assets, an order for costs against him is likely to be unenforceable, or enforceable only by significant expenditure of time and money, the defendant should be entitled to security.'

One particular instance of the syntactic complexity of legal English is the use of double conjunctions. Fowler (1991), writing generally on the topic, regards it as a fault of English usage, and Torrents dels Prats (1976) hints at ways in which the problem can be avoided. Both point to simplification of the syntax as the best way out of the difficulties posed by a sentence like the following:

> He said that the time had come for him to guarantee the future of himself and his family *if, as and when he decided to withdraw from public life.*

The point, of course, is that 'if', 'as' and 'when' individually would all ad-equately convey the notion of a hypothetical state of affairs and that the reduplication adds little or nothing to the supposition. A simplifying translation could be based on that assumption. And the same goes for the common legal pair 'unless and until', which to all intents and purposes can usually be reduced to one or the other (most often the former, since it is logically prior), e.g.:

> There should be no commitment to enter the Common Market *unless and until* clear and unequivocal safeguards for Commonwealth produc-ers are obtained.

In more subtle cases (generally when one conjunction does not preclude or include the other, as in the examples given above), it may be desirable to ex-press both. If so, the translator will often be forced into some form of extension or use of the cleft. In either case, general terms suitable for summary or apposi-tion will be found useful. Here are some examples:

> When and so long as such parties were in the throes of negotiating larger terms...' (*Cuando* *las partes se encuentren en pleno proceso de negociar la ampliación de los plazos, y mientras dure esa situación* ..., *Quand* *les parties se rencontraient afin de négocier des termes plus larges et tant que durant cette situation*)
> 'If, and only if, the accused has pled guilty...' (*Si* *el procesado se ha confesado culpable, y sólo entonces..., Si le prévenu a plaidé coupable et seulement dans ce cas*...).

7.   Thematization. Syntactic peculiarities of individual languages

Translators might find it useful to distinguish between the subject and predicate of a clause on the one hand, and the theme and rheme on the other. If we take a straightforward example like the sentence 'At home I don't do much painting', the subject is obviously 'I' and the predicate 'don't do much painting at home'; but the sentence may also be analyzed from the point of view of the priority, or privilege, given to one of its parts (the initial 'at home') over the others. In such a case we may say that the phrase 'at home' has been selected as the 'theme', whereas the rest has been relegated to the status of 'rheme'. The purpose of this selection is usually emphasis or contrast (in the present instance by opposition to a stated or implied notion like 'but outdoors...' or 'whereas in the office...').

If we apply this to our idea of the translator's duty to naturalize the syntax of the target text, we quickly see that it fits in with the obligation to preserve the syntactic spirit of the source text. Paradoxically, it once again appears that the translator must 'by indirection find directions out', i.e. faithfully retain the sense of the syntactic order of the original by artfully subverting it in the new version. Not to do so is often to *traduce* the original rather than to *translate* it, as can be seen in the following example of undesirable preservation of the source syntax:

> The restriction of insider trading is widely accepted as a principal enforcement goal under various provisions of the federal securities laws.

> *La prohibición de participar en operaciones de contratación bursátil al que posee información privilegiada cuenta con un amplio respaldo como objetivo de obligado cumplimiento, en diversas disposiciones de las leyes federales de valores.*

> [Back-translation: The prohibition on participation in stock-exchange trading operations by those who possess privileged information has wide support as principle enforcement goal, in various provisions of the federal securities laws.]

The Spanish version shows legitimate use of modulation, transposition and expansion, yet still sounds flat. The cause is not far to seek: the sentence is not naturally thematized, since the word order appropriate to the declarative sentence expressing a general truth (predicate followed by subject) has been reversed to accommodate the natural English order (subject followed by predicate). It is immeasurably better to modulate and bring forward the semantic content of 'is widely accepted' and 'under various provisions of the security laws', so that it follows the verb but precedes the subject, as in version (a), or to start with the adverbial extension and introduce an impersonal verb, as in version (b):

> *(a) Cuenta con un amplio respaldo en diversas disposiciones de las leyes federales de valores, como objetivo de obligado cumplimiento, que al que posee información privilegiada le sea prohibido participar en la contratación bursátil.*

> [Back-translation: It is widely accepted in various provisions of federal securities laws, as a principle enforcement goal, that those who possess privileged information are prohibited from participating in stock trading.]

> *(b) A tenor de lo que disponen diversas normas de las leyes federales de valores, se acepta, como objetivo de obligado cumplimiento, la prohibición de participar en operaciones de contratación bursátil al que posee información privilegiada.*

> [Back-translation: In accordance with various provisions in federal securities laws, it is accepted, as a principle enforcement goal, that there be a prohibition on participation in stock trading by those who possess privileged information.]

What this means is that the translator must be constantly alert to possible syntactic nuances that shape or frame the original utterance, and that may necessitate substantially different treatment in the target text. The question is not so much 'should we stick rigidly to the thematic order of the original sentence as a matter of fidelity?' as 'does the thematic arrangement of the original require alteration to achieve a similar effect, and hence guarantee fidelity?'. It is a question of judgement, i.e. ear and reading.

8.   Textual coherence. Lexical repetition in English legal discourse. Synonyms

It is axiomatic that well-written texts of any class must be coherently ordered. In the sense in which modern linguists use the term 'coherence', it means very much the same as it means in logic and in everyday usage, i.e. conceptual stability in the arrangement of the elements of discourse so that contradiction and ambiguity are avoided. Assuming the source text to possess this quality, part of the translator's task is to make all necessary adjustments to the target text to ensure that coherence is preserved.

Among the major textual strategies aimed at promoting coherence, we may conveniently distinguish between three types of linking terms or markers: (a) micromarkers, (b) macromarkers and (c) anaphora. Type (a), or micromarkers, includes adverbs, conjunctions and prepositional phrases indicating direction, comparison, cause, effect, purpose, etc., e.g. 'because', 'since', 'hence', 'as a result [of]', 'by comparison [with]', 'with effect from', 'in order to', 'for purposes of', and so on. The second type, which we have termed 'macromarkers' to suggest their more elaborate nature, tend to be full clauses which comment upon, explain, clarify or otherwise highlight particular elements or passages in the foregoing or subsequent text with a view to guiding the reader or hearer, or enlisting their support for what is being proposed or stated. Examples are such self-conscious expansions as 'Apart from what I have just said...', 'To summarize the positions of the parties...', 'Lest any doubt remain, let me add...', 'We would do well to remember the apt words of Lord X when he remarked that...', and so on, i.e. any kind of full-blooded and deliberate management of the surrounding text aimed at eliciting the audience's understanding or approval of what should theoretically be clear enough without it.

Finally there is type (c), or anaphora. As a rhetorical device, anaphora involves the repetition in successive clauses of a particular word or phrase, and its effects may vary from solemn emphasis, through lyrical uplift, to irony or bathos. However, in the workaday world of ordinary speech it can be applied to any form of repetition, such as the mundane use of personal and demonstrative pronouns as a simple device allowing the writer and reader of a text to link new information to old.

Perhaps unexpectedly, it is repetition of the humble pronoun that tends to give translators most trouble. Despite their greater complexity, micromarkers and macromarkers are almost always recognized for what they are and adequately dealt with. However, different languages have such different ways of handling the categories of subject, object and possessive and, most notoriously, the articulation of the persons of the verb, that problems of misalignment or ambiguity often go unnoticed. To take a simple instance, the cardinal rule in English is that the subject of a verb must be stated unless it is absolutely clear, whereas the rule in Spanish is that it should not be stated unless it is unclear, e.g. 'I gave him back the wallet and he left' (*Le devolví la cartera y se marchó*), 'I gave him back the wallet and left' (*Le devolví la cartera y me marché*). However, great difficulty can arise with a similarly simple example like 'I gave him back the wallet and she left'. To translate this as *Le devolví a él la cartera y ella se marchó* is to surrender naturalness to literal accuracy, but the alternative *Le devolví la cartera y se marchó* would almost certainly lead to confusion with the first sentence above or to perplexity as to whether he or she received the wallet and which one left. Once again, the best solution is to pay very careful heed to the context and, where necessary, reintroduce old information such as the proper names of the people involved, if they are known (*Juan*, *la señorita García*), or replace the pronouns with nouns and articles specifying gender (*el cliente*, *la camarera*).

However, there are cases where the translator simply has to apply common-sense logic to syntactic situations in which the original is itself potentially ambiguous. For example, in the sentence 'Harrelson contends now that the admission of this testimony was irreversible error because *it* had been hypnotically induced', a decision has to be made concerning the antecedent of 'it': the admission or the testimony? In the circumstances, it is likely that 'testimony' should be preferred; otherwise, the sentence would be suggesting that the judge or other relevant court official had been hypnotized, rather than the witness. Still, depending on the particular facts – and depending on the character of the judge – it has to be said that the other interpretation remains open and may well depend on external factors. In either case, the translator must take account of the whole context before arriving at a decision. Thereafter, it seems good practice to avoid reproducing unwanted ambiguity wherever possible.

Of course, the simplest way of getting rid of ambiguity of which the writer is aware is by resorting to stolid repetition, and legal and administrative texts written in English are notoriously given to this, as witness the following example:

> The SEC has reinforced the *insider trading* restrictions with promulgation of Rule 14e-3 of the SEC, an independent provision prohibiting *insider trading* in connection with tender offers. Congress has further

reinforced these *trading restrictions* by providing the SEC with the power to seek a treble penalty under the *Insider Trading* Sanctions Act of 1984 (ITSA). This legislation empowers the SEC to base enforcement actions on any recognized theory of *insider trading restriction.*

No ambiguity here, but what other language would put up with this amount of lexical repetition? Translators of this text into other languages would have to balance the stylistic undesirability of ham-fisted reiteration against the overall need for clarity, probably by resorting to devices such as approximate or partial synonyms or demonstrative or deictic summaries ('said conduct', 'activities of this kind', 'restrictive/criminal conduct of the type mentioned'). Whatever the solution chosen, the translator must ensure that the version proposed does not reintroduce the ambiguity that the repetition was intended to get rid of in the first place.

In this regard, it may not be entirely superfluous to suggest that the translator in pursuit of the ideal synonym should consult source-language as well as target-language thesauruses. For instance, if the repeated term is 'acknowledge', help may be found under target equivalents of synonyms such as 'accept', 'recognize', 'confess', 'admit', 'approve' or 'agree'. Usually it does not much matter which term in a given language is viewed as the hyperonym, or *definiens*, and in any case modern thesauruses either provide a separate alphabetical listing of hyperonyms (e.g. Roget) or repeat and cross-reference all entries without classification under a supposed *definiens* (e.g. the Spanish *Corripio* 1974/1990). 'Insider trading', as in our example, will probably not be found anywhere except in a specialist dictionary of law or financial terms, and even then it is likely to be glossed or explained rather than translated. It will therefore be up to the translator to choose a sufficiently close term for the first occurrence and to complete the remaining instances by deictic reference as we have suggested above.

References

Alcaraz, Enrique (1996) 'Translation and pragmatics', in Román Álvarez and Carmen-África Vidal (eds) *Translation, Power, Subversion*, Clevedon: Multilingual Matters, 99-115.

Álvarez, Román and Carmen-África Vidal (eds) (1996) *Translation, Power, Subversion*, Clevedon: Multilingual Matters.

Austin, John Langshaw (1962) *How to Do Things with Words*, Oxford: Clarendon Press.

Bagby, John W. (1986) 'The Evolving Controversy over Insider Trading', *American Business Law Journal* 24: 571-87.

Barnard, David (1985) *The Civil Court in Action*, London: Butterworths.

Bhatia, Vijay K. (1993) *Analysing Genre, Language Use in Professional Settings*, London: Longman.

Bird, Roger (ed) (1990) *Osborn's Concise Law Dictionary*, London: Sweet & Maxwell. 7th Edition.

Blackstone (1999) *The Blackstone's Civil Procedure Rules*, London: Blackstone Press.

Borja, Anabel (1998) *Estudio descriptivo de la traducción jurídica*, unpublished doctoral dissertation, Bellaterra: Universitat Autònoma de Barcelona.

Corripio, Fernando (1974/1990) *Gran diccionario de sinónimos*, Barcelona: Ediciones B.

Cruz-Martínez, María Soledad (1999) *El inglés jurídico. Estudio contrastivo inglés-español de términos jurídico-penales*, unpublished doctoral dissertation, Alicante: Universidad de Alicante.

Curzon, Leslie Basil (ed) (1990) *Dictionary of Law*, London: Pitman. 3rd Edition.

Davies, R. (1990) 'Record Company Cannot Apply Penalty Clause against Invoices', *FT Law Reports. Financial Times* (March 21, 1990).

Downs, S. (1985) 'Damages under the federal electronic fund transfer act: a proposed construction of sections 910 and 915', *American Business Law Journal* 23: 5-26.

Fawcett, Peter (1997) *Translation and Language: Linguistic Theories Explained*, Manchester: St Jerome.

Fowler, Roger (1991) *Language in the News. Discourse and Ideology in the Press*, London: Routledge.

Garner, Bryan A. (1987) *A Dictionary of Modern Legal Usage*, Oxford: Oxford University Press.

------ (1991) *The Elements of Legal Style*, Oxford: Oxford University Press.

Grisham, John (1989) *A Time to Kill*, New York: Dell.

------ (1991) *The Firm*, London: Arrow.

------ (1994) *The Rainmaker*, London: Arrow.

------ (1996) *The Runaway Jury*, London: Arrow.

------ (1997) *The Partner*, London: Arrow.

Hoag, Tami (1999) *Ashes to Ashes*, London: Orion

Holland, James *et al.* (1991) *Learning Legal Rules*, London: Blackstone Press.

Keenan, Dennis (1963/1989) *Smith and Keenan's English Law*, London: Pitman.

Martin, Elizabeth A. (ed) (1990) *A Concise Dictionary of Law*, Oxford: Oxford University Press. 2nd Edition.

Murphy, Peter *et al.* (1998) *Blackstones Criminal Practice*, London: Blackstone Press.

Nida, Eugene A. (1975) *Language Structure and Translation*, Stanford CA: Stanford University Press.

Norman, Guy (1999) *Cómo escribir un artículo científico en inglés*, Madrid: Azta Zeneca.

Osborne, Craig (1993/1999) *Criminal Litigation*, London: Blackstone Press.

Rabadán, Rosa (1991) *Equivalencia y traducción*, León: Universidad de León.

Solan, Lawrence M. (1993) *The Language of Judges*, Chicago: University of Chicago Press.

Swales, John M. (1990) *Genre Analysis. English in Academic and Research Settings*, Cambridge: Cambridge University Press.

Torrents dels Prats, Alfonso (1976) *Diccionario de dificultades del inglés*, Barcelona: Juventud.

Toury, Gideon (1995) *Descriptive Translation Studies and Beyond*, Amsterdam & Philadelphia: John Benjamins.

Vázquez-Ayora, Gerardo (1977) *Introducción a la traductología*, Washington DC: Georgetown University Press.

Walter, Bettyruth (1988) *The Jury Summation as Speech Genre*, Amsterdam & Philadelphia: John Benjamins.

Index